Take Flight
The Sonnets

Thomas G. Reischel

Word Art Publishing
9350 Wilshire Blvd
Suite 203, Beverly Hills, CA 90212
www.wordartpublishing.com
Phone: 1 (888) 614 - 1370

Copyright © 2025 Thomas G. Reischel.

All rights reserved. No part of this book may be used or reproduced by any means, graphic, electronic, or mechanical, including photocopying, recording, taping or by any information storage retrieval system without the written permission of the author except in the case of brief quotations embodied in critical articles and reviews.

This book is a work of non-fiction. Unless otherwise noted, the author and the publisher make no explicit guarantees as to the accuracy of the information contained in this book and in some cases, names of people and places have been altered to protect their privacy.

Because of the dynamic nature of the Internet, any web addresses or links contained in this book may have changed since publication and may no longer be valid. The opinions expressed in this manuscript are solely the opinions of the author and do not represent the opinions or thoughts of the publisher and the publisher hereby disclaims any responsibility for them. The author has represented and warranted full ownership and/or legal right to publish all the materials in this book.

Published by Word Art Publishing

ISBN: 978-1-955070-74-4 (Hardcover)
ISBN: 978-1-955070-66-9 (Paperback)
ISBN: 978-1-955070-67-6 (eBook)

DEDICATION

I dedicate this book to my late mother-in-law, Elizabeth J. Cutter, who said my poetry was "MASTERFUL," ; to young poets everywhere, those budding bards and sonneteers; and to those who love the language of poetry. May Sonnets fill your days with joy!

ACKNOWLEDGEMENT

I'd like to thank my wife, Karen Lynne (Sweetnam) Reischel, for her patience and acceptance of my time spent working on this book. Thanks to all the support staff at Word Art Publishing, for making the process simple and easy, especially Beau Brandon whose patience and persuasion over several years has gotten me here. This book would not have been possible if it were not for the site where I post all my poems, FanStory, and where each gets reviewed by my peer poets, especially from Jim Bartlett, Dean Kuch, Catherine Ginn, and Sandra Mitchell for their inspiration, support and suggestions. Some even contributed their own Sonnet formats that were then incorporated by me into the book. Most notably, Jim Bartlett created the Pantygonnet, introduced me to Pushkin, and wrote the memorable "Double Acrostic Cleaved, Petrarchan/Rondeau" format. Stephan A Carter contributed the Carrett Sonnet. Catherine Ginn added the LyriCat, and the Tiara of Sonnets. Meanwhile Nancy E. Davis created the Septillian, and Jyoti contributed the Sonnetino to the mix. Thanks to Tony Fawcus for introducing me to the Echo format. Finally I can't thank my mentor, Gungalo (who has since passed away), enough for opening my eyes to all the fabulous forms of poetry there were, as I was first starting out. Many thanks to Wikipedia as a profound source of knowledge. Plus all my other fans, family and friends. I fully appreciate your time and support.

INTRODUCTION

In this book, I have identified 74 different Configurations/Formats of the Sonnet Form, and have personally written 170 examples. All the poems and all the photographs in this book are mine. I include photographs, because I am also a Photographer. I believe that the two Genre complement each other in a way that creates a powerful Synergy. If you are familiar with my 3 book series, Picture Poems, you know then what I am all about.

My purpose in this book is many fold. I hope one can just read the Poetry and enjoy it, but particularly become emerged in the true beauty of this lovely Poetic Form. I hope the photography is enticing, and that the Synergy it adds to the Poetry is a powerful addition to the reader's enjoyment. I want the reader to grasp the flexibility, complexity, and adaptability of the Sonnet Format. I desire that the reader values learning about Poetry, and that they find something new and exciting about Sonnets in particular. I hope Students and Teachers alike can use this work in some way. So this book is meant for Poetry Lovers, Students, Teachers, budding Poets, Photography Aficionados, and avid Readers.

I must acknowledge, that much of the historical information and technical detail herein comes from Wikipedia.

In this book, I consider Major Terms of poetry, as well as descriptions of Poetry Types, to be addressable as Proper Names. Therefore, you will see them capitalized, such as: Rhyme Scheme, Stanza, Couplet, Quatrain, Free Verse, Meter, Syllable, Line, Structure and Volta. I also capitalize Themes, and sometimes do it just for emphasis. I know this will drive some people crazy, but I consider it essential to identify them as such. After all, they are the **Key Elements,** and I want them to be recognized as such. The same goes for the names of Poetic Styles and Formats. So I hope you will bear with me in this.

To understand this book of Sonnets, a number of technical items must be addressed, because I provide a lot of technical detail meant to assist other poets and students in writing their own. If you already know these things, just skip this area. If technical details are not your cup-of-tea, just read and enjoy the poems.

Let's start with a discussion of Rhyme. Poems may or may not have Rhyme. Although, most Sonnets do Rhyme. The Rhyme is usually at the end of each line and is known as "End-rhyme". If not at the end, it is known as "In-line rhyme". As you read my poetic descriptions, I may refer to the End-rhymes in an alphanumeric code. For example, the first rhyming word in a poem is referred to as the "a" Rhyme, and every line in the poem that Rhymes with it is designated the letter "a". The second Rhyme to occur would be identified as "b", the third as "c", and so on. The most common poem has 4 lines (a Quatrain). The most typical End-rhyme Rhyme Schemes for a Quatrain are:

    aabb (Coupled Rhyme)
    abab (Alternating Rhyme)
    abba (Enveloping Rhyme)
    abcb (Skipping Rhyme)

Beyond End-line and In-line Rhyme are other nuances. For example, there may be no End-line Rhymes, but lines do rhyme within the middle of each line. This is known as Hidden Rhyme. A very Welsh adaptation that is known as Cross Rhyme, where the End-line Rhyme matches to an In-line word on the following line. Rhymes can also be identified as perfect, near, or slant.

> Perfect Rhyme is where the stressed vowel sound between two words are identical, plus any subsequent sounds.
>
> Near Rhyme is a Rhyme between a stressed and an unstressed Syllable – wing/caring.
>
> Slant Rhyme is Rhyme matching Assonance (vowels) or Consonance –sh**a**k**e**/h**a**t**e** or r**a****b**ies/r**o****b****b**ers.
>
> Oblique Rhyme is Rhyme where the sounds are similar, but don't really match – one/thumb, or green/fiend.

Syllabic Rhyme is Rhyme in which the last Syllables sound the same, but are not the stressed Syllable – pitter/patter.

Mono-rhyme is where all the End-line Rhymes in a Stanza, (or even the entire multi-Stanza poem) are the same.

"No Rhyme" is known as Free Verse or Blank Verse, although Free Verse with some Rhyme is known as Free Style.

Now, let's turn from Rhymes to Line Structure. There are many other Line Structures in poetry besides the Quatrain, based on the number of Lines. Simply speaking, the most common are:

Two lines – a Couplet
Three lines – a Tercet
Four lines – a Quatrain
Five lines – a Quintain, or a Quintet, or Cinquain
Six lines – a Sestet, or Sexain, or Sextet
Seven lines – a Septet, or Septain
Eight lines – an Octave, or Octet
Nine Lines – a Nanotet, or Nonet, or a Spenserian Stanza
Ten lines – a Decatain, or Decatet, or Decastitch

Poems may contain a paragraph. These are known as Stanzas. These Stanzas may contain the same Rhyme or may vary. In order to distinguish the Rhyme Scheme, an alphanumeric code is typically employed. Here are examples of the Rhyme Scheme codes of a poem with two Stanzas.

aabb baba (Here the Rhyme was the same in both, but one was Coupled while the other was Alternating).
aabb ccdd (Here each Stanza has two different Coupled Rhymes)

Poems may also contain one or more Repeating Rhyme. That means it has the same identical Rhyme Word. This is usually identified using a capital letter, like so:

Abab Abab (Here I'm referring to the first Rhyme of each Stanza being repeated)

It could also mean a complete repeating of an entire line or Refrain. That would be identified in the author's notes. Sometimes the Refrain is referred to with the letter "R." In either case the Rhyme or Refrain may be Interlocking. Below are two examples of Interlocking Tercets. The first interlocks the Rhyme or Refrain of the first Line of each Stanza, while in the second, the middle letter creates the Rhyme for the next Stanza.

Abc Ade Afg
aBa bCb cDc ded

A similar treatment can be achieved by Interlocking Quatrains with a Couplet, as follows:

aaBa bbCb ccDc dd (See how the Capitalized letter creates the rhyme on next stanza?)

Speaking of repeated Refrains (which can be a word, an entire line, or part of a line), different treatments can create different effects. Here are as examples of some Refrain Effects you will see here in the Sonnets.

Waterfall – Abab c**A**ca ad**A**d a**A** (the A ripples through moving one position in each stanza)
Sustained – **A**bab **A**cac **A**dad **A**a (the A remains in the same first line of each stanza)
Echo – aba**B** cdc**B** ded**B** b**B** (the B remains the last line of each stanza)
Double Envelope – **AB**ab cdcd efef **AB** (first two lines become last two)
Reverse Double Envelop – **AB**ab cdcd efef **BA** (same, but Couplet reversed)
Double Summary – **A**ba**B** cdcd efef **AB** (first and last lime of stanza become last lines of poem)
Reverse Double Summary- **A**ba**B** cdcd efef **BA** (same as other, but Couplet reversed)
Stanzaic – **A**bab **C**dcd efef **AC**- First line of first two stanzas become closing Couplet)
Reverse Stanzaic –**A**bab **C**dcd efef **CA** (same, but Couplet reversed)
Rolling – **ABCD A**bab **B**cbc **C**dcd **D**ede (All first stanza lines create subsequent sequential firsts)

Poems can mix Stanza Styles. For example, an English Sonnet often contains 3 Quatrains and a Couplet (14 total lines), while an Italian Sonnet contains an Octave and a Sestet (also 14 lines).

Furthermore, poems also may contain a structured Syllable Count. This establishes the Rhythm at which the poem is read, which is known as Meter. Typically these are paired in sets of two, known as a Foot. There is a name for each type of Meter, as follows.

>Two syllables - Monometer (one foot)
>Four syllables - Dimeter (two Feet)
>Six syllables - Trimeter (three feet)
>Eight syllables - Tetrameter (four feet)
>Ten syllables - Pentameter (five feet)
>Twelve syllables – Hexameter or Alexandrian (six feet)
>Fourteen syllables - Heptameter (seven feet)
>Sixteen Syllables - Octameter (eight feet)
>The ones most common or frequently used are Tetrameter and Pentameter.

The most complex Poetic Concept focuses around Syllable accents, whether they are hard or soft, and how they are linked together. The most common of these are Iambic and the Trochaic (Trochee) Meters. As you speak a word, there is an accent on each Syllable that results in either a soft or a hard sound. For example the word "cowboy" puts the hard accent on the first Syllable – **COW**boy. The word "police", puts the hard accent on the second Syllable – po**LICE**. How you string words together determines the type of Meter. Iambic Meter alternates soft -hard, soft- hard. For example, Shakespeare's famous words –"To be or not to be" is iambic: to **BE** or **NOT** to **BE**. But the second half is not iambic – **THAT** is the **QUES**tion. Iambic is frequently defined as da-Dum, da-DUM type Meter, where each da-Dum is a Poetic Foot. Therefore, iambic Pentameter would carry a Meter of: da-**DUM**, da-**DUM**, da-**DUM**, da-**DUM**, da-**DUM**. Various dialects do tend to complicate the interpretations, however.

I should mention something here about Feminine iambic Meter. Most Iambic Meters contain an even number of Syllable Counts (2,4,6,8,10,12,14), with the hard accent on the second, or last, Syllable. But, a Feminine Line adds an extra Syllable that ends on a soft accent (for example, a one word line – e**MO**tion – is an example of Feminine Iambic Monometer). As a rule, when there is one line of Feminine Iambic Meter, there should be a matching second line paired with it in some manner.

Trochee is exactly the opposite of iambic, where each line starts with a hard Syllable accent and ends with a soft.

>**TWIN**kle **TWIN**kle **LIT**tle **STAR**,
>**HOW** I **WON**der **WHAT** you **ARE**.

An item unique to a Sonnet, Senryu, or Haiku, is a Volta, or Turn. That occurs where the poem is leading you in one direction, then suddenly surprises you with a change. In Sonnets, the usual place for a Volta is at the 9th line. Often, it is strongly demarked with words like: but, still, yet, oh, and alas. Sometimes it is more subtle. Recognizing the Volta can become an added joy in reading a Sonnet.

I hope readers will appreciate my pointing these things out as it is not my intention to bore them, but rather I hope it may bring additional depth of appreciation to the poetry. If not, feel free to skip over that part.

Well, that's about as deep as I want to get.

I welcome you to join me on this journey of 170 Sonnets, with their unique and their shared traits. Hope you enjoy them as immensely as I enjoyed writing them.

TABLE OF CONTENTS

Chapter 1. Standard Formats 17
- A. English Sonnets 18
  - Sonnet 1: Autumn's Golden Veil 19
  - Sonnet 2: Broken Door 20
  - Sonnet 3: California Fires 21
  - Sonnet 4: PPF - Pretty Pink Flower 22
- B. Shakespearean Sonnets 23
  - Sonnet 5: Bewildering Change 24
  - Sonnet 6: Blue Bachelor Buttons 25
  - Sonnet 7: Floral Fire 26
  - Sonnet 8: Pirates Plight 27
  - Sonnet 9: Rift of War 28
- C. Italian Sonnets 29
  - Sonnet 10: Blest Beauty 30
  - Sonnet 11: Investing 31
  - Sonnet 12: Outside Our Bedroom Window 32
  - Sonnet 13: These Bees 33
  - Sonnet 14: This Golden Hour 34
- D. Petrarchan Sonnets 35
  - Sonnet 15: Heaven and Hell 36
  - Sonnet 16: Reflections on the Water 37
- E. Spenserian Sonnets 38
  - Sonnet 17: Bridge Knowledge 39
  - Sonnet 18: Distracted by Beauty 40
  - Sonnet 19: Stony Gaze 41
- F. American Sonnets 42
  - Sonnet 20: Lethal Legacy 43
  - Sonnet 21: To Robin Williams 44
  - Sonnet 22: Silver Scene 45
- G. Modern Sonnets 46
  - Sonnet 23: Firebird 47
  - Sonnet 24: Frustration at Itasca 48
  - Sonnet 25: PEEPS and Company 49
  - Sonnet 26: Resolutions 50
  - Sonnet 27: The Eyes on Me 51
  - Sonnet 28: True Love 52
- H. Blank Verse Sonnet 53

    Sonnet 29: Night's Revelations 54
    Sonnet 30: OH Voyageur! 55

Chapter 2. Sonnet Form Transitions 57

  A. Acrostic Sonnet 58
    Sonnet 31: What Is This Fuss? 59
    Sonnet 32: When Your Love Is 60
  B. Kyrielle Sonnet 62
    Sonnet 33: White Bird 63
  C. Limerick Sonnet 64
    Sonnet 34: The Debate 65
  D. Pantoum Sonnet 66
    Sonnet 35: The Crowd was WOW'd 67
    Sonnet 36: Their Spirits Dance 68
  E. Quatern Sonnet 70
    Sonnet 37: Dahlia Bloom 71
  F. Rondel Sonnet 72
    Sonnet 38: Sidewalk Adorned 73
  G. Rubaiyat Sonnet 74
    Sonnet 39: The Verdant Pond 75
  H. Sestina Sonnet 76
    Sonnet 40: Golf Course Sign 77
  I. Terza Rima Sonnet 78
    Sonnet 41: Sacrificial Savior 79
  J. Triolet Sonnet (Aka: SonnTriolet, or Sonniolet) 80
    Sonnet 42: Pansies 81

Chapter 3. Famous Poet Sonnet Forms 83

  A. Byron's Sonnet 84
    Sonnet 43: Seeking Home 85
  B. Dante's Sonnet Variation 86
    Sonnet 44: Imagination Spawned 87
  C. Pushkin Sonnets 88
    Sonnet 45: Best Buddy 89
    Sonnet 46: Scurrying Squirrels 90
  D. Tirell Sonnet 92
    Sonnet 47: Enjoy a Fire 93
  E. Tuckerman Sonnet 94
    Sonnet 48: Golden Painted Sky 95

Chapter 4. Couplet Relocation Sonnets 97

  A. Alfred Dorn Sonnet 98
    Sonnet 49: The Heart in the City 99
  B. Inverted Sonnet 100
    Sonnet 50: Sunny Day Play 101
  C. Tirell Sonnet 102

	Sonnet 51: Bitter Pill	103
D.	Tory Hexatet Sonnet	104
	Sonnet 52: Geese at Peace	105

Chapter 5. Stanzaic Sonnets ... 107

A.	Alfred Dorn Sonnet	108
	Sonnet 53: Darkest Depression	109
B.	Hex Sonetta	110
	Sonnet 54: Spellbound	111
C.	Roserian Sonnet	112
	Sonnet 55: Love and Flowers	113
D.	Saraband Sonnet	114
	Sonnet 56: Minnesota Capitol Building	115
E.	Sestet Sonnet	116
	Sonnet 57: Wander With a Friend	117
F.	Tory Hexatet Sonnet	118
	Sonnet 58: Past Youth	119
G.	Tricet Sonnet	120
	Sonnet 59: Some Thoughts to Ponder	121
H.	Trilonnet	122
	Sonnet 60: Remember Him	123

Chapter 6. Added Lines ... 125

A.	Carrett Sonnet	126
	Sonnet 61: Vortex of the Dark	127
B.	Caudette Sonnet	128
	Sonnet 62: The Picnic	129
C.	Compound Sonnet	130
	Sonnet 63: Worldly Rhythms	131
D.	Dante's Version Sonnet	132
	Sonnet 64: Among the Trees	133
E.	Fusion Sonnet	134
	Sonnet 65: Humanity	135
F.	Heroic Sonnet	136
	Sonnet 66: The Yellow Mountains of China	137
G.	Septillian Sonnet	138
	Sonnet 67: Morning at Camp	139
H.	Super Sonnet	140
	Sonnet 68: Computer Industry Genesis	141

Chapter 7. Sonnets with Rhyme Variations ... 143

A.	Arabian Onegin Sonnet	144
	Sonnet 69: Winter Spell	145
B.	Asean Sonnet	146
	Sonnet 70: Bumble Bees	147
C.	Beymorlin Sonnet	148

Sonnet 71: Time to Play...149
    D. Dual Sonnet...150
        Sonnet 72: Fall, the Best..152
    E. Pantygonnet..154
        Sonnet 73: Deforestation...155
    F. Sestina Sonnet..156
        Sonnet 74: Gliding Therapy...157
    G. Shadow Sonnet..158
        Sonnet 75: Time..159
    H. Slide Sonnet..160
        Sonnet 76: Tree Top Thoughts 161
    I. Triptic Sonnet 162
        Sonnet 77: Leaf Cascade 163
        Sonnet 78: Oaken Arms...164
        Sonnet 79: OH Dandelion 165
    J. Visser Sonnet (aka. Hidden Rhyme Sonnet) 166
        Sonnet 80: Exploring Cliff Cave..168
    K. Welsh Sonnet..170
        Sonnet 81: Ghost Ship - Lady Lovibond 171

Chapter 8. Sonnets with Unusual Line Lengths..173

    A. Cornish Sonnet...174
        Sonnet 82: Fountain with Fatsia...175
    B. Faux Free Verse Sonnet..176
        Sonnet 83: The Spot...178
    C. Fusion Sonnet 180
        Sonnet 84: Cash, My Brother's Dog...181
    D. Hex Sonnetta 182
        Sonnet 85: Wayward Wings...183
    E. Japanese Sonnet...184
        Sonnet 86: Japanese Sonnet (bright decoration)..185
    F. Jazz Sonnet..186
        Sonnet 87: Groovin' 187
    G. Limerick Sonnet...188
        Sonnet 88: Crooked Trees 189
    H. Lyricat Sonnet..190
        Sonnet 89: Baby News 191
    I. Sapphic Sonnet...192
        Sonnet 90: Water Garden 193
    J. Saraband Sonnet 194
        Sonnet 91: Patterns 195
    K. Tory Hexatet...196
        Sonnet 92: The Passion of Pan (Lilac Legend)..197
    L. Tuckerman Sonnet 198

	Sonnet 93: Anticipation	199
M.	Welsh Sonnet	200
	Sonnet 94: The Bond	202
N.	Word Sonnet	204
	Sonnet 95: Meet	205
	Sonnet 96: Obsessions	206
	Sonnet 97: Rescue	207
	Sonnet 98: Sore Loser	208

Chapter 9. Sonnets with Unusual Meter 209

A.	The Curtal Sonnet	210
	Sonnet 99: Dangled Art	212
B.	Limerick Sonnet	214
	Sonnet 100: When the Rains Stop	215
C.	Pushkin Sonnets	216
	Sonnet 101: Sleeps Silently in Snow	217
	Sonnet 102: Such Souls are We	218
D.	Sapphic Sonnet	220
	Sonnet 103: Glowing Buds	221
E.	Word Sonnets	222
	Sonnet 104: Out House	223
	Sonnet 105: Moment	224
	Sonnet 106: So!	225

Chapter 10. Shortened Sonnets 227

A.	The Curtal Sonnet	228
	Sonnet 107: Hidden in the Fog	229
B.	The Sonnetino	230
	Sonnet 108: Bus Stop	231
	Sonnet 109: Eagle Perch	232

Chapter 11. Sonnets with Repeating Refrains 233

A.	The Cornish Sonnet	234
	Sonnet 110: Water's Edge	235
B.	Couplet Sonnet	236
	Sonnet 111: Rain Filled Culverts	237
	Sonnet 112: Yellow Lilies	238
C.	Echo Sonnet	240
	Sonnet 113: Sweet Music	241
D.	Kyrielle Sonnet	242
	Sonnet 114: Majestic Mountain Goat	243
E.	The Lyricat Sonnet	244
	Sonnet 115: Gathering Gloom	245
F.	Pantoum Sonnet	246
	Sonnet 116: Pink Ladies	247
	Sonnet 117: A Day by the Lake	248

- G. Quatern Sonnet...250
    - Sonnet 118: Landing Loon...251
- H. Rondel Sonnet 252
    - Sonnet 119: Pincers Probe 253
- I. Swannet Sonnet (or just Swannet) 254
    - Sonnet 120: Turning Two...255
- J. Tirell Sonnet 256
    - Sonnet 121: Dances in the Ferns 257
- K. Triolet Sonnet (aka. Sonn Triolet)..258
    - Sonnet 122: Juxtaposed Elements 259

Chapter 12. Expanded Sequence Sonnets 261
- A. Heroic Sonnet 262
    - Sonnet 123: Lush Lagoon 263
- B. Super Sonnet 264
    - Sonnet 124: Homeless Halloween 266
- C. Sonnet Trilogy 268
    - Sonnet 125: Be Careful What You Ask For 270
- D. Tiara of Sonnets 272
    - Sonnet 126: Crabapple Bloom 274
    - Sonnet 127: Rosebud in Springtime 276
    - Sonnet 128: Spring Buds 278
- E. Coronet of Sonnets 280
    - Sonnet 129: Revealed and Concealed 282
- F. Crown of Heroic Sonnets...286
    - Sonnet 130: A Pirate's Tale 288
    - Sonnet 131: Buffalo - The Great Slaughter 292
    - Sonnet 132: Minnesota Early Explorers -1600s...296
    - Sonnet 133: Robbing Paul to Pay Peter 300
    - Sonnet 134: Scientific Inquisition 304
    - Sonnet 135: Shetek Massacre at Slaughter Slough...308
- G. Wreath of Sonnets 314
    - Sonnet 136: Wreath Sonnet 7 315
- H. Sonnet Cycle..316
- I. Sonnet Sequence 317

Chapter 13. Special Complex Sonnets 319
- A. A Double Acrostic Cleaved Petrarchan/Rondeau Sonnet..320
    - Sonnet 137: The Power of Song...321
- B. An 11-9 Metered Anapestic Heroic Sonnet 322
    - Sonnet 138: Satan's Rage 323
- C. Modeled End-Line Sonnet...324
    - Sonnet 139: Sunset Passion..325
- D. Nonet/Cinquain Sonnet 326
    - Sonnet 140: Where go the Flow 327

Chapter 14. Grab Bag. 329
    A.   A Mix of Various Sonnets 330
        Sonnet 141: A Good Day - Fishing 331
        Sonnet 142: Angry Ancient Oaks 332
        Sonnet 143: All Hallows Night 333
        Sonnet 144: Cockled Whilst Away 334
        Sonnet 145: Determination 335
        Sonnet 146: Farewell 2015 336
        Sonnet 147: Ford's Fate 337
        Sonnet 148: Forest Fantasy...338
        Sonnet 149: Frozen Falls 339
        Sonnet 150: God's Gift 340
        Sonnet 151: Little People 341
        Sonnet 152: Marksman 342
        Sonnet 153 : My Temperature is Rising...343
        Sonnet 154: Proud Battle Lines 344
        Sonnet 155: Push and Pull 345
        Sonnet 156. Raindrops on Flowers 346
        Sonnet 157: Richard and Renie 347
        Sonnet 158: Season's Sight 348
        Sonnet 159: Simple Decorations..349
        Sonnet 160: Sorrow 350
        Sonnet 161: Such a Day 351
        Sonnet 162: Sweet Sleep 352
        Sonnet 163: Stumped..353
        Sonnet 164: The Dance 354
        Sonnet 165: The Falls 355
        Sonnet 166: The Signs 356
        Sonnet 167: Van Gogh 357
        Sonnet 168: War Weary Budgets 358
        Sonnet 169: Washburn Watertower..359
        Sonnet 170: The Sonnets..360
Conclusion 361
Descriptions of Sonnets. 363
Glossary of Sonnet Types...385

PREFACE

The Sonnets

The Sonnets are some of the best known, and often most beautiful, forms of poetry. Of course, Shakespeare made them famous. His works are among the best of all time. In fact, his name has become synonymous with the name "Sonnet." These are some of his better known ones: Sonnet 118, *Shall I compare thee to a summer's day?*; Sonnet 116, *Let me not to the marriage of true minds*; Sonnet 130, *My mistress' eyes are nothing like the sun*; Sonnet 104, *To me, fair friend, you never can be old*; and many more. Other famous Sonnets are: John Donne's, *Death, Be Not Proud*; William Wordsworth's, *Composed upon Westminster Bridge*; John Keats', *On First Looking into Chapman's Homer*; Percy Shelley's, *Ozymandias*; Robert Frost's, *Acquainted with the Night*; Christina Rosetti's, *Remember*; John Milton's, *When I Consider How My Light is Spent*; and, of course, Elizabeth Barrett Browning's, *How do I love thee*.

The Basic Sonnet is composed of 14 Lines usually written in iambic Pentameter, and frequently upon the Theme of love or romance. But that is not always the case. In fact, I have found an exciting adventure within the Sonnets, and I'd like to take you along this journey with me.

This journey began when I started learning to write Sonnets myself. I started researching them and finding several Variations. Wikipedia has a very good treatise on them, and there I discovered that there were many Variations. I also found the internet a treasure trove of poetry sites such as: Poetry Soup, Shadow Poetry, The Poetry Foundation, Thepoetsgarrett, Poetrymagnumopus, PoemHunter, and others. I delighted whenever I found another new Variation. I was amazed at what I found. And so, I set out to find, and then write, as many as I could, which lead me to write this book.

The thing I like best about a Sonnet is, that it is a Structured Type of poem. But that structure can be stretched in many different ways. Of course there are the 6 Standard Formats that most readers should be familiar with. Those are: the English (including the Shakespearean), the Italian (including the Petrarchan), the Spenserian, the American, the Modern, and the Blank Verse. Then there are Variations on the Sonnet made by Famous Poets. Beyond Shakespeare, Petrarch, and Spenser, whom I've already mentioned, are: Byron, Dante, Pushkin, Tirell, and Tuckerman. Of course, everyone isn't familiar with all the Poetry Formats, so I will explain each as we get to them, along with some possible commentary.

Sonnets can be created by transitioning from another Poetic Format too. Some very common Forms that one can do this with are the following: Acrostic, Kyrielle, Limerick, Pantoum, Quatern, Rondel, Rubiat, Sestina, Terza Rima, and Triolet.

A Poet can change the location of the Couplet as in the Alfred Dorn, Inverted, Tirell, and Tory Hexatet Forms. Alternatively the Stanzaic Structure may change, which occurs with the Alfred Dorn, Petrarchan, Hex Sonnetta, Rosarian, Saraband, Sestet, Tory Hexatet, Tricet, and Trilonet Sonnets. Those with unusual Meter are the Curtal, Limerick, Modern, Pushkin, and Sapphic Sonnets. Some Sonnet Types add more than 14 Lines, such as: Carrett, Caudette, Compound, Dual, Dante's Version, Fusion, Heroic, and Saraband. If that's not crazy enough, some Sonnets add more Sonnets to the Sonnet (usually Interlinked), like the Tiara of Sonnets with 3, the Coronet with 4, the Crown with 7, the Wreath with 14, the Sonnet cycle with 20+, and the Sonnet Sequence with 50+. You can, furthermore, play with Rhyme Variations as in the Arabian Onegin, Asean, Bey Morlin, Dual, Shadow, Slide, Triptic, and Visser Sonnets. Then there are those that change Line Length or the Syllable Count: the Cornish, Free Style, Fusion, Hex Sonnette, Japanese, Jazz, Limerick, Lyricat, Modern, Saraband, Sapphic, Tory Hexatet, Tuckerman, Welsh, and Word Sonnets. Some specialize is using the Repeated Refrain, such as: the Couplet, Echo, Kyrielle, Lyricat, Limerick, Quatern, Rondel Prime, Swanette, and Tirell. Others even shorten the Line Count to less than 14, like the Curtal, Sonnetino, and Word. Finally there are some very Complex Formats that I'll surprise you with when I get to that chapter.

As I provided that listing, you may have noticed that some formats fall into more than one Category. So, you can see here, the utter flexibility of this magnificent Format. After all that, you may be thinking, "Oh my, my head is spinning!"

Here's another way of explaining it. After seeing other poets stretching the limits of what it means to be a Sonnet, I discovered that there are Key Elements to any Sonnet, and that anyone of them can be stretched to accommodate a creative Variation. The Standard Elements of a Sonnet are these:

1. A structured poem of 14 Lines
2. A formalized Rhyme Scheme.
3. A structured Meter, usually iambic Pentameter
4. A structured Stanza Scheme
   a. The English version with 3 Quatrains and Closing Couplet
   b. The Italian with an Octave and Sestet (or, 2 Quatrains with 2 Tercets)
5. A Turn, or Volta
6. A developed Theme Progression (Main Theme, extended Metaphor, a Volta, closing Summary).

It can be, and has been argued, that changing one or more of the Elements does not change the essence of a Sonnet. If you can retain some, or most of the Elements, it is still a Sonnet. That is the premise of this book.

I can't wait to show them each to you.

CHAPTER 1. STANDARD FORMATS

These are the types of Sonnets that are the most common. The English and Italian Sonnets, should be familiar to most people who read poetry. All the Standard Formats have 14 Lines, and key off of one of those two forms. You'll find the English and Shakespearean Styles use the 3 Quatrain with Closing Couplet layout. While the Italian, Petrarchan, and Spenserian, key off the Octave and Sestet Motif. The American and Modern Sonnets vary the Rhyme Scheme, but maintain the typical English or Italian Format. Free Verse usually follows the English model. These 8 Styles form the bedrock of Sonnet experience, making up about 90% of all Sonnets written.

I am pleased to provide my examples of each here. But, my intent later will be to explore those regions not often visited, or even known by most. So let's explore these Standards first, then see what else might appear on our journey through THE SONNETS.

A. English Sonnets

When English Sonnets were introduced by Thomas Wyatt (1503–1542) in the early 16th century, his Sonnets and those of his contemporary, the Earl of Surrey, were chiefly translations from the Italian of Petrarch and the French of Ronsard and others. While Wyatt introduced the Sonnet into English, it was Surrey who developed the Rhyme Scheme.

A Traditional English Sonnet is a poem of 14 Lines. It follows a strict Rhyme Scheme. Purists declare that it is often about love. In the English Sonnet's 14 Lines, each contains ten Syllables and is written in Iambic Pentameter, in which a pattern of an Unstressed Syllable followed by a Stressed Syllable is repeated five times. The Rhyme Scheme in an English Sonnet is:

a-b-a-b, c-d-c-d, e-f-e-f, g-g.

The last two lines are a Rhyming Couplet.

In the following set of Sonnets, I provide four examples that demonstrate that a Sonnet can be about anything, not just love or romance. They range from a portrait of Fall colors, to Social Commentary on an abandoned building, to a current event, and finally to a flower.

In *Autumn's Golden Veil,* the Volta is subtle, but there, as it slips from description to feeling and appreciation.

Similarly with *Broken Door*, the focus slightly shifts from the tree to thoughts of a former family that lived there.

In *California Fires*, I used a unique technique by actually having three Voltas. There is one in the last line of each Stanza. While not common, it is and acceptable variation. It gives the Sonnet the feel of a Haiku.

In *PPF- Pretty Pink Flowers*, I dressed up this Ode to a flower a bit by adding a touch of Elizabethan English, making the poem sound more Shakespearean. You will find that just adding such trappings doesn't really make it a true Shakespearean Sonnet. That will come clear in the next chapter. Note here the Volta changes from delicate beauty to elegant strength.

So, here they are. I hope you like them.

Sonnet 1: Autumn's Golden Veil

What golden droplets fall from Autumn's veil
To drape in brilliant color 'cross this trail
For shoes to shuffle slowly through them all
A pleasure that's unique to only Fall

These blended hues provide a gorgeous sight
When orange and yellow tinges first ignite
To make the yards and neighborhoods invite
The passersby to marvel with delight

Then Oh, how very wonderful it feels
To have the leaflets crunch beneath our heels
To blow in swirling whirlpools in the breeze
As colors clothe those staying in the trees

Let me walk within this glowing splendor
That only finest artists ever tender.

Sonnet 2: Broken Door

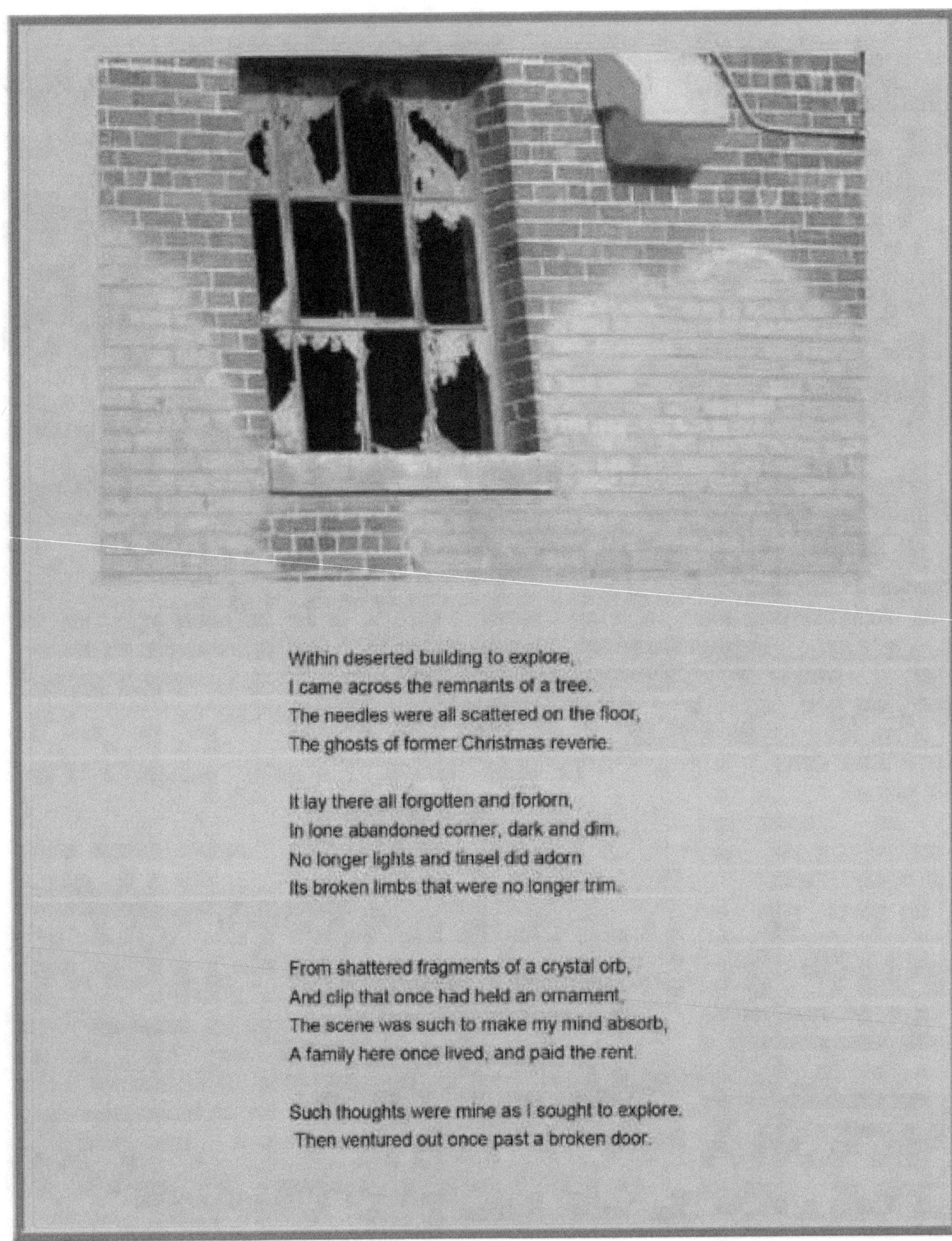

Within deserted building to explore,
I came across the remnants of a tree.
The needles were all scattered on the floor,
The ghosts of former Christmas reverie.

It lay there all forgotten and forlorn,
In lone abandoned corner, dark and dim.
No longer lights and tinsel did adorn
Its broken limbs that were no longer trim.

From shattered fragments of a crystal orb,
And clip that once had held an ornament,
The scene was such to make my mind absorb,
A family here once lived, and paid the rent.

Such thoughts were mine as I sought to explore.
Then ventured out once past a broken door.

Sonnet 3: California Fires

There's smoky tendrils carried on the wind,
From fires within the California hills.
As their expensive homes are quickly thinned,
No one laments the wildlife that it kills.

Each year it seems the story is the same,
The flames consume vast stretches of the state.
Officials wonder where to place the blame,
As owners ponder property's next fate.

Whole neighborhoods are sadly ruined by fire,
With families bereft of all they own,
Their shattered dreams consumed in burning pyre,
The victims face their tragedy alone.

Takes years before the scenery's replaced,
And lives releaved of burdens that they faced.

Sonnet 4: PPF - Pretty Pink Flower

Oh, lift thy pretty petals to bright sky,
to bathe in warmth provided by yon sun.
Pray, grace this place, where pastel pinks apply
a hue to soothe sick soul of anyone.

Thy charm is being oh so delicate,
A nymph among much larger local plants
with stem so thin, its lift is elegant.
Thy leaves are merely wisps that heaven grants

And yet, you yield commanding silhouette
that holds its own within this wild bouquet.
I ponder now, thy unknown sobriquet,
whilst viewing hence this petulant display.

Although I know not pedigree you hold,
I linger at thy countenance so bold.

B. Shakespearean Sonnets.

This Form is often named after Shakespeare, not because he was the first to write in this Form but because he became its most famous practitioner. Early Sonnets were all essentially inspired by the Petrarchan tradition, and generally treat of the poet's love for some woman. That is, until the exception of Shakespeare's sequence of 154 sonnets, where he wrote on a broad spectrum of Topics. He even included the Sonnet within his plays. The Prologue to Romeo and Juliet is also a Sonnet, as is Romeo and Juliet's first exchange in Act One, Scene Five, lines 104–117, beginning with "If I profane with my unworthiest hand" and ending with "Then move not while my prayer's effect I take." The Epilogue to *Henry V* is also in the Form of a sonnet.

A Shakespearean Sonnet is written according to the following rules:

1. The Sonnet consists of 14 Lines. The Sonnet must have three (3) Quatrains and one (1) Closing Couplet.
2. The Sonnet must be written in strict iambic Pentameter.
3. The Sonnet must follow a specific Rhyme Scheme as follows: First Quatrain: abab; Second Quatrain: cdcd; Third Quatrain: efef; and Closing Couplet: gg. Thus, this Rhyme Pattern requires seven different Rhymes.
4. The development of a Shakespearean Sonnet requires attention to detail. The Sonnet must be developed in the following Thematic Format:

...... First Quatrain: The Main Theme and main Metaphor are introduced in this Quatrain.

...... Second Quatrain: The Theme and Metaphor extended or complicated; often, some imaginative example is given.

...... Third Quatrain: Peripeteia, or Volta (a twist or conflict), often introduced by a "but" (very often leading off the ninth Line).

.......Couplet: Summarizes the Sonnet and leaves the reader with a new, concluding image and feeling, often times, one that leaves the reader pondering the Sonnet's meaning.

To distinguish it from a Standard English Sonnet, a touch of Elizabethan English adds to its feel.

Only three of Shakespeare's 154 sonnets do not conform to this Structure: Sonnet 99, which has 15 lines; Sonnet 126, which has 12 lines; and Sonnet 145, which is written in iambic Tetrameter. I have written 5 examples here.

The first is *Bewildering Change* about a love turned sour.

The second, *Blue Bachelor Buttons*, is about true love and separation by war. A Romance.

The third, *Floral Fire*, brings to life the vibrant color of Fall. But winter awaits.

The fourth, *Pirates Plight*, is an adventurous story poem about a condemned Pirate, and lady who frees him. But the scallywag is true to form, and runs off after a night of passion. I added an Envoi as a closing farewell, just for fun.

Finally, Rift of War, provides a commentary on War, good and bad. It uses Feminine iambic Pentameter.

Sonnet 5: Bewildering Change

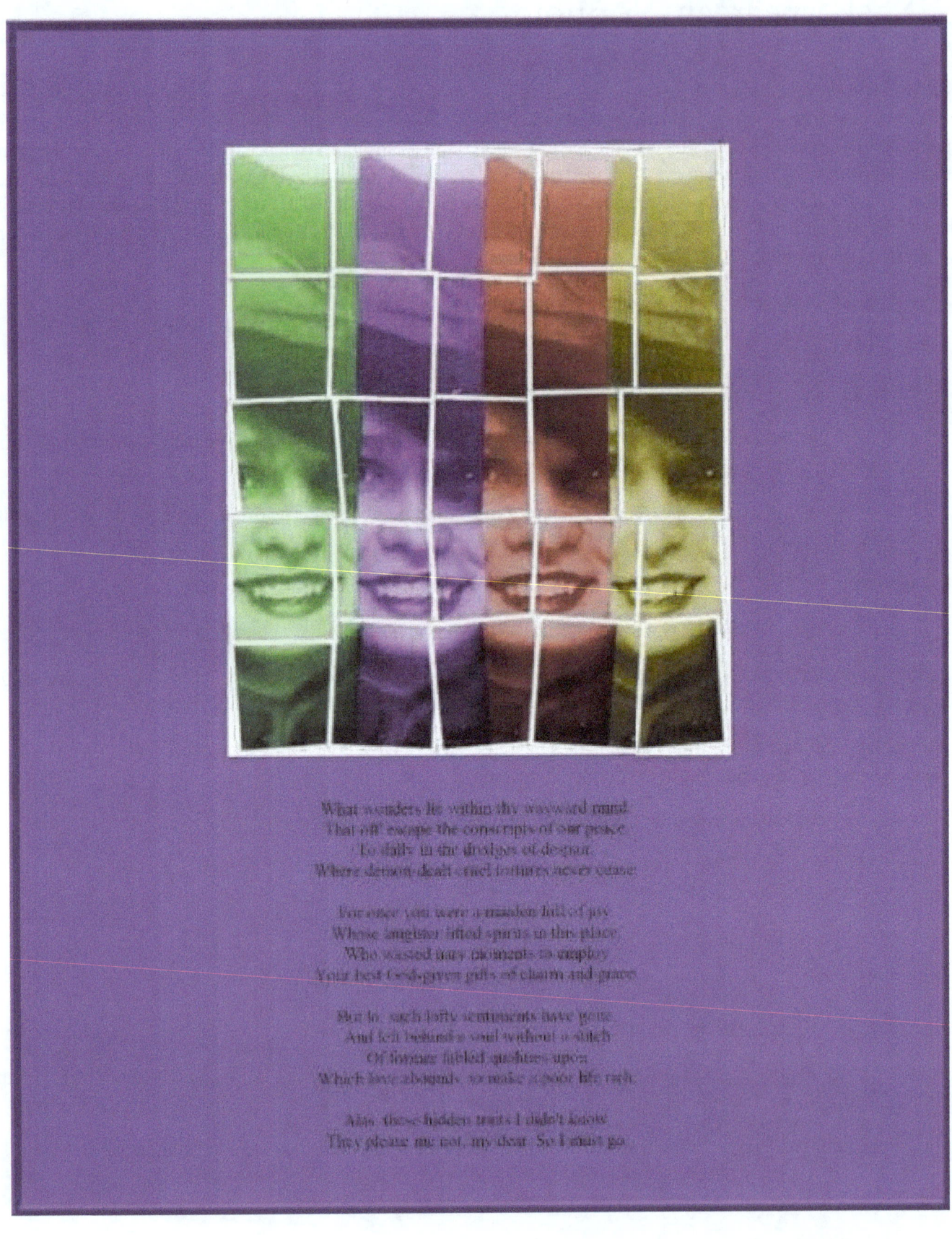

What wonders lie within thy wayward mind,
That oft escape the conscripts of our peace
To dally in the dredges of despair,
Where demon death's cruel tortures never cease.

For once you were a maiden full of joy,
Whose laughter lifted spirits in this place,
Who wasted nary moments to employ
Your best God-given gifts of charm and grace.

But lo, such lofty sentiments have gone,
And left besides a soul without a stitch
Of innate fabled qualities upon
Which love abounds, to make a poor life rich.

Alas, these hidden traits I didn't know,
They please me not, my dear. So I must go.

Sonnet 6: Blue Bachelor Buttons

Our fairest maid was so in love with him,
Her shining knight, who off to battle rode.
He carried her bright ribbons on his trim,
They traveled close to him where ere he strode.

When Kingly battles took him 'cross the sea,
Would she still wait forever and a day?
He picked Blue Bachelor Buttons, just to see,
How quick the deep blue color'd fade away.

And when each day he'd find the shade stayed true.
He'd fight with heart to make the journey end,
And one day as he found the fighting through,
He hastened home to find true love ascend.

He found Blue Bachelor Buttons had been right
She melted in his arms at her first sight.

Sonnet 7: Floral Fire

Beneath thy veil of Summer's green attire,
Adorning trees with leaves of red and gold,
'Tis Autumn's bursting glimpse of floral fire,
Magnificent displays to oft' behold!

Whence sunlight spreads its rays into its boughs,
Thy hidden colors have become revealed.
What splendor! Causing passions to arouse
Where'er they once were ever well concealed.

But oh, so short thy season of the leaves,
When soon thy remnants rustle in the breeze,
As Mother Nature grants nought one reprieve
But drops in pastel piles 'neath naked trees.

For Lo, we know yon season hath an end,
As Winter lurks just 'round the barren bend.

Sonnet 8: Pirates Plight

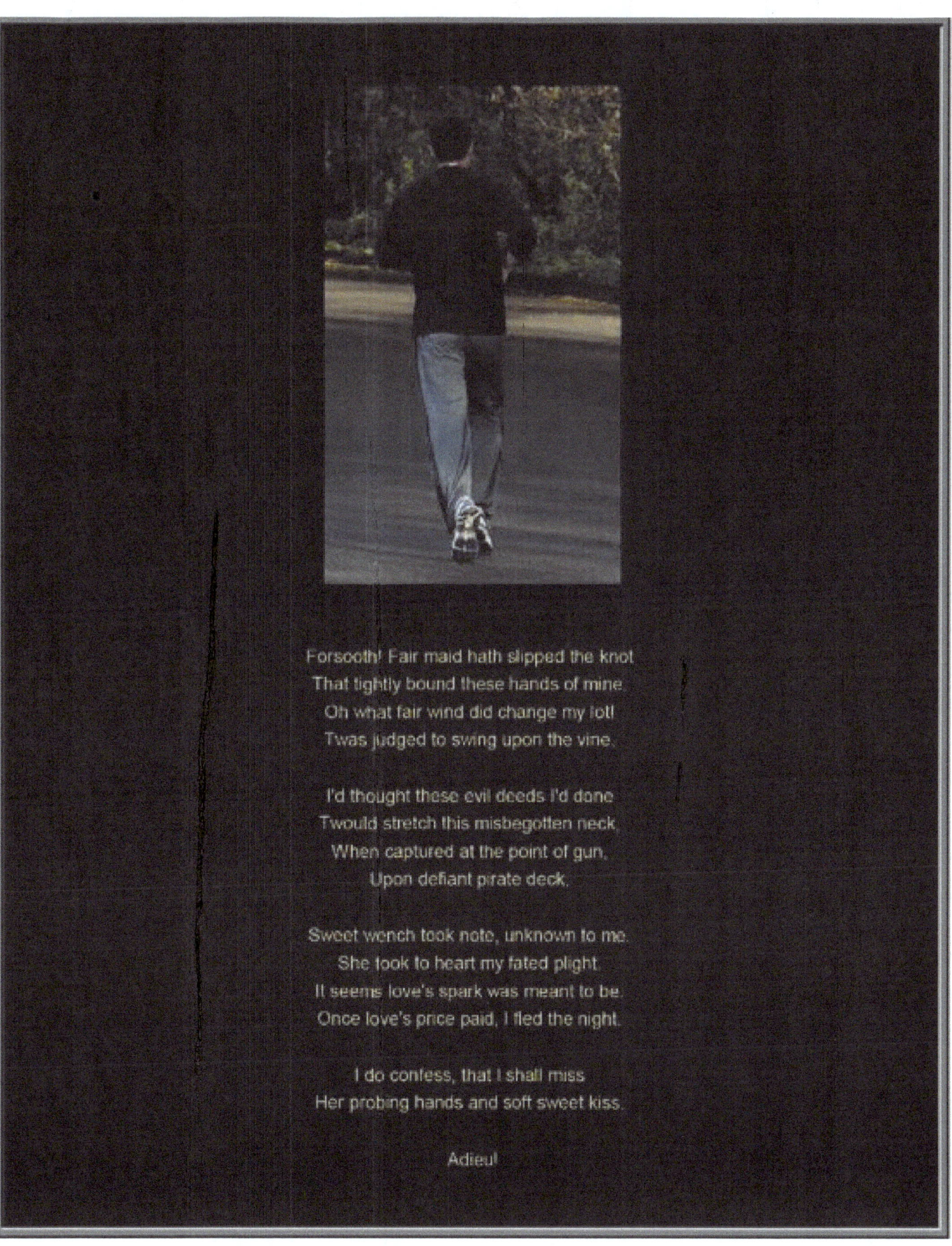

Forsooth! Fair maid hath slipped the knot
That tightly bound these hands of mine.
Oh what fair wind did change my lot!
Twas judged to swing upon the vine.

I'd thought these evil deeds I'd done
Twould stretch this misbegotten neck,
When captured at the point of gun,
Upon defiant pirate deck.

Sweet wench took note, unknown to me.
She took to heart my fated plight.
It seems love's spark was meant to be.
Once love's price paid, I fled the night.

I do confess, that I shall miss
Her probing hands and soft sweet kiss.

Adieu!

Sonnet 9: Rift of War

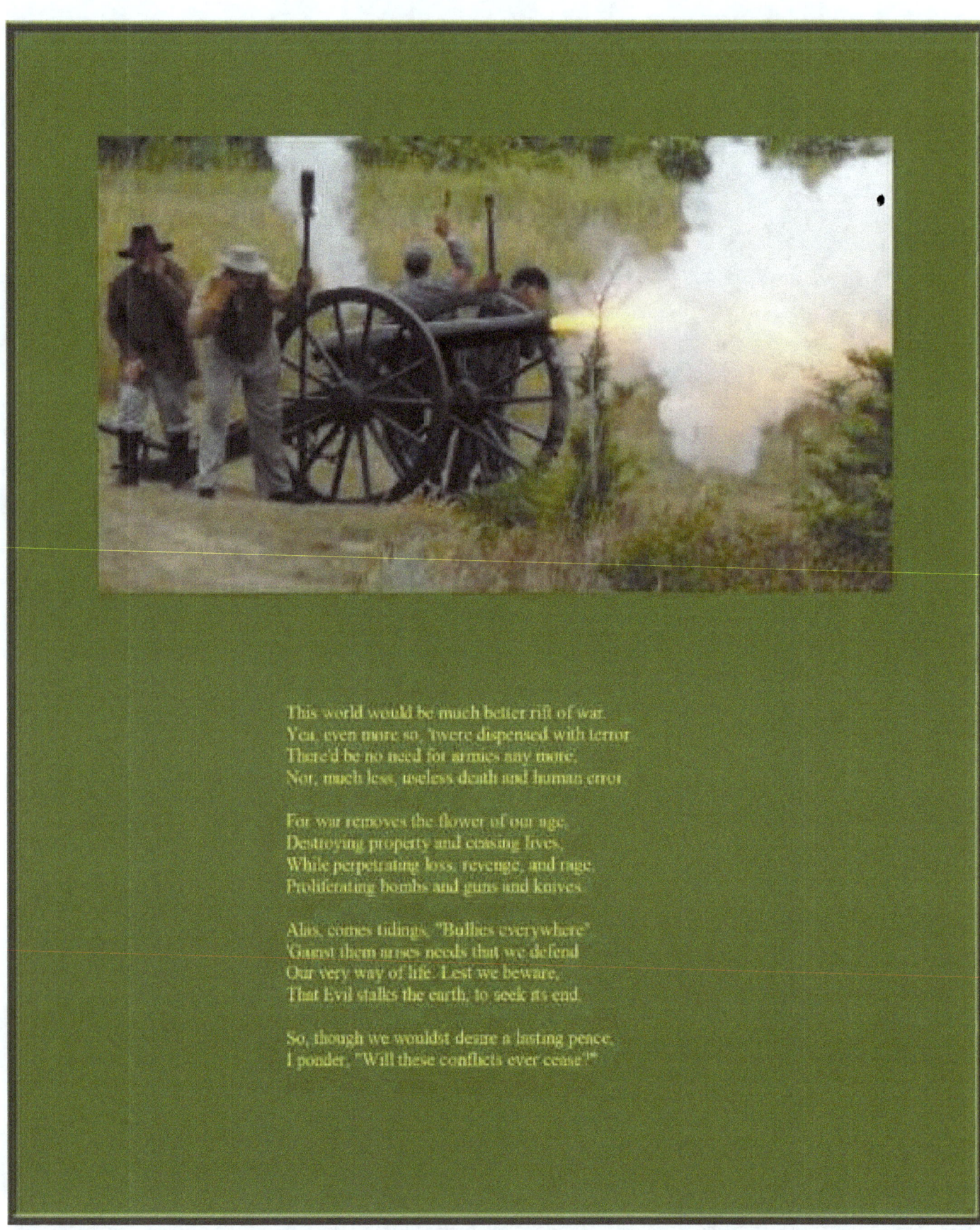

This world would be much better rift of war,
Yea, even more so, 'twere dispensed with terror.
There'd be no need for armies any more,
Nor, much less, useless death and human error.

For war removes the flower of our age,
Destroying property and ceasing lives,
While perpetrating loss, revenge, and rage,
Proliferating bombs and guns and knives.

Alas, comes tidings, "Bullies everywhere"
'Gainst them arises needs that we defend
Our very way of life. Lest we beware,
That Evil stalks the earth, to seek its end.

So, though we wouldst desire a lasting peace,
I ponder, "Will these conflicts ever cease?"

C. Italian Sonnets

The Italian Sonnet originated in Italy; Giacomo da Lentini is credited with its invention. The term *Sonnet* is derived from the Italian word *Sonetto* (from Old Provençal *Sonet* a little poem). .

An Italian Sonnet is composed of an Octave, Rhyming abbaabba, and a Sestet, Rhyming cdecde or cdcdcd, or in some Variant Pattern, but with **no** Closing Couplet.

The Italian Sonnet is divided into two sections by two different groups of Rhyming Sounds. The first 8 lines is called the Octave and rhymes:

a b b a a b b a (note the Enveloping Rhymes, if broken into Quatrains would be abba abba)

The remaining 6 Lines are called the Sestet and can have either two or three Rhyming Sounds, arranged in a variety of ways:

c d c d c d
c d d c d c
c d e c d e
c d e c e d
c d c e d c

The one thing that is to be avoided in the Sestet is ending with a rhyming Couplet (dd or ee), as this was never permitted in Italy, and Petrarch himself (supposedly) never used a Couplet Ending; in actual practice, Sestets are sometimes ended with Couplets (Sidney's "Sonnet LXXI is an example of such a terminal Couplet in an Italian Sonnet). So if it is, the Form is Italian, but not Petrarchan.

Thus, the poem is divided into two sections by two differing Rhyme Groups. In accordance with the principle, a change from one Rhyme Group to another signifies a change in subject matter. This change occurs at the beginning of Line 9 (L9) here, and is called the Volta, or "Turn"; the Turn is an Essential Element of most Sonnet Forms. At the Volta the second idea or conflict is introduced.

I have provided five examples here.

The first is *Blest Beauty*, and Ode to beauty that transitions from an Ode to a flower to a Romance. The Sestet is cdccdc.

In the second, *Investing*, I turn to the Stock Market, of all things. I separated the Octave to two Quatrains and demarked the Sestet in a separate Stanza. Sestet is cdecde. See if you can find the In-line Rhymes.

The third one, *Outside Our Bedroom Window*, separates the Octave and Sestet. It has a picture of my house too. A touch of Romance ensues. How best to enjoy a winter's day? Sestet is cddcdc.

The fourth, *These Bees,* provides no Stanzas. a description of pollination and flower appreciation turns to a typical daisy dally. Note the use of Feminine Rhyme. Sestet is cdecde.

The final Sonnet, *This Golden Hour*, has atypical Meter. I intentionally deviated from iambic and went with Anapestic Meter. So note the difference in the Rhythm. It describes a photographer's ideal, and demonstrates it with a photo. Sestet is cdccdc.

Sonnet 10: Blest Beauty

As I perceive blest beauty of the rose,
Its aura flows from many colored hues.
Oft' seen adorned in reds and pinks and blues,
There's even peach, whose center nearly glows.
Delight abounds where e'er one finds it grows.
You can't go wrong whichever bloom you choose.
Then wiff a waft, as from it fragrance ooze
To fill the air and titillate the nose.
But, even with these formidable things,
Amazing assets set second-to-none:
The smells, the hues, the beauty that it brings,
Yet there's another charming chime that rings
Adoring notes, the best under the sun.
It's precious you, my Dear, whom my heart sings.

Sonnet 11: Investing

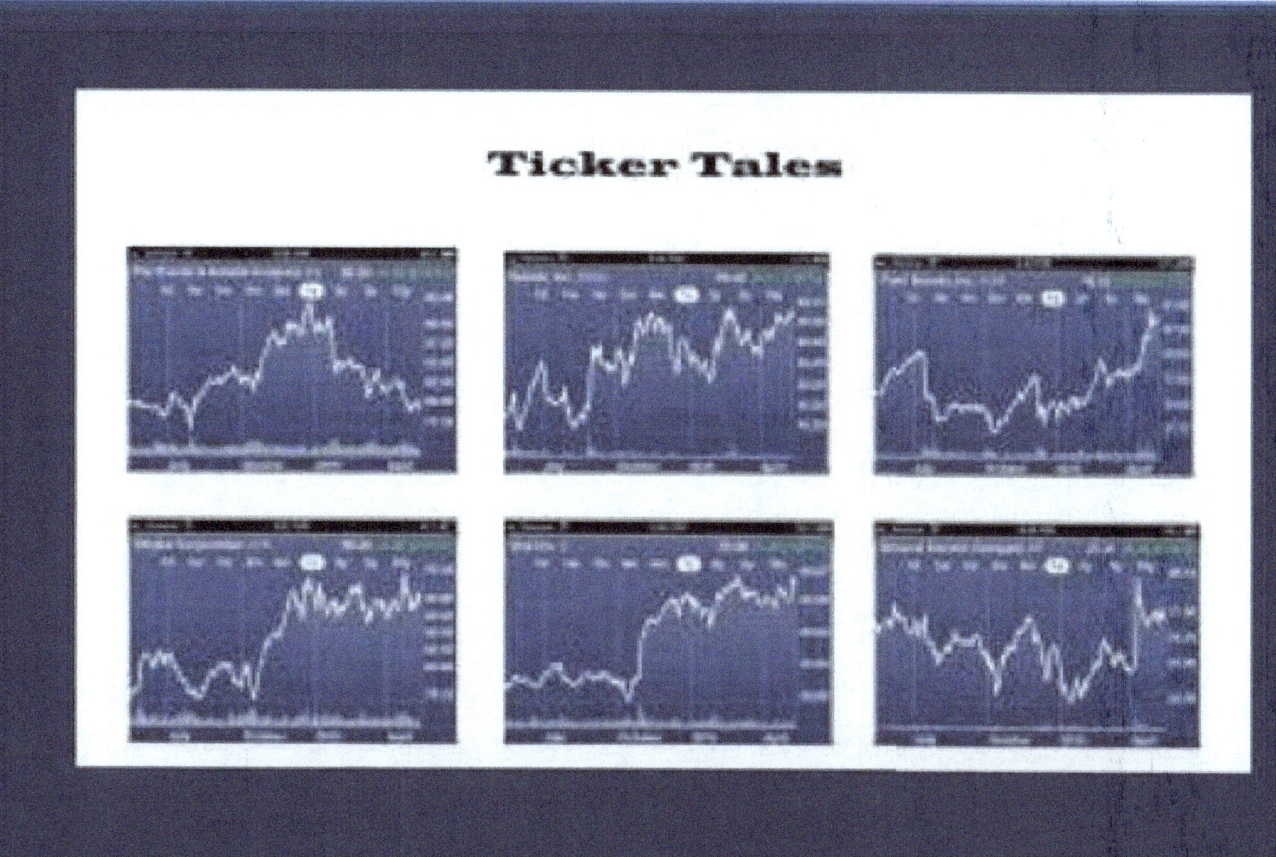

The ticker ticks its ups and downs,
Enchanted by the Market's call.
Investor's fortunes rise and fall
Upon the whims of kings and clowns.

They often wear misfortune's frowns
When all their dreams fall off the Wall,
And find it isn't good for all
When Lady Luck makes daily rounds.

But, if you dabble wisely when
You need a place for funds to grow,
Your fortunes may rise up again
To please, more than you've ever been,
When guided by those men who know
Stock Market's secret stratagem.

Sonnet 12: Outside Our Bedroom Window

We are so warm and cozy in our bed.
We love to snuggle 'neath the comforter,
where I can share my body warmth with her,
as sweet endearments wander through my head.
Outside I see the snowflakes swiftly spread.
The window shows a white and nasty blur,
Where only silent snowdrifts dare to stir.
I see a lovely languid day ahead.

Although the air outside contains a chill,
and our thermometers are far below
that zero mark, where winters often go.
It's warm beneath our cozy goose-down fill,
and temp'ratures are rising to a glow,
regardless what's beyond our window sill.

Sonnet 13: These Bees

Two bees that flutter on white flower's face
Are drawn as sights and smells intoxicate,
Assisting bloom's attempt to pollinate
On sticky grains their tiny legs encase
That help to transfer true genetic trace,
Allowing flowered plants to propagate.
These bees are born, in part, to instigate
A complex process that is commonplace.
But oh, what beauty lies in fabled flower!
Such petals are adorned in purest white,
The center blessed with brightest yellow spot.
Romantics ask if love's true "here and now" were
But answered with a petal's picking plight,
Declaring "Does she love me, love me not?"

Sonnet 14: This Golden Hour

The Golden hour is a magical time,
It comes at dusk, near the end of the day,
Where shadows all grow longer as they play
In mystical moments, so sweet, sublime,
As rays of sunshine softly reach decline,
They set a golden glow upon the bay.
The golden hour, as photographers say,
Is just the perfect time, when light is prime.

So then, I sought out this magical place,
To see myself whether those tales were true,
And searched about for such a special space
Where Midas' touch had left his golden trace.
Became impressed, as my amazement grew
From glorious sight in golden embrace.

D. Petrarchan Sonnets.

Petrarch developed the Italian Sonnet pattern, which is known to this day as the Petrarchan Sonnet, a true Subset of the Italian Sonnet. Francesco Petrarca (Petrarch in English; July 20, 1304 -July 19, 1374) was a scholar and poet in Renaissance Italy. Petrarch's Sonnets were admired and imitated throughout Europe during the Renaissance and became a model for lyrical poetry. He is also known for being the first to develop the concept of the "Dark Ages". Because of the Structure of Italian, the Rhyme Scheme of the Petrarchan Sonnet is more easily fulfilled in that language than in English. The original Italian Sonnet Form divides the poem's 14 Lines into two parts, the first part being an Octave and the second being a Sestet. The Rhyme Scheme for the Octave is typically:

a b b a a b b a.

The Sestet is more flexible:

c d d c e e and c d c d e e are most used. See Italian Sonnets for other Variations.

The entire poem is written in iambic Pentameter.

The Octave and Sestet have special functions in a Petrarchan Sonnet. The Octave's purpose is to introduce a problem, express a desire, reflect on reality, or otherwise present a situation that causes doubt or conflict within the speaker. It usually does this by introducing the problem within its first Quatrain (unified four-line section) and developing it in the second. The beginning of the Sestet is known as the Volta, and it introduces a pronounced change in tone in the Sonnet; the change in Rhyme Scheme marks the Turn. The Sestet's purpose as a whole is to make a comment on the problem or to apply a solution to it. The pair are separate but usually used to reinforce a unified argument - they are often compared to two strands of thought organically converging into one argument.

So, what distinguishes a Petrarchan Sonnet from just an Italian Sonnet? Nothing really. In fact most people use the terms interchangeably. I think that in the Petrarchan, the Turn may be more pronounced. Furthermore, a Sestet ending with a Rhyming Couplet is Itallian, but never Petrarchan.

To that end, I provided two examples. The first, *Heaven and Hell*, provides a clearly pronounced Volta. I even used color to make it more so. It also features a picture of my grandson Isaac.

The second poem, *Reflections on the Water*, is not Petrarchan, as the Sestet is cddcee (the forbidden Rhyming Couplet). I provided it to show the distinction between Petrarchan and just an Italian Sonnet. Although, it makes a fine statement about the environment.

Sonnet 15: Heaven and Hell

On high thy angels sing songs to their Lord
In pure white garb, radiantly attired,
Bright presence of the King of Kings inspired
To praise Him in His glory, Christ adored,
By they who hath attained their just reward
In all the heavenly hosts, He be admired,
A model of pure righteousness desired
By souls who want to seek a true accord.
Alas, there are those who cannot relate.
Their stone cold hearts are driven to rebel;
Consuming passion oft seals bitter fate
They can't control their hungers very well
And so, they turneth backs on Heaven's gate.
To soon become the denizens of hell.

Sonnet 16: Reflections on the Water

On water, fine reflections reign supreme,
With mirrored images that float in sight,
Of colors - purple, green, with red and white.
This tableau that sits simply so serene
Beside a building looking most pristine,
Through shining glass-clad windows, such delight
That fills the mind with thoughts of fancy flight,
A vision placed as if it were a dream.

Yet, were the water to be swiftly drained,
Too soon would these reflections disappear.
Might quickly kill the plants and mar our cheer.
The elegance of art would be profaned.
So, let us pray those waters stay in place,
This circumstance must never be the case.

E. Spenserian Sonnets

The Spenserian Sonnet was named for Edmund Spenser 1552-1599, a 16th century English Poet. It is a third Major Type of Sonnet, (along with the Shakespearean and Petrarchan) that creates a Subset to the basic English and Italian Sonnets. It has the same Structure as the English Sonnet, but it employs a uniquely different Interlocking Rhyme Scheme of:

abab, bcbc, cdcd, ee,

which links the Couplets within the three Quatrains together. Note how the "b" Rhyme carries into the second Stanza, and the "c" Rhyme bridges into the third. This reduces the number of rhymes from the typical 7, to 5, and puts less pressure on the final Couplet at the end to resolve the argument. The three Quatrains develop separate ideas, but they are closely related to each other. The Couplet then simply provides a different idea or Closing Commentary.

The Spenserian Sonnet is written in iambic Pentameter, like the other two major Sonnet forms.

It is interesting to note here that Shakespeare and Petrarca gave their names to Sonnet forms due to their sheer volume and celebrity. Here Spenser, also used a consistent Deviation from Traditional Rhyme Meter to gain celebrity. This foreshadows the creativity of the Formats that I will highlight in the upcoming pages. He shows that Elements of the Form can be changed.

Here I provide three examples. I structure them in three different ways to exhibit how simple adjustments to the Stanzaic Structure impacts the result.

In the first poem, *Bridge Knowledge*, I write about how Man's creative skill has an impact on the environment, likely driven by early natural phenomenon. The separation of the Closing Couplet highlights the commentary. Lots of Alliteration.

The second poem, *Distracted by Beauty*, demarcates the Quatrains separately, so the Rhyme Scheme is more easily seen. It is clearer to see the distinct concepts present in each Stanza – beauty, distraction, realization, prior commitment. Just a touch of humor here.

The third and final example, *Stony Gaze*, is shown in the most Typical way a Spenserian Sonnet is written, with no Stanzas, but the Couplet indented. I used an inanimate stone formation to take on foreboding aspects.

Sonnet 17: Bridge Knowledge

I wonder at wide water's engineers,
With skillful knowledge of long span techniques,
That settle steel or stone on several piers
Creating mighty structures, quite unique,
That bridge across a river or a creek.
They oft' display the useful Roman arch.
Their methods bear a measure of mystique,
As graceful curving columns stately march
Across the current meant to overarch.
Where do these geniuses obtain such skills?
They seem to have the wisdom Titans parch,
To keep mankind conjoined between two hills.

It likely was a fallen tree we owe
That bridged the gap above first water flow.

Sonnet 18: Distracted by Beauty

The prettiest flowers I've ever seen,
have caught my eye, with multi-colored hue.
They laid upon a luscious bed of green,
with hearts of white, but crowned in royal blue.

To me, they seemed so gloriously new.
The blooms all teamed, to overflow the pot.
Such beauties! Likes of these are very few.
Their photograph was taken on the spot.

But, taken by their charms, almost forgot,
I had to carry on my purposed walk.
Although I want to stay transfixed, a lot,
my promise was to meet her at the dock.

So I must set this dalliance aside,
for I committed first to meet my bride.

Sonnet 19: Stony Gaze

An angry spirit lingers in the rock
Imprisoned there since long forgotten time
To some it seems a simple sandstone block
That's coated with some centuries of grime.
A guardian where people often climb,
Although the effort's difficult and steep,
Because the views up there are so sublime.
You share them with the likes of Bighorn Sheep.
Beware! As there are secrets those stones keep,
You're being watched by wizard's evil eye,
With stare whose glare may make your neck skin creep
It's said that spirit has caused some to die.
    So, if you don't respect that sacred ground,
    It may be you'll no longer be around.

F. American Sonnets

The American Sonnet brings European artistic tradition to New World innovation and expansiveness. The Themes and Rhyme Schemes, as well as the history become something new, fresh, and characteristically American. The most familiar American Sonneteers are: Emily Dickinson, Longfellow, Tuckerman, Frost, Wylie, and Millay. These are perhaps our Petrarchs and Shakespeares.

The American Sonnet is a derivation of the English Sonnet. It takes the Typical 14 Line Configuration with three Quatrains and a Closing Couplet. The difference, much like the Spenserian, is in the Rhyme Scheme. Here, instead of using the Alternating Rhyme of abab cdcd efef in the Quatrains, it uses Coupled Rhyme of aabb ccdd eeff. Besides that, an American Sonnet may break with traditional iambic Pentameter, going with other Meters, such as: Hexameter, or Tetrameter.

I have written three examples here. They range from a Commentary on the Crusades, to a Tribute to a famous comedian, and finally to an Ekphrastic Vision of a morning on Lake Superior.

The first is *Lethal Legacy*. It is written in iambic Hexameter. The Commentary bridges the Crusade history to today's ongoing terrorism.

What is more American than writing a Tribute to a TV personality? In the second Sonnet, *To Robin*, I create just such a poem about Robin Williams, written in iambic Tetrameter.

The third poem, *Silver Scene*, was inspired by a photograph I took one fine morning on Lake Superior near Duluth, Mn. The lake shimmered like silver stardust, as I captured a fishing boat in silhouette.

Sonnet 20: Lethal Legacy

Those beating hearts once driven, to the pounding drums,
With flags unfurled and snapping, to the battle hum.
No-man's land between them, two armies that have come
To prove in battle, whose God is the chosen one.

Pope Urban set in motion, with words -"It's God's Will",
Unleashed crusades for Holy Land, loosing bloody spill.
He granted an indulgence to forgive all sin,
To take Jerusalem back, greatest prize to win.

And so we find two armies, here on holy ground,
Where reaper's grim destruction will too soon abound.
With endless seeds of hatred sown on blood-soaked soil
Now carried over eons, fueled by faith and oil.

And so the lines stand ready, it's so sad to say,
That hatred planted then, is still in play today.

Sonnet 21: To Robin Williams

Oh, Robin Williams, Rest in Peace
From Inner turmoil, no surcease
Such deep depression, suicide
Has brought you to the darker side

We won't forget your Mork from Ork
Or all your brilliant other work
There's never been a sharper mind
To craft a quip, act unconfined

We'll miss your wit, we'll miss your style
It's hard for us to reconcile
Your sudden end, our funny friend
Whose spirit now from Earth ascends

When you greet God, I hope you do,
He'll laugh with you -- Nanoo Nanoo!

Sonnet 22: Silver Scene

The sunlight on the water shines,
Creating bright wave top designs,
That flash and dance before my eyes,
To decorate the morning skies.

It sets this scenic water show,
As lake-borne traffic come and go,
That launches as the sun comes up,
A scene shared with my coffee cup.

I sit on shore and watch it all,
With splashing waves and seagull calls.
A breakfast in the lakeside breeze,
With view as pretty as you please.

Delight imbues this silver scene
With memories so seldom seen.

G. Modern Sonnets

Modern Sonnets reflect a rebel aspect of poetry that breaks with any convention as desired. No Volta, any or variable Meter, variable Line Lengths, odd or unusual Syllable Counts, Mixed Meter, macabre Subjects, and family photographs, may all be fair game in the Modern Sonnet. . They don't necessarily follow the same rules as the more Traditional Sonnets. While there were once Strict Rules about how many Lines could be in a Sonnet, how many Syllables had to be in every line, and the acceptable Rhyme Scheme that a Sonnet had to follow, the writers of Modern Sonnets have much more freedom when it comes to Structure and Rhyme. It can be difficult to distinguish different types of Modern Sonnets because the purpose of the modern poetry writers who write these types of poems is often to break the rules. In fact, Modern Sonnets have a lot in common with Free Form, also known as Free Verse, poetry. However, while similar to Free Form poetry in many ways, Modern Sonnets tend to have a bit more Structure and will have certain Characteristics that will classify it as a Sonnet.

So I have provided six examples here to give you a flavor of the Genre.

The first poem, *Firebird*, utilizes a very simple Rhyme Type that only Rhymes two lines of a Quatrain instead of four, Skipping Rhyme (abcb). This would be anathema to the classical poets, but is very common in Modern Sonnets. To accommodate an iambic Meter, requires one to pronounce the Word "fire" as two syllables (**FI**-er), which can be dialectic. Note here also, that I used a tree stump to provide an image of a bird and smoke, when it is actually an inanimate object. Look closely, you'll see the bird's wing.

The second poem, *Frustration at Itasca*, uses Variable Line Lengths and Variable Meter to tell a true story.

I threw in some A typical Capitalization too. While unconventional, I think it works.

The third one, *Peeps and Company*, throws iambic Meter out the window, and uses a short 7 Syllable Motif. There is no Volta either.

The fourth, *Resolutions*, is an example of Mixed Meter, alternating between iambic and Trochee. I dressed it up with Elizabethan dialect. A Commentary on New Year's resolutions is the theme.

In the fifth, *The Eyes on Me*, I used an ice wall to imagine faces staring out. The long iambic Heptameter allows for creative use of In-line Rhyming on a Macabre Theme.

I close the last one, Poem 6 of this group, *True Love*, with a Romance, which could easily be classified as Shakespearean, except for the Coupled Rhyme Scheme, and use of a family photograph (of me and my wife dating in our twenties). Yes, I was a hippie in the 1960s. The poem has a nice iambic Pentameter, and Elizabethan sway.

Sonnet 23: Firebird

Oh Firebird of myth and ash,
Your purpled plumes rise from the flames
And like the heat returning sun,
Renewal forms your mythic claims.

Oh Phoenix formed from fire's force,
Your legend burns across the sky,
In trails of smoke and glowing arch,
On toasted wings that make sparks fly.

Oh Benu glyph of ancient myth,
In resurrection of the soul,
Set free the purgatory lost
Their spirit cleanse to make them whole.

And once their essence has renewed
Feed them with your spiritual food.

Sonnet 24: Frustration at Itasca

Up North we go, to the legendary Land of Snow
Where Eagles soar high, and the Owls hoot after dark,
Where the Lakes are Blue, and the cold rivers flow,
Sits the famous Itasca. It's a Beautiful, Bountiful State Park.

Entered the Gate anxious to see the mighty river's source.
The East Entryway was miles away: Winding, Narrow, and Long.
Anxious to see the mighty Mississippi, encountered delay, Of Course!
Newlywed pair, Nose in the Air, is plodding slowly along.

Vacation, you know! Family in tow. Needing to make Time.
Labor Day crowd, Laughing and Loud, filled the Park today.
Groan, Gripe, Glower, 3 Mile Hour, is a thoughtless Crime
A Twenty car row, Nowhere to go, Hours frittered away.

Horse drawn Carriage makes me Disparage its plodding pulling works.
The Oblivious Two, Terrible Traffic Queue, really are just Jerks.

Sonnet 25: PEEPS and Company

If they are craving candy,
Fam'lies love to visit PEEPS.
Sweet choices are all dandy,
Tempting all to purchase heaps.

Mike and Ike are so chewy,
Hot Tamales make you roar,
And others that are gooey,
Found in this favorite store.

Bring the kiddies in to see
What sweet goodies they might like.
Choices pondered happily
Smiles on faces of each tyke.

Friendly staff there always keeps
Pleasant place at pop'lar PEEPS.

Sonnet 26: Resolutions

'Tis breaking dawn of coming year
Wouldst strive to make the future clear,
Consulting through a crystal ball,
Or Gypsy fortune telling all.

Perchance magical solutions
Dost aid setting resolutions.
Prithee, that faire intentions caught,
Insures these plans shant go for naught.

Alas, past history has cast
A shadow 'pon my will to last.
Hark, take tidings with great sorrow.
All's been broken by the morrow.

Still, like unto a ruined romance,
I'll vie to take another chance.

Sonnet 27: The Eyes on Me

These chilly canyons strange companions hide, to my surprise.
I hear the cackle hidden in the crackle of the ice.
And I despise that feel of eyes my senses realize.
The ghosts are there, must be somewhere, I felt it once or twice.

Behind each boulder, eyes upon my shoulder, are so vague.
But will he show, this man of snow, who's hidden in the wall?
It seems he blends where ice suspends from every little crag.
What I can't see, I want to flee, I don't like this at all!

Oh! There he is, that mug of his, I see him hiding there.
His hollow eyes can't be disguised, so large they point him out.
That toothless mouth was facing south, I really didn't care
To see him there, up in the air, just hanging all about.

I see now other ghosts among those frozen posts, but you,
Whose voice annoys with creepy noise, continue showing through.

Sonnet 28: True Love

'Tis true love's smitten touch which I espound,
Elusive, yet a treasure when it's found.
For I put forth, no finer beauty lies,
Than here within thy shining love-filled eyes.

Thy soul resides within those glist'ning jewels.
I propose that nay-sayers are fools.
For silent succor deep within me cries,
"Without true love thy soul most surely dies!"

But verily, with grace I find it here.
The sense of it anon, so deep, so dear,
It leaves me breathless, lost in total bliss.
I rush ahead to seal it with a kiss.

Oh time! I lock away this moment dear,
Prithee, this dream remains forever clear.

H. Blank Verse Sonnet

We can't leave out the final Sonnet Type under the category of Standard Formats. Any self-respecting poet knows about Blank Verse.

A Blank Verse poem is written without Rhymes. It does have a specific set Metrical Pattern of iambic Pentameter. But it is a flexible Form that is often used in narrative and dramatic poetry. It was popularized by William Shakespeare. This Format can also take the Form of a Sonnet (only Unrhymed), having 3 Quatrains with a Closing Couplet, totaling 14 Lines. If written well, one almost doesn't notice the lack of Rhyme, but due to that, more attention needs to be made to other Poetic Techniques, such as Imagery, Alliteration, Onomatopoeia, and Metaphor. See if you can detect some.

I've put forth two examples in this section.

The first is *Night's Revelations*. While there are no End-rhymes, I did include some In-line Rhymes, which the purists will say is a no-no.

The second poem is *Oh Voyageur*. I've written this from personal experiences of traversing Minnesota's Boundary Waters Canoe Area (BWCA) when I was younger. OH yeah, that is a picture of me back then too, on the portage trail.

So, with these last two. I've completed an overview of those Sonnet Types that most poetry lovers (and anyone interested in Sonnets specifically) should be, or become, familiar with – The Standard Formats (English, Shakespearean, Italian, Petrarchan, Spenserian, American, Modern, and Blank Verse).

Sonnet 29: Night's Revelations

So often I'll go walking in the dark,
To listen to the rhythms of the night,
Without the blind distractions of the day,
The only light produced by moon and stars.

The moon will cast its glow upon the path,
And pull the waves that crash upon the shore.
I watch the twinkling sky put on a show
And hear the breeze blow gently in the trees.

For then, is when I feel it once again,
The pulse of something vital that's in me.
I sense the vastness of the universe,
That sends mysterious vibrations out.

I have a sudden sense of feeling small
But part of it, in some strange mystic way.

Sonnet 30: OH Voyageur!

You ride the waves, Oh Voyageur!
Sun beating on your leathered back,
As muscles strain 'gainst breaking waves
In deep uncharted wilderness.

While as you toil, there comes a tune,
When dipping paddles to the song.
A shanty sung as you traverse
Vast waters of this wild bold land.

Between the lakes you portage packs,
Along a twisting rooted trail,
Past cascade falls that would deny
Swift passage any other way

These grizzled veterans of the North
Delighted in their labor's fruits.

CHAPTER 2. SONNET FORM TRANSITIONS

Here we start on a new adventure, away from familiar territory into Sonnets that take on a new perspective on what the Form is capable of. It begins with other Poetic Formats that have been melded into a Sonnet. These are the Forms that poetry lovers will recognize as Standards in their own right, such as : Limericks, Kyrielles, Pantoums, Triolets, Acrostics, Rondels, Sestinas, Rubiats, and Terza Rimas. Those should all be familiar to most poets and their fans. However, if you are not familiar with them, fear not! For I will explain them as we go.

In writing these, I delighted in recognizing the Characteristics of the Primary Form and the creativity of bending it into the Sonnet Layout. I hope that those familiar with the original Poetic Style, will enjoy these transitions too, and that those new to them will learn to love and enjoy them as well.

A. Acrostic Sonnet

An Acrostic is a Poem (or other Form of writing) in which the First Letter (or Syllable, or Word) of each Line spells out a Word, Message or the Alphabet. The word comes from the French "*acrostiche*" and from post-classical Latin "*acrostichis*", These Acrostics even occurred in the Bible, in the first four of the five songs that make up the Book of Lamentations, and in several Psalms (Psalms 9, 10, 25, 34, 37, 111, 112, 119 and 145). Acrostics are common in medieval literature, where they usually serve to highlight the name of the poet or his patron, or to make a prayer to a saint. They are most frequent in Verse works but can also appear in Prose.

Often the ease of detectability of an Acrostic can depend on the intention of its creator. In some cases an author may desire an Acrostic to have a better chance of being perceived by an observant reader by use of color, text size, bolding, hyphenating, or other method to make the Message stand out. However, Acrostics may also be used as a form of Steganography, where the author seeks to conceal the message rather than proclaim it. This might be achieved by making the Key Letters uniform in appearance with the surrounding text, or by aligning the Words in such a way that the relationship between the Key Letters is less obvious.

An Acrostic Sonnet takes all the Standard Features of a Regular Sonnet's 14 Lines of three Quatrains and Closing Couplet, along with any of the Typical Sonnet Rhyme Schemes. What makes it unique is characteristic of any Acrostic Poem in which the First Letter of each Line contributes to spell out the Words that make up the Title of the poem (either a Word, Words, or Phrase).

In this section I provide two examples.

In the first Sonnet, *What is the Fuss*, the Words define the Stanza length, so the typical Quatrain and Couplet Layout of a Typical Sonnet is changed. I do have 3 Quatrains and a Couplet, but instead of closing the poem, the Couplet becomes the Second Stanza. I changed the Key Letters to a slightly different color in order to show them better. The poem is my commentary on Global Warming. The Rhyme Scheme is Alternating (abab).

The second Poem, *When Your Love Is*, takes on the more usual Sonnet Structure. Here I really made the Phrase stand out with white on a dark background. Family portrait here, of my daughter, Aisha, and her husband, Jeremy, beside my brother, Richard, his wife, Corrine, and their grandson, Landon. I use a Coupled (aabb) Rhyme Scheme.

Sonnet 31: What Is This Fuss?

What now, is all this Global-warming fuss?
Has Earth not often waffled hot and cold
As Ice Ages have often cycled thus,
That underwent reverses very bold?

I think we give our impact overplay,
Since Nature trumps our efforts any day.

Ten thousand times worse is volcanic ash
Hurled high into our open atmosphere,
Inhibiting all sunlight in a flash.
So many times that thing has happened here.

Forever Earth has undergone such change.
Unlikely is our chance to rearrange.
So worry 'bout the weather, if you must.
Still, Earth will keep recurring boom and bust.

Sonnet 32: When Your Love Is

When your love is really true
Happiness comes passing through
Everything that you may do,
No matter what troubles brew.

Young people don't understand
Other gifts at their command
Until they've had to withstand
Ravages that lay at hand.

Loving couples have a bond
Only death can go beyond.
Very often they respond
Enduring they grow fond.

It's a lasting testament
Such a strong development.

B. Kyrielle Sonnet

The Kyrielle is a Poetic Form that originated in troubadour poetry. The name Kyrielle derives from the *Kýrie*, which is part of many Christian liturgies. The original Kyrielles were written in Rhyming Couplets or Quatrains, where the Repeated Refrain was religious, using the phrase "Lord, have mercy", or a variant of it, as the Second Line of the Couplet, or Last Line of the Quatrain. In less strict usage, other Phrases, and sometimes single Words, developed to be used as the Refrain. Each line within the poem consists of only eight Syllables. There is no limit to the number of Stanzas a Kyrielle may have, but three is considered the accepted minimum. Now-a-days, the religious aspect has been lost.

This Sonnet is made up of three Rhyming Quatrains and a Non-rhyming Couplet. Just like the Traditional Kyrielle poem, the Kyrielle Sonnet also has the Repeating Line, or Phrase, as a Refrain (usually appearing as the Last Line of each Stanza).

While each Line within the Kyrielle Sonnet consists of only 8 Syllables, French Forms have a tendency to link back to the beginning of the poem. So common practice is to use the First and Last Line of the first Quatrain as the Ending Couplet. This would also reinforce the Refrain within the poem.

Therefore, a good Rhyming Scheme for a Kyrielle Sonnet would be:

AabB, ccbB, ddbB, AB - or AbaB, CbcB, dbdB, AB,

where the capital letters indicate the Repeated Lines.

In my Kryielle Sonnet, *White Bird*, I write an ode to a Great White Egret.

Sonnet 33: White Bird

On twisted branch the white bird stands,
A specter in the hinterlands.
Through mists of time its story's told
Its ancient countenance is bold.

Some say it carries dragon blood,
Predating even Noah's flood.
For sure, its origin is old.
Its ancient countenance is bold.

It looks impressive as it soars,
Like Pterodactyl dinosaurs,
With legs behind, broad wings unfold
Its ancient countenance is bold.

On twisted branch the white bird stands,
Its ancient countenance is bold.

C. Limerick Sonnet

Since I found none, I created this Format myself.

The Format uses the signature Limerick Syllable Count and Rhyme Scheme. A Limerick is a Form of Poetry which is sometimes obscene with humorous intent. The oldest attested text in this Form is a Latin prayer by Thomas Aquinas of the 13th century. The Form appeared in England in the early years of the 18th century. It was popularized by Edward Lear in the 19th century, although he did not use the term. Gershon Legman, who compiled the largest and most scholarly anthology, held that the true Limerick, as a Folk Form, is always obscene, and cites similar opinions by Arnold Bennett and George Bernard Shaw, describing the clean Limerick as a "periodic fad and object of magazine contests, rarely rising above mediocrity". From a folkloric point of view, the Form is essentially Transgressive. Violation of taboo is part of its function. Of course that's all debatable. But at the very least, they should be fun.

According to a dictionary, a Limerick Form consists of 5 Lines (two long, followed by two short, and closed by 1 long). The first, second and fifth Lines must have matching lengths of seven to ten Syllables (8 or 9 is most typical). The third and fourth Lines only have between five and seven matching Syllables. Hence, there is a bit of flexibility.

So, that is the Form I modified to create this Sonnet Format.

Since the Limerick uses a Quintet (5 Line) Structure, I elected to give it two Closing Couplets rather than one, in order to achieve the classic 14 Lines. For the First Stanza, I mixed 9 with 5 syllables. In the Second Stanza, I used 8 with 5. The Volta comes at the first Couplet (lines 11 and 12).

The Rhyme Scheme is: aabba ccddc ee ff.

The Syllable Count is: 9,9,5,5,9 – 8,8,5,5,8- 9,9 – 5,5.

The Long Cadence is is either: da DUM da da DUM da da DuM da; or, da DUM da da DUM da da DUM.

The Short Cadence is either: da DUM da da DUM; or, da DUM da da DUM da

What better topic for a Limerick than the 2016 Republican Political Debates? That is the topic of my representative example, *The Debate*. This Republican Debate was very contentious among the following Candidates: Donald Trump, Marco Rubio, Chris Christie, Mike Huckabee, Jeb Bush, Ted Cruz, Ben Carson, John Kasich, Rand Paul, and Scott Walker. There were lots of fireworks, with Trump stealing the spotlight. Sort of reminds me of this photograph I took one July 4th.

Sonnet 34: The Debate

I watched the political debates,
With all Republican candidates
Neatly aligned in rows,
So their true color shows,
When grilled by Media heavyweights.

A boost to the TV rating slump,
As viewers tuned in for Donald Trump.
He didn't disappoint,
As he lit up the joint.
His language dominated the stump.

Should the women and immigration
Dominate the poll's conversation?
The prospects of war
Could lead to much more.
Providing public stimulation

D. Pantoum Sonnet

The Pantoum is a Poetic Form derived from the "Pantun," a Malay Verse Form: specifically from the *pantun berkait*, a series of Interwoven Quatrains. It is a Form of Poetry similar to a Villanelle in that there are Repeating Lines throughout the poem. it is a Two Line Refrain Type. It is composed of a series of Quatrains; the Second and Fourth Lines of each Stanza are repeated as the First and Third Lines of the next Stanza. The pattern continues for any number of Stanzas, except for the Final Stanza, which differs in the Repeating Pattern. The First and Third Lines of the Last Stanza are the Second and Fourth of the Penultimate; the First Line of the Poem is the Last Line of the Final Stanza, and the Third Line of the First Stanza is the Second of the Final. Ideally, the meaning of Lines shifts when they are repeated although the Words remain exactly the same: this can be done by shifting punctuation, punning, or simply recontextualizing.

A Pantoum Sonnet combines the characteristics of the two Formats. While a Pantoum is a Repeating Poem who's Second and Fourth Lines become the First and Third lines of the next Stanza for any number of Stanzas, the Typical Sonnet is a 14 Line Poem with 12 Lines of abab Rhyming Quatrains and two Closing Rhymed Lines, Couplets. Both Forms can be combines into the Sonnet's Contemporary Structure of three Quatrains with closing Couplet, of the traditional way of 14 lines together with the Reapeaing Sequence of the Pantoum. (as done here). In either case, the Rhyme Scheme for a Pantoum Sonnet is:

A1/B1/A2/B2/ B1/C1/B2/C2/ C1/D1/C2/D2/ A2/A,

where the capital letters indicate Repeating Lines, and the numbers differentiate between two or more of those Lines.

I have written two examples.

The first is *The Crowd was Wow'd*. It reiterates an event that I attended where some eagles were released back into the wild by the Minnesota Raptor Center. I captured this photograph using a 300mm lens and high speed Sony camera. Although this form has a lot of repeats, I tried to make the transitions as smooth as possible.

The second poem, *Their Spirits Dance*, was inspired by a fountain at Bemidji, Minnesota. A couple of copper Indians cavort in the pool.

Sonnet 35: The Crowd was WOW'd

He lofted injured raptor to the air.
A flash of furtive feather flaps ensued,
As freedom was released from deep despair
The crowd was wow'd as broken health renewed.

A flash of furtive feather flaps ensued,
Those gathered gasped as nurtured bird arose.
The crowd was wow'd as broken health renewed,
Anticipating paths this eagle chose.

Those gathered gasped as nurtured bird arose.
When sudden burst of energy let loose.
Anticipating paths this eagle chose,
They picked their spot the best they could deduce.

As freedom was released from deep despair
He lofted injured raptor to the air.

Sonnet 36: Their Spirits Dance

Their spirits dance on water's waves,
Delighting in refreshing spray,
As droplets pelt these prancing braves,
On sacred pond bronzed warriors play

Delighting in refreshing spray,
They flop atop the lily pads
On sacred pond bronzed warriors play,
These ghosts of long past native lads

They flop atop the lily pads,
Reminders of what once had been
These ghosts of long past native lads,
Someday their hopes may rise again.

As droplets pelt these prancing braves,
Their spirits dance on water's waves.

E. Quatern Sonnet

The Quatern (Latin meaning "4 each") is a French Verse Form, possibly from the Middle Ages since it is so close to the Retourne and Kyrielle which also came from that period. The Quatern like so many other French Forms employs a Refrain. It is a One Line Refrain Type. The defining feature is the movement of the Refrain within the Quatrain from Stanza to Stanza.

A Quatern is a Poem consisting of four Quatrains, where the First Line of the poem Ripples through each Stanza. It becomes the Second Line of the second Stanza, the Third Line of the third Stanza, and the Last Line of the fourth. So it is a Progression that makes for a lovely Waterfall Effect as the line Ripples from beginning to end of the poem. This creates a Rhyme Scheme of:

Abab bAba abAb babA, or

Abab CAca adAd eaeA,

where the capital letter signifies the Repeated Line. The first choice uses only two Rhymes, while the second uses five. See where the "A" Refrain falls in each Stanza.

Written in Tetrameter.

Therefore, to make a Quatern Sonnet, you merely turn the last Quatrain into a Rhymed Couplet, using the Repeated Line as the Last Line of the Poem, but retaining the Waterfall Effect. The trick is to use the Repeated Line in various ways, changing its aspect, while still being a repeated Refrain. The Rhyme Scheme becomes:

Abab bAba abAb aA.

I have one written here. It is *Dahlia Bloom*. My photograph was taken at the Minnesota Arboretum in Chanhassen, Minnesota. I thought it is spectacular. Notice how "the delicate Dahlia bloom" Phrase moves through the Stanzas, beginning and ending the Poem.

Sonnet 37: Dahlia Bloom

The delicate Dahlia bloom
With circles of lovely florets
Will brighten most any a room.
There's beauty wherever it sets.

It's certain one never forgets
The delicate Dahlia bloom
With petals that turn prosuettes
Creating a colorful plume.

They give off a lovely perfume.
Aroma that often begets
The delicate Dahlia bloom
Finds love of enthused Baronets.

It moves many florists to groom
The delicate Dalia bloom.

F. Rondel Sonnet

A Rondel is a Verse Form originating in French Lyrical Poetry of the 14th century. It was later used in the Verse of other languages as well, such as English and Romanian. It is a Variation of the Rondeau.

A Rondel is a Two Line Refrain Type Poem with two Quatrains followed by a Sestet where the First Two Lines of the Poem become repeated as the Last Two Lines of the next two Stanzas (the second Quatrain and the Sestet). Sometimes the second line is dropped in the last Stanza. It is usually in Tetrameter, but is always iambic.

So, the Rhyme Scheme would be:

ABba abAB abbaAB (Prime),

or

ABba abAB abbaA (Classic).

The conversion to a Sonnet is quite simple. Change the Meter to Pentameter and separate the last two Lines of the Sestet to make it a Couplet. In actuality the Rondel Prime, as introduced in France about 1544 by Clermont Marot, was a Sonnet. But the Classic Form became more popular. The Rhyme Scheme then for the Sonnet becomes:

ABba abAB abba AB.

For this book, I wrote one, *Sidewalk Adorned*. Just a simple Poem about a sidewalk and a flower pot. Note the easy two line transitions.

Sonnet 38: Sidewalk Adorned

This sidewalk's splayed with flowers in a pot.
Their elegance provides a touch of charm,
With floral sights that make the setting warm
To those who travel by this lovely plot.

For usually, more often than it's not,
An unembellished concrete is the norm.
This sidewalk's splayed with flowers in a pot.
Their elegance provides a touch of charm.

But I believe I like it quite a lot!
It sets a sense of peace without alarm,
Where lovers walk together arm-in-arm.
In fact, it may become their fav'rite spot.

This sidewalk's splayed with flowers in a pot.
Their elegance provides a touch of charm.

G. Rubaiyat Sonnet

The Rubaiyat Poem is a Persian Form of several Quatrains. Its name derives from the Arabic plural of the word for "Quatrain". This, in turn, comes from the Arabic Rubá, meaning "four." This Persian Form of Poetry presents a series of Rhymed Quatrains that Interlink. In each Quatrain, all lines Rhyme except the third, leading to this Pattern: a,a,b,a. Then the "b" Rhyme establishes the Primary Rhyme for the next Stanza: b,b,c,b, while the "c" Rhyme does the same for the next, and so on, and so on.

The most famous Rubaiyat Poem is *The Rubaiyat of Omar Khayyam*, which is the title that Edward FitzGerald gave to his translation of a selection of poems, originally written in Persian and numbering about a thousand, attributed to Omar Khayyam (1048–1131), a Persian poet, mathematician and astronomer.

To make a Sonnet, combines the Attributes of a Sonnet, having 3 Quatrains and a Closing Couplet, with a Rubiyat, having Quatrains that Interlink Rhymes. The Rubiyat Mono-rhymes line 1, 2, and 4 of each Stanza, while line 3 creates (establishes) the Rhyme for the following Stanza, thus Interlinking them. The "d" Rhyme establishes the Rhyming Couplet, rather than continuing a Quatrain. So, the Rhyme Scheme for the Sonnet is:

aaba bbcb ccdc dd.

Here I wrote just one, *The Verdant Pond*. The image is from a pond in my brother Richard's back yard. I tried to bring the picture to life with the ripples and trickles.

Sonnet 39: The Verdant Pond

A pond amidst the verdant moss,
Where ripples ring the mirrored gloss,
Attracts the most aesthetic eye.
A pleasant scene to look across.

A gentle trickle falls nearby
To bring the pool its cool supply.
Of most refreshing water fill,
In lovely liquid lullaby.

The flowage dribbles down a hill,
Between the mossy foliage spill,
To sunshine dappled lily pond,
Where two bright aspen leaves lie still.

But when such visions lie beyond,
Could any person not respond?

H. Sestina Sonnet

The invention of the Sestina Form is usually attributed to Arnaut Daniel, a troubadour of 12th-century Provence, and the first Sestinas were written in the Occitan language of that region. The Form was cultivated by his fellow troubadours, then by other poets across Continental Europe in the subsequent centuries. The earliest example of the Form in English appeared in 1579, though they were rarely written in Britain until the end of the 19th century.

A Sestina is unusual in that it doesn't use Rhyme, but instead uses the Same Words repeated in different, yet set, Sequences for each Stanza. So it Mimics Rhyme by repeating (or parroting) the Same Words, only in a very specific Sequence. Normally, the Sestina has 6 Repeated Words Sequences over six Verses and a Closing Tercet that uses all Six Words. But, in order to accommodate a Sonnet, it has been modified to have only 4 Words ending each line of a Quatrain repeated over three Verses, plus a Closing Couplet that incorporates all four of the Key Words. It is not necessary to choose words that Rhyme, but I like to, as it then gives a nice Rhymed Sequence. Note also that the Fixed Sequence causes the last Word of each Sanza to repeat as the First End-word of the next Stanza.

So, if you identify the Four Words with the letters A, B, C, and D, the Word Sequence for the Sonnet is:

ABCD DCAB BADC (BC)(DA),

Where the letters in parens represent Two Words in each Line of the Couplet.

I have written one example, *Golf Course Sign*. For this poem, I chose the 4 Words as:

A - stone

B – strange

C - grown

D - range

You'll note that I deliberately chose two sets of words that Rhyme. That is not a requirement, but I like Rhyming Poems, and did that here, to show how such an Effect can be achieved, even in a Sestina. Most are **not** rhymed. See how the Words are also integrated into the Couplet?

Sonnet 40: Golf Course Sign

Directions on this chiseled stone
Create a setting very strange
Where groups of purple leaves have grown
Nearby the golf course driving range.

Where benches placed upon the range
Are visible above what's grown
Around the words upon the stone
That steel spikes are considered strange.

But then again it's not so strange,
For greens are never made of stone
And solid cleats may ruin the range
Of cultured grasses that were grown.

Is it so strange highlights are grown
'Round driving range's message stone?

I. Terza Rima Sonnet

Terza Rima is a Rhyming Verse, Stanzaic Form that consists of an Interlocking Three-line Rhyme Scheme. It was first used by the Italian poet Dante Alighieri, who wrote The Inferno. The literal translation of Terza Rima from Italian is "third rhyme". Terza Rima is written in a Three-line Stanza using Chain (Interlinking) Rhyme in the pattern A-B-A, B-C-B, C-D-C, D-E-D. There is no limit to the number of Lines in the Standard Poem, but Poems or sections of Poems, written in Terza Rima end with either a Single Line or Couplet repeating the Rhyme of the middle line of the Final Tercet. The two possible endings are d-e-d, e; or d-e-d, e-e. There is no set Rhythm for Terza Rima, but in English, iambic Pentameter is generally preferred.

So, a Terza Rima Sonnet combines that Rhyme Pattern into only 4 Stanzas of 3 Lines each (giving 12 Lines), then using the Couplet option to create the signature 14 Lines of a Traditional Sonnet. The Sonnet's Rhyme Scheme, therefore is:

aba bcb cdc ded ee.

I have provided one example here, *Sacrificial Savior*. Of possible interest is the image, which is of a Paint-by- Number painting of Jesus in the Garden, which I painted when I was 10 years old. It hangs in my home office. I thought a Spiritual poem appropriate. I did deviate from the standard Meter by using iambic Tetrameter instead. But as noted, that is OK.

Sonnet 41: Sacrificial Savior

When I contemplate reflection
On the evils of mankind,
There is only one direction

Where we are headed, that I find.
Its location isn't pleasant,
And it's really quite confined.

For the demons that are present
Are so destructively obsessed,
And their tortures are incessant.

But be glad that we've been blessed
With a sacrificial Savior,
Who keeps Satan's work depressed.

For no act of love was braver,
When He died for our behavior.

J. Triolet Sonnet (Aka: SonnTriolet, or Sonniolet)

This form is another of my own invention, after seeing other poets stretching the limits of what it means to be a Sonnet. While developing this book, I discovered that there are Key Elements to any Sonnet, and that anyone of them can be stretched to accommodate a creative variation. The Standard descriptions of a Sonnet are these:

1. A Structured Poem of 14 Lines

2. A formalized Rhyme Scheme.

3. Iambic Pentameter

4. A Structured Stanza Scheme

 a. The English version with 3 Quatrains and Closing Couplet

 b. The Italian with an Octave and Sestet (or, 2 Quatrains with 2 Tercets)

5. A Turn, or Volta

6. A developed Theme Progression: Main Theme, extended Metaphor, a Turn (twist or conflict), and Closing Summary.

It can be, and has been argued that, changing one or more of the Elements, does not change the Essence of a Sonnet. If you can retain some, or most of the Elements, it is still a Sonnet.

In this Format, I changed Elements 3 and 4, in order to adopt the Structure of a Triolet. So instead of three Quatrains and a Couplet, I have 3 Octaves and a Couplet. It still has 3 Stanzas followed by a Closing Couplet (blending English with Italian). It still has a formal Rhyme Scheme - that of the Triolet.

A Triolet is a French Form with a double Refrain. It consists of 8 Lines (an Octave) with a Rhyme Scheme of:

ABaAabAB,

where the capital letters represent the Repeated Lines. It can be written in any Meter. but being French in origin, iambic Tetrameter is the favorite, while iambic Pentameter is a favorite of the Sonnet form. So I propose that this Format should be either one or the other.

To convert to a Sonntriolet, requires three Triolet followed by a Rhymed Couplet.

The example I provide here is *Pansies*. The Format allowed me to write about three phases – planting, growing, fully bloomed. I used iambic Pentameter in this one.

Sonnet 42: Pansies

Those tiny seeds I placed deep in the ground
Were watered all freely and left to grow.
Then nurtured soil weekly to keep them sound.
Those tiny seeds I placed deep in the ground.
I dreamt they'd be the best flowers around.
Those tiny seeds I placed deep in the ground
Were watered all freely and left to grow.

Then from the fertile earth a shoot did sprout,
A delicate sprig with a promise of joy.
I tended the dirt to keep the weeds out,
Then from the fertile earth a shoot did sprout,
A wondrous miracle without a doubt,
A beautiful blossom, each to enjoy.
Then from the fertile earth a shoot did sprout,
A delicate sprig with a promise of joy.

Now blessed with a dash of white, yellow, blue,
The color burst forth from my new pansies.
They proudly displayed color, tint, and hue,
Now blessed with a dash of white, yellow, blue.
With smashing smile, it's beaming right at you,
They flash pizzazz like little dandies.
Now blessed with a dash of white, yellow, blue,
The color burst forth from my new pansies.

I cherish each little tinted treasure.
Their graceful presence gives me much pleasure

CHAPTER 3. FAMOUS POET SONNET FORMS

Beyond those poets already mentioned (Shakespeare, Petrarca, and Spenser), there are other poets who left their imprint on the Sonnet Form as well. These icons will be investigated within this chapter.

By virtue of their fame and creativity, their impact was felt and absorbed. They are: Byron, Dante, Pushkin, Tirell, and Tuckerman. I'll introduce you to their work, one by one. Some may lend their attention to the Rhyme Scheme. Others my expand the Form, or play with the Meter. The Stanzaic Structure becomes fair game for one, while all rules are thrown to the wind by another.

These rebels demonstrated that the Sonnet Format can be changed without out destroying the Essence of the Genre. They are the pioneers who set the stage for those who follow. So it is only right that we begin our journey beyond the Standard Forms with these men who lent their genius and stature.

I delight in introducing them to you.

A. Byron's Sonnet

George Gordon Byron, 6th Baron Byron, (22 January 1788 – 19 April 1824), commonly known simply as Lord Byron, was an English poet, politician, and a leading figure in the Romantic Movement. Among his best-known works are the lengthy Narrative Poems, *Don Juan* and *Childe Harold's Pilgrimage*, and the short Lyric Poem, "*She Walks in Beauty*".

Byron is regarded as one of the greatest British Poets and remains widely read and influential. He travelled extensively across Europe, especially in Italy, where he lived for seven years with the struggling Poet Percy Bysshe Shelley. Byron is considered to be the first Modern-style celebrity. His image as the personification of the Byronic Hero fascinated the public, and his wife Annabella coined the term "Byromania" to refer to the commotion surrounding him

Lord Bryon wrote several Sonnets. Byron's Sonnets are obviously influenced by the Italian Form rather than the English and possess an Octave with a Sestet. The Eight Lines of the Octave comprises a Progression of three Rhymes: a. b. b. a. - a. c. c. a, but it's the Six Lines of the Sestet that makes it unique, with its Pattern of d. e. d…e. d. e. This was his favorite and signature Rhyme Scheme. The total Interweaving Rhyme Scheme is:

abba acca ded ede.

So you can see, he was a great fan of Enveloping and Interlocking Rhyme. The Form is written in iambic Pentameter. Volta at line 9.

The example I have written here is *Seeking Home*. It demonstrates that , even such a mundane activity as rush hour, when expressed with his signature Rhyme Scheme, can be lovely. His mark is truly with the Rhyming.

CHAPTER 3. FAMOUS POET SONNET FORMS

Beyond those poets already mentioned (Shakespeare, Petrarca, and Spenser), there are other poets who left their imprint on the Sonnet Form as well. These icons will be investigated within this chapter.

By virtue of their fame and creativity, their impact was felt and absorbed. They are: Byron, Dante, Pushkin, Tirell, and Tuckerman. I'll introduce you to their work, one by one. Some may lend their attention to the Rhyme Scheme. Others my expand the Form, or play with the Meter. The Stanzaic Structure becomes fair game for one, while all rules are thrown to the wind by another.

These rebels demonstrated that the Sonnet Format can be changed without out destroying the Essence of the Genre. They are the pioneers who set the stage for those who follow. So it is only right that we begin our journey beyond the Standard Forms with these men who lent their genius and stature.

I delight in introducing them to you.

A. Byron's Sonnet

George Gordon Byron, 6th Baron Byron, (22 January 1788 – 19 April 1824), commonly known simply as Lord Byron, was an English poet, politician, and a leading figure in the Romantic Movement. Among his best-known works are the lengthy Narrative Poems, *Don Juan* and *Childe Harold's Pilgrimage*, and the short Lyric Poem, "*She Walks in Beauty*".

Byron is regarded as one of the greatest British Poets and remains widely read and influential. He travelled extensively across Europe, especially in Italy, where he lived for seven years with the struggling Poet Percy Bysshe Shelley. Byron is considered to be the first Modern-style celebrity. His image as the personification of the Byronic Hero fascinated the public, and his wife Annabella coined the term "Byromania" to refer to the commotion surrounding him

Lord Bryon wrote several Sonnets. Byron's Sonnets are obviously influenced by the Italian Form rather than the English and possess an Octave with a Sestet. The Eight Lines of the Octave comprises a Progression of three Rhymes: a. b. b. a. - a. c. c. a, but it's the Six Lines of the Sestet that makes it unique, with its Pattern of d. e. d...e. d. e. This was his favorite and signature Rhyme Scheme. The total Interweaving Rhyme Scheme is:

abba acca ded ede.

So you can see, he was a great fan of Enveloping and Interlocking Rhyme. The Form is written in iambic Pentameter. Volta at line 9.

The example I have written here is *Seeking Home*. It demonstrates that , even such a mundane activity as rush hour, when expressed with his signature Rhyme Scheme, can be lovely. His mark is truly with the Rhyming.

Sonnet 43: Seeking Home

A golden light has settled on the day,
While people in their cars are heading home
No matter where their efforts make them roam;
They seek it, whether near or far away.
And so, they'll brave the traffic's frantic fray
That tests them to outrun the setting sun
And often tattered tempers have begun,
Beyond what soothing music can allay.

But finally, their residence is reached,
Where they receive the comfort of their mate.
Although their nerves and senses have been breached,
There's someone there to whom they can relate,
And bring about the prayers that were beseeched,
As sun was setting, day was getting late.

B. Dante's Sonnet Variation

Another shining star in the pantheon of Famous Poets is Dante. His full name is Durante degli Alighieri, simply called Dante (c. 1265 – 1321). He was a major Italian Poet of the Late Middle Ages, famous for his *Inferno*. His other famous work, *Divine Comedy,* is widely considered the greatest literary work composed in the Italian language, and a masterpiece of world literature. It has been referred to as the Greatest Poem of the Middle Ages.

The most common Italian Sonnets are written in the Petrarchan Format of a 14 Line Set consisting of two Quatrains (or an 8 Line Octave), with two Closing Tercets (or a Sestet), having the Rhyme Scheme: abba abba cdc cdc.

Dante wrote a 20 Line Deviation to this Style. Most Sonnets in Dante's La Vita Nuova are Petrarchan. Chapter VII gives Sonnet "*O voi che per la via*", with two Sestets (aabaab aabaab) and two Quatrains (cddc cddc), and Ch. VIII, "*Morte villana*", with two Sestets (aabbba aabbba) and two Quatrains (cddc cddc). That's quite a departure from the Typical Sonnet, but who's to question the immortal Dante?

I am recreating his Variation using the "aabbba" Form of his Chapter VIII. I chose that because, I personally like 3 consecutive Repeated Rhymes. So this intrigued me when I read about it. Thus, the total Rhyme Scheme is:

aabbba aabbba cddc cddc

Done in iambic Pentameter, of course.

With only 4 unique Rhyme choices (a,b,c,and d) covering 20 Lines, the choice of Rhymes is crucial.

My contribution to his Form is *Imagination Spawned*. It is a work describing how human imagination creates civilization. An Ode to the gift of imagination. It certainly is not equal to the *Inferno,* but I tried to capture the Essence of the Form. I used a doctored image of myself as the artwork for this Poem.

Sonnet 44: Imagination Spawned

A gift - to travel visions of the mind,
Imagining all things of every kind,
To travel to the most exotic places,
Encountering hosts of alien faces,
Or following paths of those who left traces,
Uncovering the truths yet undefined.

Uncommon things the mind has just divined,
The likes of visions yet to be refined,
Until they've gone and touched a sensing soul,
Or met the challenge of a leading role
That was so tense emotions lost control.
Then, only then, have particles aligned

For that is what the Masters all desire –
Achievement touched by blessed inspiration,
With extraordinary mood elation,
The likes the Grecian gods would oft' admire.

These geniuses of yesterday's empires,
Who dreamed and brought about civilization,
With such a gifted strong imagination,
Are those whose spark lit ancient worlds on fire.

C. Pushkin Sonnets

Alexander Sergeyevich Pushkin was a Russian Poet, Playwright, and Novelist of the Romantic Era who is considered by many to be the greatest Russian Poet and the founder of modern Russian literature. Critics consider many of his works Masterpieces, such as the poem *The Bronze Horseman* and the drama *The Stone Guest*, a tale of the fall of Don Juan. His poetic short drama *Mozart and Salieri* was the inspiration for Peter Shaffer's movie *Amadeus*. The Russian Poet, Alexander Pushkin, was best known for his Sonnets through his novel in Poetic Verse, *Eugene Onegin*. The work was mostly written with each Verse in **iambic Tetrameter**. His works have been rendered in both English and Italian Versions.

Pushkin Sonnet written in the English version.

The Pushkin Sonnet (aka: Onegin Sonnet), also called the Pushkin Stanza, contains a couple of unique features. The first is in its Meter, and the second is in its Layout. The English Format features the Pushkin signature Rhyme Scheme:

aBaBccDDeFFeGG,

where the lowercase letters represent Feminine endings (i.e., with an additional Unstressed 11th Syllable) and the uppercase representing the typical Masculine Ending (i.e. Stressed on the final 10th Syllable). So that is the first Feature mentioned. However, the English version is written in iambic Pentameter

The second unique Feature involves the lack of Stanzas. Unlike other Traditional Forms, such as the Petrarchan Sonnet or Shakespearean Sonnet, the Pushkin Sonnet does not divide into smaller Stanzas of four Lines or two in an obvious way. If analyzed in a Stanzaic Format the Structure would look like this:

abab ccdd eff egg,

which reveals some interesting Aspects. Note that the Quatrains shift Rhyme Scheme from Alternating (abab) to Coupled (ccdd). Furthermore, the two Tercets contain an Interlocking "e" Rhyme. A Tercet of effegg is a very Italian Feature.

Pushkin Sonnet done in the Italian format.

The Italian Version is written in Verses of **iambic Tetrameter,** with the Rhyme Scheme:

aBaBccDDeFFeGG,

where the lowercase letters represent Feminine Endings (i.e., with an additional Unstressed 9th Syllable) and the uppercase representing the typical Masculine Ending (i.e. Stressed on the final 8th Syllable).

So that is the First Feature mentioned, making the Italian Version recognizable by the Tetrameter, but the Rhyme Scheme is identical to the English Version. .

The second unique Feature remains the lack of Stanzas. Thus, the entire Poem is referred to as a Stanza. Therefore comes the designation as the Pushkin Stanza.

So I have rendered an example of each type.

The first example is *Best Buddy*. It is an Italian Version. I thought I'd add a bit of humor in this one, about man and dog. I used some Slant Rhyming too.

The second poem is *Scurrying Squirrels*. It is an English Version.

Note the Feminine Lines. Otherwise, pretty subtle difference from other Sonnets.

Sonnet 45: Best Buddy

What better buddy than a doggy
To get you out to exercise,
And set the pace for when you're jogging,
As healthcare pundits emphasize.
A great companion everywhere, when
He enjoys any time you share, then
A dog can raise your spirits high
To be your body's best ally.
Not everything is loads of fun, no.
There's several things that owners do,
Like picking up the doggy poo.
When everything is said and done, so
Unlimited the love you get,
Along with nose both cold and wet.

Sonnet 46: Scurrying Squirrels

It's up and down, all day
To find their food around the autumn trees.
Just watching them, seems they're in a hurry
To store up food before the winter freeze.
Such active guys, their moves are acrobatic
When scampering with motions so dramatic.
They'll run straight up the trunks, then down with ease.
Then jump from limb to limb like a trapeze.
Then suddenly, they'll stop, as if they're frozen,
And blend into the bark's dark camouflage
To predators a silhouette mirage
That disappears when hindrance has been chosen.
They hurry, scurry up and down a tree
Their playfulness is wonderful to see.

D. Tirell Sonnet

A Tirrell Sonnet was created by Robert Tirrell Leonard, a Poet from Woburn, MA, who is also a Politician and Author of several Poetry Collections.

The Tirrell Sonnet (an American Model), is quite different and has a unique feel to it. It starts with a Couplet followed by a Tercet, followed by a Quatrain, adding the Turn with a following Tercet and then reversing the order of the Repeated Couplet as a Refrain. So it is: Couplet + Tercet + Quatrain + Tercet + Reversed Couplet. See the Progression, 2 Lines, 3 Lines, 4 Lines, then back down to 3 Lines, then 2 Lines (2,3,4,3,2). It utilizes Stanzaic Symmetry. A broad departure from the Standard, with its two Couplets.

It features only 3 Rhymes (a,b,and c). It is written in iambic Pentameter, with Interlinking Rhyme.

This can create an introspective feel to the whole Poem.

The Rhyme Scheme is:

A1, A2 - b,c,b - c,b,b,c - b,c,b - A2, A1,

where the capital letters indicate the Repeated Verses and the numbers provide identification.

My example is *Enjoy the Fire*.

In this one, the Volta is a bit subtle, but it moves away from a description of the fire itself, to the connection with location.

Sonnet 47: Enjoy a Fire

I love to sit about, enjoy a fire,
To watch those dancing flames is my desire.

To be entranced by open flick'ring flame
That draws my gaze into its very heart,
Where hidden mysteries remain unclaimed.

Aromas of that burning wood impart
A feeling that the fragrances proclaim,
Of camping reveries that often came
With woodland explorations from the start.

These places, much too numerous to name,
Have left impressions as the fondest part,
As each new pyre reminds me why I came

To watch those dancing flames is my desire,
I love to sit about, enjoy a fire.

E.   Tuckerman Sonnet

Frederick Goddard Tuckerman (February 4, 1821 - May 9, 1873) was an American Poet, remembered mostly for his Sonnet Series. Tuckerman wrote Sonnets with free abandon and with virtually no regard for any kind of Pattern at all. His Sonnets burst from the gate in a flurry of Rhyme, without any Stanzas, then, after the first few Lines, Rhymes fall seemingly at random, as in his "*Sonnets, First Series*," which Rhymes:

a b b a b c a b a d e c e d, with a Volta at L10.

He was a reclusive contemporary of Emily Dickenson, Nathaniel Hawthorne, Ralph Waldo Emerson and Henry Wadsworth Longfellow, and acquaintance of Alfred, Lord Tennyson, but remained in relative obscurity, even with several published works.

My example here is *Golden Painted Sky*. The Meter is close to iambic, but the Syllable Count is erratic at: 12,13,14,11,10, 10, 12, 9, 10, 12, 13. There is lots of Enjambment and Alliteration, and a touch of In-line Rhyme.

Sonnet 48: Golden Painted Sky

As sun was going down, I made a mystic turn,
and suddenly I beheld a sky so very bold,
beside a burnished, glowing lake, reflecting gilded gold,
with its colors so intense, it seemed to burn.
Believing it a blessing to behold,
I stopped, bewitched, and made a silent prayer
of gratitude, while skepticisms churn.
I learn! For this meets any masterpiece of old,
a priceless gem, as any educated judge discern.
Yet, here it was, this golden painted sky,
as dusk devoured restless remnants of the day.
A tinted lake, amber colored air
aloft, was spread about in radiant display.
By-the by, it caught the muse of grateful poet's eye.

CHAPTER 4. COUPLET RELOCATION SONNETS

One very simple Variation upon the Sonnet Form is to change the location of the Rhyming Couplet. Whether you put it on top, like the Inverted Sonnet; in the middle, as the Alfred Dorn does; between the Octave and the Sestet, like the Tory Hexatet; or even have two as Tirell does it; the impact is immediate and distinctive. So here they are.

A. Alfred Dorn Sonnet

The Alfred Dorn Sonnet originated in a Formalist Publication Contest. Each year the Formalist runs a Sonnet contest where the applicants make up their own Form of Sonnet. The Sonnet Form is named after the winning applicant, and in this case Alfred Dorn was the winner and the Sonnet he devised named after him. He is a Contemporary Poet and this Form now appears on several Poetry Websites.

An Alfred Dorn Sonnet is distinguished by two Sestets bridged by a Couplet. The first one is an Italian Sestet, having a Rhyme Scheme of: abcabc (Rolling Rhyme). The second one is a Sicilian Sestet, taking the Scheme of: aeaeae (Alternating Rhyme). So the entire Rhyme Scheme becomes:

abcabc dd aeaeae.

Note that the "a" Rhyme is a Linking Rhyme between the 2 Sestets. Written in iambic Pentameter. The Turn (or Volta) is at Line 9, as in most Sonnets.

The Sonnet of this Type that I have written is *The Heart in the City*. The photograph is of downtown St. Paul, Minnesota. If you look closely at the rising smoke, you'll see a heart. That was not doctored, it actually formed naturally. Both the buildings and the heart formed the Muse for this poem.

Sonnet 49: The Heart in the City

I traveled down the central city street
in downtown, where the buildings frame the sky,
where architecture reigns, like mountain peaks,
and cars roam canyons made from formed concrete,
as trains and buses often wander by
the buildings bonded using bridge techniques.

These manmade monuments consume the scene,
and green's a color seldom ever seen.

And yet, there's beauty that your eyes may greet!
An ordered chaos sets this sight apart.
Unique detail provides esthetic treat,
while "ancient" often meets "state-of-the-art."
Now note that smoky statement in the heat
that says that "Even cities have a heart."

B. Inverted Sonnet

An Inverted Sonnet is one of what is known as one of the Modern Sonnets. A specific Type of Modern Sonnet, most famously penned by Elizabeth Bishop, is the Inverted Sonnet.

Elizabeth Bishop (February 8, 1911 – October 6, 1979) was an American Poet Laureate and short-story Writer. She was Consultant in Poetry to the Library of Congress from 1949 to 1950, the Pulitzer Prize winner for Poetry in 1956, the National Book Award winner in 1970, and the recipient of the Neustadt International Prize for Literature in 1976.

While the Traditional Sonnet is classified as having exactly 14 Lines and a strict Rhyming Scheme, an Inverted Sonnet will also have 14 Lines, but with an Opening Rhyming Couplet rather than a Closing Couplet. It may start with an Opening Couplet, but the remaining Lines could be written in Free Form as well, rather than Rhymed. A Sonnet that's been split in half, with each section having its own Tone and Style, might also be referred to as an Inverted Sonnet. The Meter and Line Length may vary in this Format. Source: The WiseGEEK and Wikipedia.

For this Poem I used iambic Tetrameter. I also structured a Rhyme Scheme so that the Rhyme of the Opening Couplet blended into an abba Type, Enveloping Scheme in the Last Stanza. But that is not a requirement. So, for this poem, the Rhyme Scheme is:

aa bcbc dede agga,

where a traditional Sonnet Rhyme Scheme would be:

abab cdcd efef gg

My example is *Sunny Day Play*. The picture is of Carver Lake beach in Woodbury, Minnesota. You can just see the playground off to the right background.

Sonnet 50: Sunny Day Play

There are so many ways to play
On delightful, warm, and sunny day

It may be on a sandy beach
Where sunlight turns a body tan,
Or in the water's cooling reach,
To splash and swim the best you can.

Or maybe it's a playground slide
That seems to draw the summer's child
With promise of a swing or glide
That keeps them happy and beguiled.

But it's the cooling shade, I say,
Where breezes gently kiss the skin
On fresh cut grass I wallow in,
That yields the peace for which I pray.

C. Tirell Sonnet

Here again is another example of the Tirell Sonnet, which we introduced in the last Chapter as a Form named for a well known Poet. Here we highlight its Structure, specifically the location of the Couplet.

The Tirrell Sonnet (an American Model), is quite different and has a unique feel to it. It starts with a Couplet followed by a Tercet, followed by a Quatrain, adding the Turn with a following Tercet and then reversing the order of the Repeated Couplet as a Refrain.

So it is: Couplet + Tercet + Quatrain + Tercet + Reversed Couplet.

It features only 3 Rhymes (a,b,and c). It is written in iambic Pentameter.

The Rhyme Scheme is:

A1, A2 - b,c,b - c,b,b,c - b,c,b - A2, A1,

where the capital letters indicate the Repeated Verses and the numbers provide identification.

For this chapter I wrote *Bitter Pill*. It is a poem about rejection and personality change.

Sonnet 51: Bitter Pill

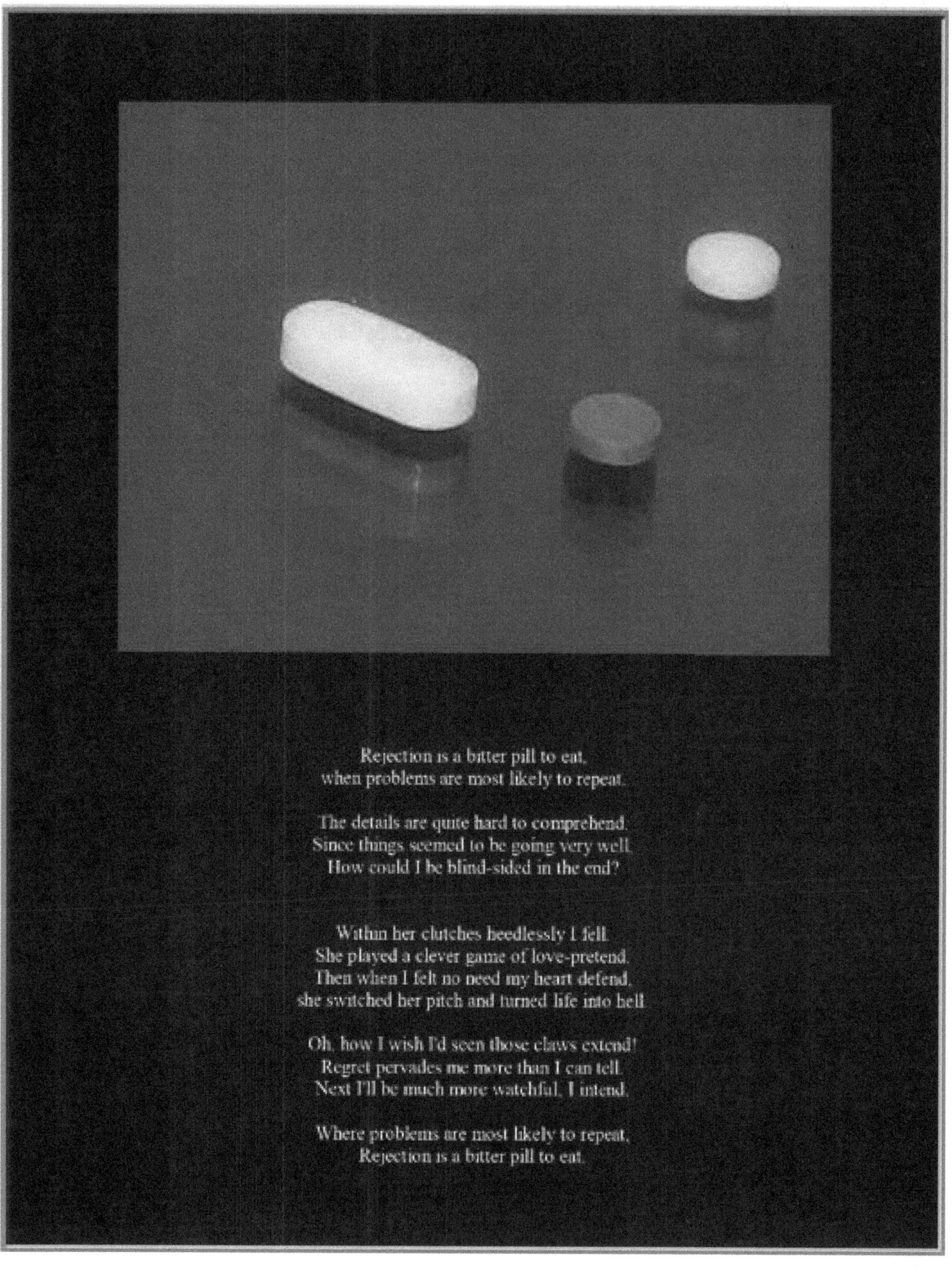

Rejection is a bitter pill to eat,
when problems are most likely to repeat.

The details are quite hard to comprehend.
Since things seemed to be going very well,
How could I be blind-sided in the end?

Within her clutches heedlessly I fell.
She played a clever game of love-pretend.
Then when I felt no need my heart defend,
she switched her pitch and turned life into hell.

Oh, how I wish I'd seen those claws extend!
Regret pervades me more than I can tell.
Next I'll be much more watchful, I intend.

Where problems are most likely to repeat,
Rejection is a bitter pill to eat.

D. Tory Hexatet Sonnet

This is a Sonnet form created by Victoria Sutton (aka. PassionsPromise) and named by Larry Eberhart (aka. Lawrencealot). They are two contemporary Poets. Her works are often published on the Poets Collective Website under that pseudonym.

Like the Alfred Dorn Sonnet, it places the Couplet in the middle of the Poem. But instead of separating two Sestets, she divided an Octave and a Quatrain. The Sonnet consists of an Octet + Couplet + Quatrain, with a Rhyme Scheme of:

ababcdcd ee ffgg.

The Format features the first eight Lines (the Octet, or Octave) in 12 Syllable iambic Hexameter, but the Rhyming Couplet holds to eight Syllables (iambic Tetrameter), located at Line 9, rather than at the end (like a Typical Sonnet's Couplet). The last four Lines of the closing Quatrain revert back to 12 Syllables. So the Poem retains the signature total 14 Lines of a Typical Sonnet.

The Couplet in the center provides the "changing point", or Volta. Its shorter Meter provides a visual, as well as oral impact, embedded as it is between two Hexameter Stanzas. Thus, it makes a direct statement and could be read by itself.

My contribution is *Geese at Pease*. I couldn't resist capturing a picture of these little puff balls, then writing a poem about it.

Sonnet 52: Geese at Peace

A lazy summer day on lush pastoral hill
Provides a pleasant backdrop artists contemplate,
That gives a feathered family of geese their fill
Of seeds in fresh-cut grass upon a large estate.
The parents both provide examples, what to choose
Their youngsters follow, looking like some yellow puffs.
It's such a treat to watch these gratifying views,
To see all these small geese in fuzzy downy fluff.

We love babies of any kind
They help to set a tranquil mind.

For when we see these youngsters with their mom and dad
They represent simplicity we wish we had.
It's plain to see these birds all seem to have such peace.
I wish we all could be as happy as those geese.

CHAPTER 5. STANZAIC SONNETS

Another method of Sonnet Variation is through the Stanzas. You see, the Standard English layout of three Quatrains, or the Italian Model of Octave and Sestet, can be abandoned for other Models. I've already introduced you to two – The Alfred Dorn and the Tory Hexatet. In this chapter, you'll meet five others: The Hex Sonnetta, the Rosarian, the Saraband, the Sestet, the Tricet, and the Trilonet. Each added their own character to the Format, yet retains enough Elemental Integrity to be recognized as a Sonnet.

A. Alfred Dorn Sonnet

In the previous Chapter, the Alfred Dorn Sonnet was highlighted for where it located its Couplet. In this chapter, the focus is on the other Elements of a Sonnet, mainly the Stanzas. What holds its status as a Sonnet, is the adherence to a total 14 Line structure, and loyalty to iambic Pentameter.

An Alfred Dorn Sonnet is distinguished by two Sestets bridged by a Couplet. The first one is an Italian Sestet, having a rhyme scheme of: abcabc (Rolling Rhyme). The second one is a Sicilian Sestet, taking the Scheme of: aeaeae. Six plus six equal twelve, plus the two Couplet lines brings the total to fourteen. So the entire Rhyme Scheme becomes:

abcabc dd aeaeae.

Note that the "a" Rhyme is a Linking Rhyme between the 2 Sestets. Written in iambic Pentameter. The Turn (or Volta) is at Line 9, as in most Sonnets.

I've written another one for this chapter. It is *Darkest Depression*. It was written when I was depressed, incorporating a doctored image of myself.

Sonnet 53: Darkest Depression

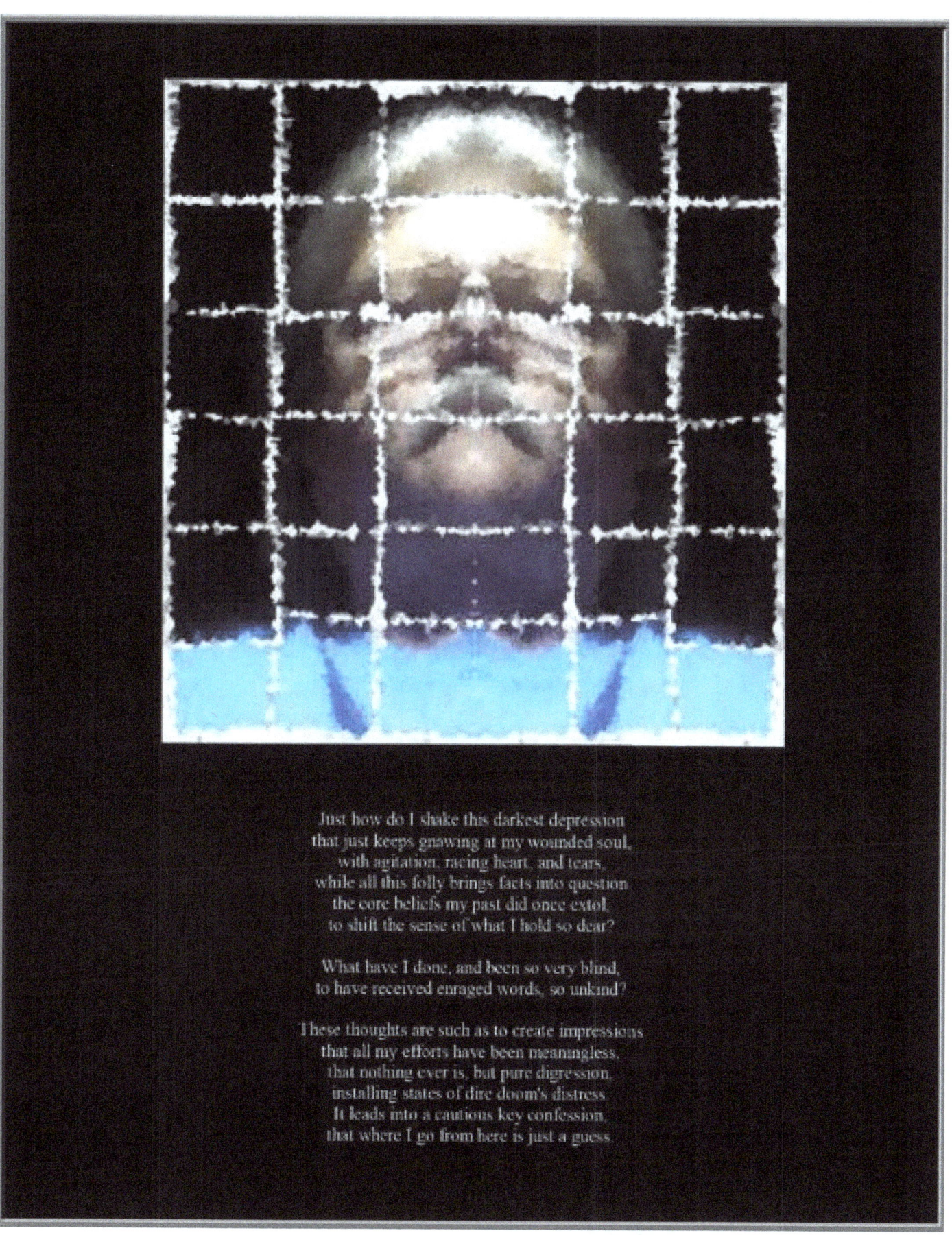

Just how do I shake this darkest depression
that just keeps gnawing at my wounded soul,
with agitation, racing heart, and tears,
while all this folly brings facts into question
the core beliefs my past did once extol,
to shift the sense of what I hold so dear?

What have I done, and been so very blind,
to have received enraged words, so unkind?

These thoughts are such as to create impressions
that all my efforts have been meaningless,
that nothing ever is, but pure digression,
installing states of dire doom's distress.
It leads into a cautious key confession,
that where I go from here is just a guess.

B. Hex Sonetta

The Hex Sonnetta was created by Andrea Dietrich. She is a contemporary Poet who often posts her work on the Poetry Soup Website. Like the Alfred Dorn, it features Stanzas that are Sestets, but places the Couplet at the usual end of the Sonnet, but the Meter is atypical.

It consists of two Six-line Stanzas and a finishing Rhyming Couplet with the following set of rules:

Meter: Iambic Trimeter (6 Syllables)

Rhyme Scheme: abbaab cddccd ee.

This particular Form uses Six Syllables of iambic Trimeter per line. Thus, the name Hex Sonnetta, as it keys off the number 6. The first part of the Form's name refers to the Syllable Count per line, as well as Six Lines per Stanza. The second part of the name, Sonnetta, is to show this to be a Form similar to the Sonnet, yet with its shorter lines and different Rhyme Scheme, it is not the Typical Sonnet. Not only does this poem have Six Syllables per Line, it also has a set of two Six-line Stanzas, giving an extra "Hex" to the meaning of Hex Sonnetta. The Rhyme Scheme, with the two 6-line Stanzas has more of an Italian feel. The Rhyming Couplet completes the Classic 14 Line Format of the Sonnet.

The one I present here is *Spellbound*. The picture is of the Sunken Garden area at the Como Park Conservatory in St. Paul, Minnesota, where flower shows are given every season, and where weddings often take place.

Sonnet 54: Spellbound

Bright flowers placed with pride,
all set in patterned rows,
or drifting water flows,
where oft' I go inside,
as senses may collide
between my eyes and nose.

This lovely plant tableau
of colors most profuse,
is perfect poet's muse.
For there the mind lets go,
to wander to and fro,
while passions are let loose.

To sense the sights, the smells,
Is felt like magic spells.

C. Roserian Sonnet

The Roserian Sonnet was created by Jose Rizal M. Reyes of the Philippines. He is a contemporary Poet who often posts on various internet sites.

The Sonnet consists of two Quintets or Quintrains (5 Line Stanza) plus a closing Quatrain. The two Quintrains are Interlinked with a shared Rhyme in the third Line (middle) of each. So there are two Rhyming Couplets in the first Stanza with another Rhyme sandwiched between them that matches the one in the center of the second Stanza. It's almost like a Peek-a-Boo Rhyme. The closing Quatrain uses an Enveloping Rhyme. It's usually written in iambic. Volta somewhere after Line 8.

So it's a Quintet + Quintet + Quatrain, using a Rhyme Scheme of:

aabcc ddbee fggf

So, its big departure from the usual Sonnet Format is the lack of a Closing Couplet, but it still maintains the integrity of 14 Lines, and requires an iambic Meter.

My example is *Love and Flowers*. The picture was taken in my brother, Richard's back yard.

Sonnet 55: Love and Flowers

What speaks more love than flower's bloom?
They fill the air with sweet perfume,
and give the eye a vivid view
that sets the scene with bright display.
Such beauty spreads in every way.

There's some presenting ruffled edge,
to grace an ornamental hedge,
with inner charm of subtle hue.
While other buds will burst with flair,
to fan out, sleek and debonair.

In either case, when picked with pride,
or purchased from a floral shop,
love's true intentions never stop,
when given to your lovely bride.

D. Saraband Sonnet

This Sonnet Form is taken from a musical dance form which has an Alternate Meter of: 3 – 4. What could be more fitting than having a Sonnet ("little song") derived from a dance. The original Saraband was a dance of Asian origin introduced into Spain in the 16th century and later to the courts of France and Italy.

A Saraband Sonnet is a Form that consists of a Tercet + Quatrain + Tercet + Closing Quatrain. So here it mimics the 3-4-3-4 character of the dance., but lacks a Couplet. It can be configured in various Styles: English, Italian, Spanish or French, making it extremely flexible. Each Stanza can be unique, but here are the basic rules.

Stanza 1: a Tercet, Rhyme: aba or aaa.

Stanza 2: a Quatrain, any Quatrain Form or Rhyme.

The Stanza Format may be mixed, taking on any of the Classic Forms as shown below.

English: abab or abcb.

Italian: baab.

Spanish: bcbc.

French/American: bbcc.

Stanza 3: a Tercet, but must be same Tercet Form as Stanza 1, and requires at least Line 2 of both Tercets to Rhyme.

Stanza 4: a Quatrain, any Quatrain Form and Rhyme.

Any Metrical Foot.

Any Metrical Line.

Some authorities insist on eight Syllables but this is not cut and dried.

Rhyme Scheme: depends on the form chosen.

The Volta is in the first Line of the second Tercet.

My contribution is *Minnesota Capitol Building*. I took that shot from the front steps of the St. Paul Cathedral.

Sonnet 56: Minnesota Capitol Building

The seat of government is physical.
When comes the time to build a capitol
Designs all tend to turn to classical.

With domes and arches meant for regal show
Of Greek and Roman architecture frills,
Where stone and marble decorations go
Upon the walls, the floor, and window sills.

Where all the shapes and forms are geometrical,
Aesthetic possibilities are practical,
Resulting in a building that is magical.

Then gild the topmost cupola in gold,
And any other spots where it's allowed,
Providing classic statement that is bold
To make the residents of this state proud.

E. Sestet Sonnet

The Sestet is a very Italian Poetic Stanza. There are even many Long Poems written in Sestets. However, it is most commonly the last Stanza of an Italian Sonnet. But here we use it in both the first and second Stanza.

A Sestet Sonnet still has the 14 Lines, like the Traditional Sonnet, but instead of the first 12 being done in 3 Quatrains (4 Line Stanzas), this Format uses 2 Sestets (6 Line Stanzas). The poem is then closed with a traditional Rhyming Couplet. The Rhyme Scheme of a Sestet Sonnet is:

abcabc cdecde ff.

With the Rhymes spaced a little further apart, they are a bit more subtle. Some think this adds to the eloquence of the Format.

My example is *Wander with a Friend*. I wrote this in a bit of a different Cadence to imitate the Rolling Rhyme Scheme of "abcabc". Instead of iambic, I used the more waltz-like Meter of Anapestic. So, instead of a marching "da Dum da Dum" of the iamb, I have a more skip-like "da da Dum, da da Dum" here. .An Anapest consists of three Syllables where the first two are Unstressed and the last one is Stressed. I blended it into a 10 Syllable line.

Sonnet 57: Wander With a Friend

At the end of the day that's forever,
When the weight of the world feels so heavy,
On the edge of the night you may wander,
In the hope to release day's endeavors
You may meet with a friend at the levee
And discuss what philosophers ponder.

For the path may be dark that you travel,
When a pal and her dog, who come along,
Make it easiest to see, when there's three;
That the knots of the day may unravel
All because they just shouldn't belong.
And with friends you become more carefree.

There is nothing better than evening time walks
With a frisky dog and with friendly talks.

F.   Tory Hexatet Sonnet

In the last chapter, the Tory Hexatet was introduced to you due to the Form's location of the Couplet in the middle, rather than the end of the Sonnet. In this chapter, we focus on its Non-traditional Stanzaic Structure.

The Format features the first eight Lines (the Octet, or Octave) in 12 Syllable iambic Hexameter, but the Rhyming Couplet holds to eight Syllables (iambic Tetrameter), located at Line 9, rather than at the end (like a Typical Sonnet's Couplet). The last four Lines of the Closing Quatrain revert back to 12 Syllables. So the poem retains the signature total 14 Lines of a Typical Sonnet.

The Couplet in the center provides the "changing point", or Volta. Its shorter Meter provides a visual, as well as oral impact, embedded as it is between two Hexameter Stanzas. Thus, it makes a direct statement and could be read by itself.

For this chapter, I wrote *Past Youth*. It features a beefcake picture of me when I was in my early twenties.

Sonnet 58: Past Youth

Recalling all my younger days is bittersweet.
The glow of youth was carried then so easily,
and possibilities were endlessly replete
with boundless energy. The future seemingly
to hold the key to our enchanting destiny.
Where nothing was impossible to those who try,
unlimited where things deserving scrutiny,
and my horizons were as open as the sky.

The mirror shows more wrinkles now
and time has slipped away somehow.

Still yet, the boy has grown and now become mature,
and tackled all the problems life makes souls endure.
When I recall the circumstances known back then,
and overcome, I'd surely do it all again.

G. Tricet Sonnet

Never heard of that? Well, that's because I recently created it. At least, to the best of my knowledge and research. You see, I like poems that have Triple Consecutive Rhymes. I feel that really brings the Rhyme to life. So, I incorporated that here in this Sonnet Format. The name Tricet derives from Triple-Rhymed Tercet (Tri-cet). So this Form does not use Quatrains at all, and deviates significantly from iambic.

A Tricet Sonnet has the usual 14 Lines, but consists of four Tercets with a Rhyming Couplet, and a Volta at Line 10. The Lines of each of the Tercets Mono-rhyme. What is also unique is the Meter. The Rhyme Scheme is:

aaa bbb ccc ddd ee

It is written in Dactylic Dimeter. A Dactyl is a Meter with a Hard Stress followed by two Soft Stresses. This Poem repeats it twice in each line.

The one I wrote for this book is *Some Thoughts to Ponder*. This one also uses an image of the author, but more recent. I used the Technique of Capitalization here, to provide impact. The picture was modified with an Emboss Technique.

Sonnet 59: Some Thoughts to Ponder

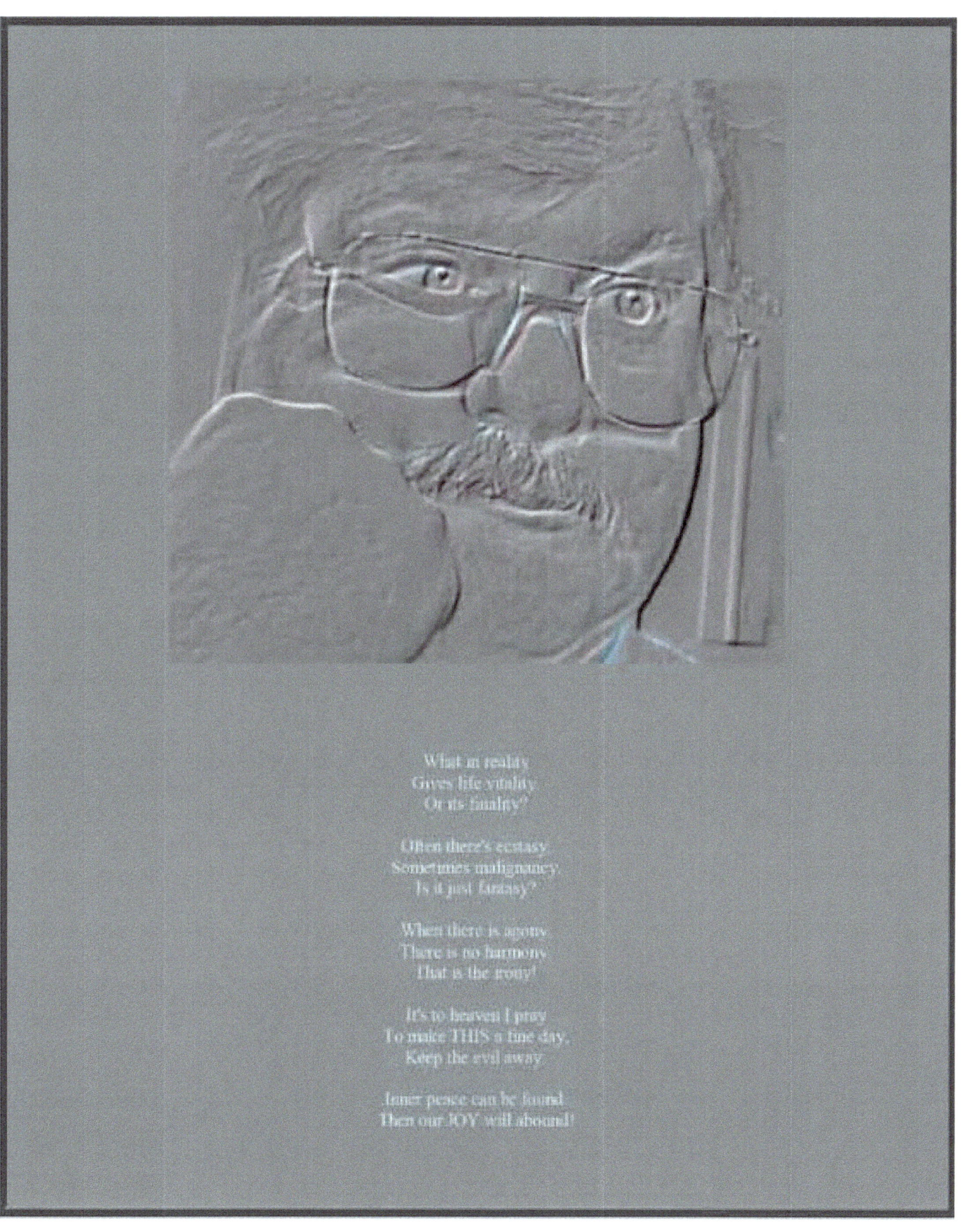

What in reality
Gives life vitality,
Or its finality?

Often there's ecstasy,
Sometimes malignancy,
Is it just fantasy?

When there is agony,
There is no harmony,
That is the irony!

It's to heaven I pray
To make THIS a fine day,
Keep the evil away.

Inner peace can be found,
Then our JOY will abound!

H. Trilonnet

The Trilonet, created by Shelley A. Cephas (aka. Shelley A). She is a contemporary Poet, Librarian, and a corporate Documentation Specialist, from Connecticut, now living in New York, who posts her work on the AllPoetry Website. She also created the Decuain.

Like my Tricet, she uses Tercets, rather than Quatrains to achieve the Structure. The Meter is more conventional. The Trilonnet is a 14 Line poem made up of four each Three-line Verses (Tercets) of 8 Syllables (iambic Tetrameter) and one Rhyming Couplet, or alternately, four each Three-lined Verses of 10 Syllables (iambic Pentameter) and one Rhyming Couplet.

Each 3 Line Verse is an Unrhymed Triplet. Each Triplet has a Rolling Rhyme Scheme of "abc". It is a Sonnet in that it made up of 14 Lines, although the Volta may occur on a Line other than Line 9. There are 2 possible Rhyme Schemes for this Form:

abc abc abc abc dd (here the Rhyme repeats).

or,

abc cba abc cba dd (here the Rhyme rolls, or undulates)

This Form is written in either iambic Tetrameter or iambic Pentameter.

I wrote *Remember Him* as my example. It is a commentary on the true meaning of Christmas. I chose iambic Tetrameter on this poem. The tree is a picture on my sister Marilee's tree.

Sonnet 60: Remember Him

December's here, with Christmas cheer,
And it's now time to celebrate
With family and closest friends.

Unwrapping toys that Santa sends,
The children all anticipate
Receiving gifts this time of year.

It's also time meant to revere
The Christ-child born upon this date,
Who died to make our sin amends.

An act of love whose gift transcends
All other gifts you contemplate.
His sacrifice was most sincere.

Enjoy the season's festive trim.
Then go to church. Remember Him.

CHAPTER 6. ADDED LINES

The most shocking departure from the Standard Sonnet Format is, I think, a break from the Traditional 14 Lines. That seems like Sonnet heresy. But here, I provide a group that demonstrates that even that Deviation can be tolerated. I'll introduce you to: the 15 Line Carrett Sonnet, the 20 Line Caudette Sonnet, the 28 Line Compound Sonnet, Dante's 20 Line Version, the 21 Line Fusion Sonnet, the 18 Line Heroic Sonnet, the 17 Line Septillian Sonnet, and finally, the 16 Line Super Sonnet.

After you have read all these, and your head stops spinning, make up your own mind as to whether these qualify as Sonnets, or not.

A. Carrett Sonnet

The Carrett Sonnet was created by my good friend, and an accomplished Canadian poet, Stephen A Carter (Carter + Sonnet equals Carrett). Who says a Sonnet has to be closed with a Rhyming Couplet? Isn't a Tercet an equally valid Stanzaic Element? Steve is a fellow FanStory Site college. He has published several books focusing on historical subjects. His Sonnet creation is a 15 Line Sonnet consisting of 3 Quatrains (a certainly recognizable Sonnet Element) with a Closing Tercet. It has an Inter-twining Rhyme Scheme, as follows:

abab cdce dfef fef

It requires a Meter of 10 beats per line in iambic Pentameter (another recognizable Standard Element).

My contribution is *Vortex of the Dark*. It was inspired by the image I captured. Just written as a bit of the Macabre Genre. I think I wrote this around Halloween. The leaves blowing off the twisted branches reminded me of bats.

Sonnet 61: Vortex of the Dark

The sun is setting, things start stirring free,
Beginning preparations for the dark.
These evening actions are what's meant to be,
When creatures of the nighttime make their mark.
The wind starts blowing, howling at the moon,
A vortex forms of things that want to roam,
Releasing to the heavens very soon,
The beasts of Hell that seek unwary souls,
And those that tarry long to make it home,
May very much regret their tardiness,
As misery and death creep from their holes
To reap the havoc only some may guess.

So heed the words Samaritans may stress,
To stay inside. Outside madness controls
The fate of those these creatures may possess.

B. Caudette Sonnet

The invention of this Form is credited to Francesco Berni (1497/98 – May 26, 1535) who was an Italian poet. So the Form has been around a long time. Berni is credited for beginning what is now known as "Bernesque poetry", a Serio-comedic Type of Poetry with Elements of Satire. Thus, according to the *Princeton Encyclopedia of Poetry*, the form is most frequently used for Satire, such as the most prominent English instance, John Milton's "*On the New Forcers of Conscience Under the Long Parliament*". Gerard Manley Hopkins used the Form in a less Satirical Mood in his "*That Nature is a Heraclitean Fire*". That Poem is one of many in which Hopkins experimented with Variations on the Sonnet Form. Hopkins explored the possibility of such a Coda in a series of letters exchanged with Robert Bridges, from whom he learned of the centrality of Milton's example in the Form. With its 6 extra Lines, including 2 Couplets, it certainly is a departure from the Standard Sonnet.

So, a Caudate Sonnet is another Expanded Version of the Sonnet. It consists of the 14 Lines of the Standard Italian Sonnet Form followed by a Coda (Latin "Cauda" meaning "tail", from which the name is derived). It starts with the Petrarchan Sonnet and adds a Three-foot Tail, then adds a Heroic Couplet, then another Tail, then another Heroic Couplet. The origin is Italian. The Rhyme Scheme is:

abbaabba cdecde e ff f gg

The Tail echoes the Rhyme of the previous Line (thus a Tail) with a 6 Syllable Meter. The rest of the lines are in iambic Pentameter.

Here is my example, *The Picnic*. It really allows the Poet you explore a Topic in more depth, and creates a lovely Effect.

Sonnet 62: The Picnic

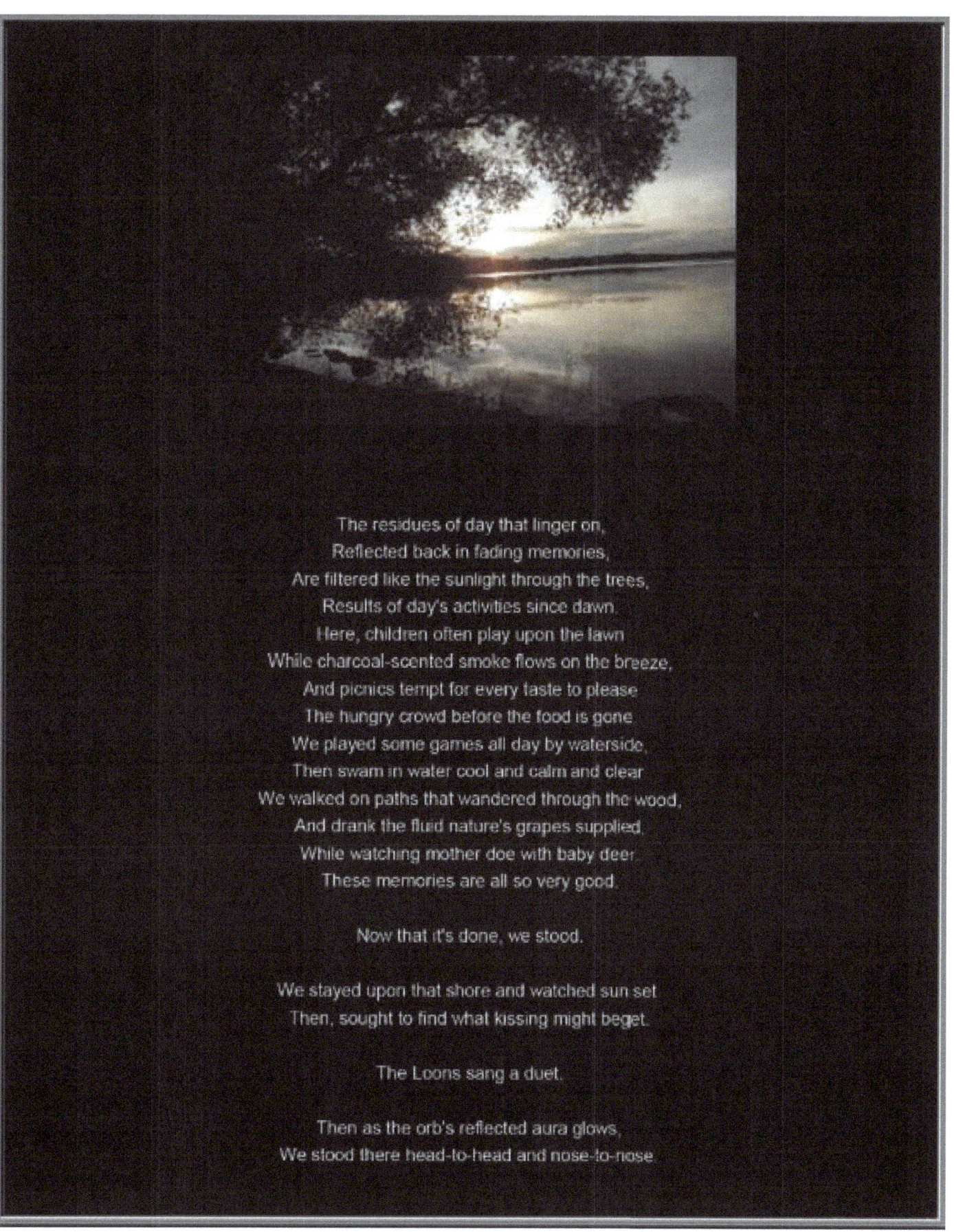

The residues of day that linger on,
Reflected back in fading memories,
Are filtered like the sunlight through the trees,
Results of day's activities since dawn.
Here, children often play upon the lawn
While charcoal-scented smoke flows on the breeze,
And picnics tempt for every taste to please
The hungry crowd before the food is gone.
We played some games all day by waterside,
Then swam in water cool and calm and clear
We walked on paths that wandered through the wood,
And drank the fluid nature's grapes supplied.
While watching mother doe with baby deer
These memories are all so very good.

Now that it's done, we stood.

We stayed upon that shore and watched sun set
Then, sought to find what kissing might beget.

The Loons sang a duet.

Then as the orb's reflected aura glows,
We stood there head-to-head and nose-to-nose.

C. Compound Sonnet

A Compound Sonnet is basically a Sonnet with everything Doubled or Compounded. Compound Sonnets have: 28 Lines of iambic Pentameter composed of three Octaves and a concluding Quatrain. Rhyme Pattern is: aabbaabb for the first Octave, ccddccdd for the second, eeffeeff for the third and gggg for the Quatrain. So you have 3 Double Qutrains (an Octave), plus a double closing Couplet (a Quatrain). The pattern is there, only twice Normal. I could find no reference to who created.

My example is *Worldly Rhythms*. One dark night I got a really crisp image of the moon. The poem transitions from night to day and back again.

Sonnet 63: Worldly Rhythms

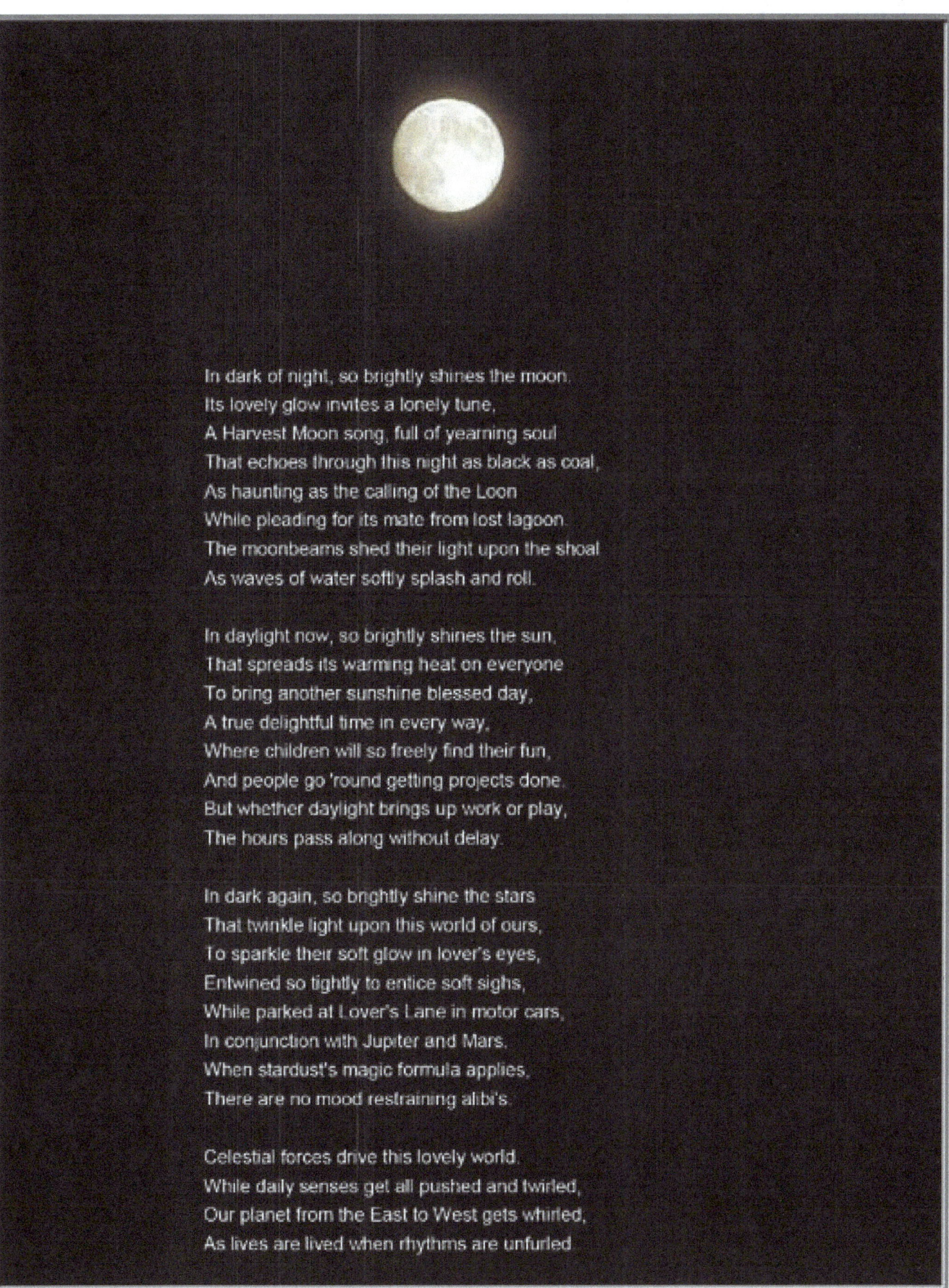

In dark of night, so brightly shines the moon,
Its lovely glow invites a lonely tune,
A Harvest Moon song, full of yearning soul
That echoes through this night as black as coal,
As haunting as the calling of the Loon
While pleading for its mate from lost lagoon.
The moonbeams shed their light upon the shoal
As waves of water softly splash and roll.

In daylight now, so brightly shines the sun,
That spreads its warming heat on everyone
To bring another sunshine blessed day,
A true delightful time in every way,
Where children will so freely find their fun,
And people go 'round getting projects done.
But whether daylight brings up work or play,
The hours pass along without delay.

In dark again, so brightly shine the stars
That twinkle light upon this world of ours,
To sparkle their soft glow in lover's eyes,
Entwined so tightly to entice soft sighs,
While parked at Lover's Lane in motor cars,
In conjunction with Jupiter and Mars.
When stardust's magic formula applies,
There are no mood restraining alibi's.

Celestial forces drive this lovely world,
While daily senses get all pushed and twirled,
Our planet from the East to West gets whirled,
As lives are lived when rhythms are unfurled

D. Dante's Version Sonnet

I introduced you to Dante's Version back in Chapter 3, as a Format created by a Famous Poet. Here we focus on its Unusual Length. The most common Italian Sonnets are written in the Petrarchan Format of a 14 Line Set consisting of two Quatrains (or an 8 line Octave), with two closing Tercets (or a Sestet), having the Rhyme Scheme: abba abba cdc cdc.

Dante wrote a 20 Line Deviation to this style. Most Sonnets in Dante's *La Vita Nuova* are Petrarchan. Chapter VII gives sonnet "*O voi che per la via*", with two Sestets (aabaab aabaab) and two Quatrains (cddc cddc), and Ch. VIII, "*Morte villana*", with two Sestets (aabbba aabbba) and two Quatrains (cddc cddc). That's quite a departure from the Typical Sonnet, but who's to question the immortal Dante?

I am recreating his Variation using the "aabbba" Form of his Chapter VIII. I chose that because, I personally like 3 Consecutive Repeated Rhymes. So this intrigued me when I read about it. Thus, the total Rhyme Scheme is:

aabbba aabbba cddc cddc

Done in iambic Pentameter, of course.

With only 4 unique Rhyme choices (a,b,c,and d) covering 20 Lines, the choice of Rhymes is crucial.

The one I wrote for this chapter is *Among the Trees*. It's an Ode to the outdoors.

Sonnet 64: Among the Trees

I always yearn to be among the trees
enticed by scents and sounds upon the breeze
that tell me, once again, that I am free
in places that I'm truly meant to be.
Where all around the beauty that I see
is such, it always puts my mind at ease.

For often, life is paced to tense degrees,
in ways that start to cause upright disease
from schedules full of ambiguity,
from stresses of a shock you can't foresee,
from overreaching opportunity.
It all adds up to bring you to your knees.

But there are places that have stayed pristine,
where wanderers can still take timeless walks,
engaging friends in confidential talks
or taking in the essence of the scene.

So heed my words: Seek out the most serene
in places where there's eagles, red-tailed hawks,
with deer and rabbits in some trees and rocks.
It's there you'll find the air is fresh and clean.

E. Fusion Sonnet

The Fusion Sonnet was invented by the contemporary Greek Poet, Yannis Livadas (born in 1969), and popularized by Sonnet Modal. In Sonnet Modal's collection *Twenty One Lines: Fusion Sonnets of 21st Century*, the Poet introduces this new Poetic Form for the Sonnet. The book presents 70 sonnets. Sonnet Mondal writes from India and is the founder of *The Enchanting Verses Literary Review*. He has authored eight books of Poetry and is on the editorial board of the multilingual magazine *Levure littéraire* based in Paris, France. I was drawn to this one by the Triple Rhymes imbedded in it.

This falls under the auspices of the Modern Sonnet Genre. As such, it breaks several Sonnet Rules. Most notably, it has 21 Lines rather than the Typical 14. The Fusion comes from blending in of 4 Lines of Free Verse at Lines 11 through 14. It has a Strict Structure and Rhyme Scheme, but is more flexible in the area of Meter. Here are the complex rules:

14 Line Poem followed by a Half Sonnet of 7 Lines acting as a Coda or Tail to add additional stability to the Poem. No particular Meter is followed, Fusing it with the modern Free Verse style.

First Fourteen Lines:

Same Rhyme in 1st,5th,9th & 10th Lines.

Same Rhyme in 2nd,3rd & 4th Lines.

Same Rhyme in 6th,7th & 8th lines.

Rhetorical Questions in 9th & 10th lines.

Negative and Pessimistic note in the first 10 lines.

Free Verse carrying Optimistic Tone in 11th, 12th,13 & 14th Lines.

Volta gradually through 9th, 10th and 11th lines.

Next Seven Lines:-The Half Sonnet acting as a Coda.

Same Rhyme in 16th and 17th lines.

 Same Rhyme in 18th and 19th lines.

Volta in the 20th line.

For this poem the Rhymes Scheme, as laid out above is:

A1, b,b,b, A2, c,c,c, (4 Lines Free Verse)--- A1, d,d,e,e,A2, where the capital letters indicate Repeated Lines.

This is the second instance of a Sonnet adding a Coda. Like the Caudatte Sonnet, it adds a Tail.

My contribution is *Humanity*. The picture was taken at the Minnesota State Fair, which runs at the end of every August. The poem is a commentary on resource conservation.

Sonnet 65: Humanity

Humanity is all about.
The numbers cannot be denied.
The trend is on an upward glide,
Where our resources soon collide,
And there are some things we can't do without.
Like any fresh water supply.
Our reservoirs are going dry.
We soon may just be getting by.
How long will it take for food to run out?
Is our survival in some long-term doubt?

We seem a very resilient lot,
And some resources are renewable.
We can learn conservation and practice
All the ways to consume within reason.

Humanity is all about.
Our intelligence has no real limit
When inspiration resides within it.
Add in our science and necessity,
We'll find ways to save our society.
For the need is great to forge the right route,
And there are some things we can't do without.

F. Heroic Sonnet

The Heroic Sonnet is the Cornerstone Format of the Crown of Heroic Sonnets, which links a string of seven of them together. This Form (to be further developed in Chapter 8) was invented by the Siena Academy, which was formed in 1460. Unlike other Sonnets this Format does not require a Volta (or Turn), in that it is meant to convey large amounts of information, or a story. It consists of four Quatrains typically in iambic Pentameter, using one of two Classic Rhyme Schemes throughout, either "aabb" or "abab." It is closed with the usual Rhyming Couplet. So it contains 18 Lines, rather than the usual 14 Lines of a Sonnet, in order for it to tell a longer story. That's where the "Heroic" designation comes from, that extra Quatrain.

My version is *The Yellow Mountains of China*. Here I give a Treatise on the region in China, with some History as well. Li Bai, who is mentioned in the Poem, is famous for the artistry of the Asian Poetic Form. Around a thousand Poems attributed to him are extant. His Poems have been collected into the most important Tang Dynasty Poetry Anthology. This image is not the Yellow Mountains of China. They are yellow sandstone cliffs near St. Paul, Minnesota at Battle Creek, but you get the idea.

You can see how this Form is good for transmitting information.

Sonnet 66: The Yellow Mountains of China

The Yellow mountain range of Chinese lore
can glow in sunset's shine, like purest gold.
What beauty has brought culture to the fore?
Its very vistas, beautiful and bold.

Huang Di, China's leader who was known
as "Yellow Emperor" of ancient fame --
Has legends he ascended heaven's throne
from there, which gave that mountain site his name.

Huangshan, "Yellow Mountain" in Chinese,
gained fame -747 AD.
Li Bai described it in a poem treatise,
which brought attention as a sight to see.

The sixty thousand steps carved in its side,
were dug out fifteen hundred years ago
Unesco's designation brings great pride,
with twenty thousand poems been penned, or so.

These mountains rise unto majestic heights
as one of China's most artistic sites.

G. Septillian Sonnet

The Septillian Sonnet was created by a contemporary Poet and fellow Fanstorian, Nancy E. Davis. It is an Elongated Version of the Basic Sonnet Format, having 17 Lines versus the Typical 14 Lines. Nevertheless, it carries all the features and recognizable Structures of a Standard Sonnet, with: three Stanzas followed by a Closing Couplet, in iambic Pentameter, and a Volta (but at line 11, rather than 9). The Elongation is due to using Quintains (5 line Stanzas) instead of Quatrains. The Rhyme Scheme is set at a strict "aabbb" Scheme. The name is derived from the 17 Lines, "Sept" being "7" in French, and "tillian" being a play on "teen". The total Rhyme Scheme is therefore:

aabbb ccddd eefff gg.

I wrote one called *Morning Camp*. The picture was taken one early morning at Lake Carlos, a Minnesota State Park near Alexandria, Minnesota. Hope you can feel my mood.

Sonnet 67: Morning at Camp

Down by the lakeshore, early in the day,
the rising sun was burning fog away.
What was remaining, was a thinning mist.
Like tendrils, drifting smoke would slowly twist
in silent scene no poet can resist.

The morning coffee, brewing in the pot,
was wafting fragrance, getting nice and hot.
The perfect way to chase the morning chill
I poured a cup, prepared to drink my fill.
Then found a bench, to gather in the still.

A Loon had landed, out upon the lake.
An eerie song proceeds to overtake
the silent setting, with its mournful call,
and yet its echo blended with it all,
to make that moment perfectly enthrall.

Within this instance, found profound release,
and drank my coffee in idyllic peace.

H. Super Sonnet

A Super Sonnet is composed of several Quatrains closed by a Rhyming Couplet. It is meant to provide for very long Poetic Expression, or even book chapters. It generally utilizes all four of the Primary Rhyme Schemes:

Alternate Rhyming - abab

Coupled Rhyming - aabb

Enveloping Rhyme - abba

Skipping Rhyme - abcb

So, the Poem writes in a Set of the Four Types, and then Repeats them as many times as the Author wishes. The Four Sets are necessary in every four Stanza Series, but not necessarily in the same Sequence. One required feature though, relates to the very Last Stanza, which is always the "abcb" Skipping Rhyme Type. The Unrhymed Third Line of that Stanza sets the Rhyme for the Final Rhyming Couplet, thereby linking the last Quatrain to the Couplet. The creator of this Format in unknown, but there are many examples of this Form around. It really stretches the Boundries of the Format, but when the Closing Couplet is finally reached, it provides a point of recognition and comfort.

My example is *Computer Industry Genesis*. For this poem I used only Two Sets of the Four Types. In the First Four, I used - Alternating, Coupled, Skipping, then Enveloping. For the Second Set, I went - Alternating, Enveloping, Coupled, and then Skipping.

I kept the Meter as iambic Tetrameter. I give a touch of business history. Since I worked is this industry for 44+ years, I lived it. The early computers took up whole rooms.

Sonnet 68: Computer Industry Genesis

A spark, a thought, a draft design,
Desire to meet a certain need,
A mind alert to help define -
All elements to plant the seed.

Then from a noble nebulous,
A dream that was ambiguous,
Took on its own reality,
Creating opportunity.

John Mauchly and John Eckert gave
A gift to the entire world.
Turned on the first Eniac 1,
As digital readouts unfurled.

For thus it was, they turned the page
From 1's and 0's the men bestowed
What ushered the Computer Age
With magical binary code.

They formed the firm of Univac,
Put first commercial use to it,
For government's need, keeping track,
And turned a profit - just a bit.

In Nineteen Fifty census counts,
The Univac machine worked out
To prove efficiency throughout,
Reducing time by large amounts.

From something that was so benign,
Some software tools became divine.
The world was soon completely changed,
Amazed, improved, and rearranged.

And from it sprang a whole new way
Of doing complicated tasks.
It should rank high celebrity
Whenever survey question asks.

This joins historic tapestry.
They founded whole new industry.

CHAPTER 7. SONNETS WITH RHYME VARIATIONS.

The Bedrock of the Sonnet Format is iambic Pentameter, followed by iambic Tetrameter, but not for the writers of these Sonnets. OH no! For these Pioneers, that is too boring. The Rhyme Scheme is beefed up is some manner. In this chapter, I'll introduce you to Arabian Onegin, where every Stanza is Mono-Rhymed; the Asean, that makes the Entire Poem Mono-Rhymed (not just each Stanza); the Beymorlin, with Mirrored Rhyme; The Dual Sonnet, using In-line Rhyme to match the End-line Rhyme; The Pantygonet, where Interlinked Feminine Rhyme is used; the Sestina Sonnet, that eschews Rhyme for matching Repeated Words; the Shadow, that knows Duplicate, even Homophonic Words; the Slide Sonnet, where the First Half of the First Line of each Stanza, Slides to become the Second Half of the Third Line; the Triptic, that plays with Interlinking Triple Rhymes; the Visser, that Hides the Rhymes; and the Welsh, which uses Cross-Rhymes. Now that's some Variation. Catch your breath as we journey through these Sonnets.

A. Arabian Onegin Sonnet

An Arabian Sonnet is simply one that is comprised of two Quatrains followed by two Tercets, where each Stanza is Mono-Rhymed. Written in iambic Pentameter. The Onegin aspect adds a touch of complexity to the Rhyme Scheme by repeating End Rhymes (rather than Refrain lines) in the following Rhyme Scheme:

A,a,A,a - B,B,b,b - C,c,C - D,D,d.

The Capital letters indicate the Rhymes that are Repeated. The trick here is to write the Repeats so that they sound Unique and the Theme flows smoothly. Not sure why it was named that or who named it, as it doesn't resemble the Pushkin Sonnet in any manner.

I am not particularly enamored with the Format, as without the Author Notes, a reader could assume the Poet is a Sloppy Rhymer. Usually, Rhyming a Word with itself is a "no-no", but not in this Format. In fact, it's a Requirement.

My example is *Winter Spell*. I took the picture one winter morning at Harriet Island, located in the Mississippi just across from downtown St. Paul, Minnesota. It tried to capture the Essence of the Image within the Verse. I hope you agree.

Sonnet 69: Winter Spell

When winter covers walks in layered snow,
there's still a track to show you where to go,
by following impressions in the snow,
on footprints that will wander to and fro.

That path may be a challenge for your feet.
You might engage another's booted feet,
that tracked a trail that people can repeat,
where you could even chance to take a seat.

Then oh, what winter wonders will be seen,
where white snow leaves a veil so crisp and clean.
Let's linger there to see what can be seen.

As shadows cast a spell in twilight glow,
the sparkles in the snow begin to glow,
like sprinkled dust the fairies might bestow.

B. Asean Sonnet

The Asean Sonnet was created by Jose Rizal M. Reyes. This renowned Sonneteer of the Philippines has suggested that there are Three Classes of Sonnets; namely Sonnets of the head, of the heart, and of the hand. Sonnets of the hand are those with some mechanistic feature or formulation that differentiates the Sonnet by Rhyme Pattern, Meter, Line Length, or Volta placement. Sonnets by head are merely a matter of content. Sonnets of the Heart are romantic in nature, dealing with love. He is a contemporary Poet, who considers himself the only Sonnet Grandmaster of the world; author of 1500 Sonnets. The Poem's name refers to the geographic region of South East Asia.

The Asean Sonnet's two unique features are; that it contains a Format of an Octave (8 lines), plus a Quatrain (4 lines), closed by a Couplet (2 lines); and it is completely Mono-Rhymed for all 14 Lines. The Rhyming is what I am focusing on here in this chapter. It makes for a Poem where a Single Rhyme throughout requires a very careful choice of Rhyme Words and Subject Matter. Volta begins at Line 9.

My contribution is *Bumble Bee*. The image is one I captured of common clover with a bee on it. All the Rhymes match the word "bees," with no Repeats. Note the Alliteration and In-line Rhymes too.

Sonnet 70: Bumble Bees

I often watch the humble bumble bees
That glide and swoop with ease upon the breeze.
Their presence on the clover guarantees
The propagation of its properties.
It's easy here to spot the likes of these.
Their bodies are distinctive when one sees
The black and yellow furred extremities,
Or hear clear buzzing wing-borne frequencies.

With nests that might be found in ground or trees,
Disturbing them can cause extreme unease
From stings applied by frequent pain degrees
Which lead to dire health emergencies.

So, watch these bees carefully, if you please.
Their actions bolster our economies.

C. Beymorlin Sonnet

Beymorlin Sonnet is called "a Shakespearean Sonnet in the Italian form" probably meaning it is a Cross between a Shakespearean and Italian Sonnet. The Distinguishing Feature of this Sonnet is that there is a Double Rhyme Pattern occurring simultaneously. This Verse Form was introduced into US by Carl Morton, Alabama State Poet Laureate in the 80s. The Beymorlin Sonnet may be the 1976 creation of the collective effort of American Poets Richard Beyer, Carl Morton and Marjorie Lees Linn (Bey-Mor-Lin).

The Beymorlin Sonnet is unique in its Mirrored Rhyming. It is Structured within the Conventional 14 Line Format of a Sonnet, but it requires the **second syllable** of each Line to Rhyme with the End-rhyme of each Line, in addition to carrying an overall Rhyme Scheme of the Author's choosing.

My example is *Time to Play*. For this one, I chose an Overall Rhyme Scheme of:

ababcdcd efef gg.

I bolded the Rhymes to make it easier for you to see. The Poem includes a family portrait of my grandson Isaac, granddaughter Skylah, and Son-in-law Jeremy, playing and mugging.

Sonnet 71: Time to Play

Today, we found sufficient time to **play**,
To **take** the time to share the fun kid's **make**,
As **they** so innocently can portray
A **break** from things we grownups may foresake,
To **smile** and just be silly for a **while**,
To **hug** and just cavort upon a **rug**,
To **pile** upon each other with some **style**,
And **mug** some funny faces, looking **smug**.

Oh **how** delightful, living in the **now**!
It's **real**, how children's joy can make you **feel**,
Allowing peals of laughter to endow
A **healing** tonic touch of such appeal.

So go enjoy them, they so quickly **grow**,
And **show** them love. They're gone before you **know**.

D. Dual Sonnet

The Dual Sonnet was invented by Allan R. Emery (aka Joe King), a contemporary Poet who posts his work on AllPoetry.com.

A Dual Sonnet is very similar to the Beymorlin Sonnet that I published earlier, in that both contain In-line Rhyming, The Beymorlin requires the Second Syllable to match the End-line Rhyme, as I noted before. The Dual Sonnet requires a Rhyme Scheme in the Center of the Hexametered Lines of the Stanza, but not necessarily matching the End-line Rhyme Scheme. In fact, there are Two Separate Intertwining Rhyme Schemes within the Poem. There is a Rhyme Scheme at the Center of the Poem, and another at the End. The two Schemes are as follows:

Stanza 1	Stanza 2	Stanza 3	Couplet
a - a	a - c	c - e	e - g
b - b	b - d	d - f	e - g
b - a	b - c	c - e	
a - b	a - d	d - f	

So the Center Scheme is:

abba abba cdcd ee.

The Back Scheme is:

abab cdcd efef gg

My Version for this book is *Fall, The Best*. Since this may be hard to detect in the poem, I repeated it with the rhymes bolded so that you can see the Rhyme Scheme in detail better. I did use a bit of Slant or Near Rhyme in Rhyming: seem/between and include/attitude.

Sonnet 72: Fall, the Best

Enjoy the leaves when Autumn comes for then the world becomes
A landscape-painter's dream, where all the colors are extreme.
Where a pretty pigment scheme provides such vivid outcomes.
The day at once succumbs unto the beauty of the scene.

When adding up the sums, another aspect to include,
Bright sunlight, it would seem, adds its own vibrancy to all,
And houses in between complete the urban attitude.
The pulse of Nature hums within the Season we call Fall.

The squirrels may soon intrude, as they scurry for their nuts.
A soul may hear the geese call, flying over, heading south.
All creatures, big and small, prepare their Winter huts.
You'll see some storing food -- a chipmunk, acorns in its mouth.

So, if you're asking, "What's the finest Season to attest?"
There are no IFs, or ANDs, or BUTs, it's Fall that seems the best.

(Poem repeated with rhymes bolded)

Enjoy the leaves when Autumn **comes** for then the world **becomes**
A landscape-painter's **dream**, where all the colors are **extreme**.
Where a pretty pigment **scheme** provides such vivid **outcomes**.
The day at once **succumbs** unto the beauty of the **scene**.

When adding up the **sums**, another aspect to **include**,
Bright sunlight, it would **seem**, adds its own vibrancy to **all**,
And houses in **between** complete the urban **attitude**.
The pulse of Nature **hums** within the Season we call **Fall**.

The squirrels may soon **intrude**, as they scurry for their **nuts**.
A soul may hear the geese **call**, flying over, heading **south**.
All creatures, big and **small**, prepare their Winter **huts**.
You'll see some storing **food** -- a chipmunk, acorns in its **mouth**.

So, if you're asking, **"What's** the finest Season to **attest**?"
There are no IFs, or ANDs, or **BUTs**, it's Fall that seems the **best**.

E. Pantygonnet

This Format is a Variation of the Standard Sonnet and was created by contemporary and fellow Fanstory Site Poet, Pantygynt (James Bartlett), by modifying his Form – the Pantygynt. The primary aspect is the use of Feminine Meter, and the break from Typical Pentameter. The original Pantygynt Poem consists of a Quatrain in Ballad Meter and Rhyme followed by a Rhyming Tercet in iambic Tetrameter. The cycle concludes with a Single Line of iambic Tetrameter on the "b" Rhyme. So the Rhyme Scheme of the Poem is:

abab, ccc, b.

By running the Eight Lines together and putting the whole thing into Tetrameter a Typical Octave, not too unlike that in a Petrarchan Sonnet, is created. Two Tercets are run together to create the Sestet with one of the many Rhyme Schemes acceptable in the Petrarchan form. The Rhyme Scheme in the Octave is:

a B a B c c c B, where the "B" Rhyme is Feminine.

The Petrarchan Sestet can be any of the following, where:

c d d c e e, or

c d c d e e,

are most used. So the total; Rhyme Scheme of the Sonnet would be:

a B a B c c c B – c d d c e e, or

a B a B c c c B – c d c d e e

I wrote my example as *Deforestation*, a commentary on use of resources. However, for this Sonnet I deviated a bit, for fun, and carried the "B" Rhyme down into the Sestet as follows:

B d e e d B

So the entire Rhyme Scheme is: a B a B c c c B - B d e e d B.

Sonnet 73: Deforestation

Once forests covered all the land,
the crowning glory of creation,
Each tree a process where they stand,
producing much oxygenation,
And the ground was firm where they stood,
alive with creatures in the wood,
For all concerned, it was quite good,
achieving balanced acclimation.

Before any deforestation,
when mankind happened on the scene,
to dominate, impose his will,
by cutting trees, so he could till,
all Nature's laws to contravene,
oblivious to devastation.

F. Sestina Sonnet

You were originally introduced to this Format back in Chapter 2 as a Transition from a well-known popular Type of Poem that is turned into a Sonnet. Here it is highlighted as Type of Poem that Deviates from the Typical Rhyme Scheme they usually take. In fact, it doesn't Rhyme at all.

A Sestina is unusual in that it doesn't use Rhyme, but instead uses the same Words Repeated in different Sequences for each Stanza. So it Mimics Rhyme by Repeating (or Parroting) the same Words, only in a specific Sequence. Normally, the Sestina has 6 Repeated Words Sequences over six Verses and a Closing Tercet that uses all six Words. But, in order to accommodate a Sonnet, it has been modified to have only 4 Words ending each Line of a Quatrain repeated over three Verses, plus with a Couplet that incorporates all four of the Key Words. It is not necessary to choose Words that Rhyme, but I like to, as it then gives a nice Rhyme Sequence. Note also that the Fixed Sequence causes the last Word of each Stanza to Repeat as the first End-Word of the next Stanza.

So, if you identify the four words with the letters A, B, C, and D, the Word Sequence for the Sonnet is:

ABCD DCAB BADC (BC)(DA),

Where the letters in parens represent two Words in each Line of the Couplet.

The example that I wrote here is *Gliding Therapy*. It was inspired as I walked along the Mississippi River and watched some University of Minnesota students rowing a skiff. For this Poem, I chose the 4 Words:

glow
outside
row
glide

Sonnet 74: Gliding Therapy

Fine days upon the Mississippi flow
are wonderful sweet times to be outside,
to take a chance to be in boats that row,
to exercise on working gear that glide.

Oh, what a thrill, to feel that sleek craft glide,
while passing lovely landscape as you row,
to pull upstream or race down with the flow,
experiencing wonders found outside!

It seems we're at our best when we're outside.
I know for me, it makes my juices flow.
It yields that place to let our problems glide,
or sort them, like ducks swimming in a row.

Outside brings therapy with row, row, row-
a healthy glide to help go with the flow.

G. Shadow Sonnet

I must recognize Anthony Fawcus (aka. tfawcus), because Tony, a colleague and fellow Fanstorian, led me to find and research this Format.

The Shadow Sonnet was created by Amera M. Andersen. It is a fairly recent invented Form found at All Poetry.com and Shadow Poetry. She is a contemporary Poet. Her biographical profile reads, "Amera is a classically-self-taught Poet, award-winning Author, Social-butterfly and Renaissance Thinker who leads from the heart toward a world of unlimited possibilities," The form may be written in any Sonnet Style. The Shadow takes place at the Beginning and Ending of each Line as the words may be identical or even Homophonic. Since all Poetry was originally meant to be sung or recited out loud, Homophonic words are acceptable. They are words that sound alike such as "see and sea," or "be and bee." The trick is to repeat the words as creatively as possible to convey meaning without being clunky or intrusive.

The rules for a Shadow Sonnet are:

A Poem written in the usual 14 Lines,

The Meter uses either 8, 9 or 10 Syllables per Line.

The Poem should have a Volta or Pivot.

Iambic Pentameter is not necessary, allowing wiggle room on what Syllables are Stressed or Unstressed.

My contribution to this Style is *Time*. I used a Meter of 8 Syllables (Tetrameter). I have two Homophonic Lines using no/know and our/hour. There is Enjambment between line 10 and 11.

Sonnet 75: Time

Hark unto me, listeners hark!
Time waits for none, fast fleeting time.
Dark in the night, it drags in dark.
Sublime then, when rest is sublime.

Fast, as the years blur by, so fast.
Slow, when you're waiting, it goes slow.
Last to mind, when coming home last.
No wait, when there's a need to know.

So keep clocks handy, keep them so.
Our lives are organized as our
Flow of day's rhythm sets the flow.
Our time is numbered by the hour.

Time waits for none, fast fleeting time.
Chime every hour, sweet sounding chime!

H. Slide Sonnet

The Slide Sonnet is another Format created by Victoria Sutton (aka. "PassionsPromise"), a contemporary Poet. Her works are often published on the Poets Collective Website under that pseudonym. You were originally introduced to her other layout, the Tory Hexatet, in Chapters 4 and 5. This is another creatively unique Form.

Like most Sonnets, it has 14 Lines. It is composed with an Author's choice of eight, ten, or twelve Syllables to each Line. The unique feature of this Format is, that the First Half of the First Line of each Stanza, "Slides" to the Last Half of the Third Line, creating a unique Poetic Repetition, and raising havoc with the Rhymes. The Rhyme Scheme may be in any of the Standard Sonnet Rhyme Schemes, either:

aabb ccdd eeff gg (Coupled), or
abab cdcd efef gg (Alternating), or
abba cddc effe gg (Enveloped).

It is typically done in iambic. The Volta, or Turn, occurs at Line 9.

My Version is *Tree Top Thoughts*. I took that photograph of an eagle in its nest with a telephoto lens from about 200 yards away. To me, the nest looks quite uncomfortable. I used iambic Hexameter (12 Syllables , or six Metric Feet). I highlighted the Phrases that Slid, to identify them more clearly. Note how this Technique creates Cross Rhyming. I also used some Elizabethan Dialect, and a touch of Humor.

Sonnet 76: Tree Top Thoughts

Where e'er thou buildest nest, best not to build with twigs,
Unless an eagle be, who decorates with sprigs.
For comfort be thy goal, where e'er thou buildest nest.
Unless thee thrive in trees, a softer nest is best.

A home is meant to be a place where most relax.
Not likely, when thy rump is sitting on sharp tacks.
That's not the common way a home is meant to be.
But then again, most are not living in a tree.

Did nature compensate for giving birds their wings?
To gain command of air, did give up other things?
I oft' have wondered thus. Did nature compensate?
When given gift of flight, is treetop home thy fate?

'Tis just this observation, so subtly profound,
When God was making plans, we humans lived on ground.

I.   Triptic Sonnet

Never heard of that? Well, that's because I created it. So here is another Format of my creation. At least, to the best of my knowledge and research. You see, I like Poems that have Triple Consecutive Rhymes. I feel that really brings the Rhyme to life. So, I incorporated that here in this Sonnet Format. The name Triptic derives from the Triple Rhyme Scheme.

A Triptic Sonnet has the usual 14 Lines, consisting of three Quatrains with a Rhyming Cuplet, and a Volta at Line 9. What distinguishes it is the Rhyme Scheme and Meter. The First Line of each Quatrain Rhyme with each other, Interlinking the Stanzas. The next 3 Lines of the Stanza all Rhyme, creating a elegant Echo Effect. The Rhyme Scheme is:

abbb accc addd ee.

It is written in any iambic Meter.

I have written three for this book, one in each of the three Meters.

The first is *Leaf Cascade*. I chose iambic Pentameter here. It's an Ode to the green colors that dominate nature. I used a touch of Onomatopoeia in the first Stanza. The image is a wall of weeping willow trees.

The second is *Oaken Arms*, written in iambic Tetrameter. I took this picture to show the grace of oak trees, even without their leaves. I have the image of the St. Paul Cathedral framed by their limbs. In this one, I used the First Line of each Stanza as a Repeated Refrain.

The third is *Oh Dandelion*, done is Hexameter. I tried to capture their Essence in both the flower as well as the seed phase. I added a touch of Elizabethan Dialect to dress it up a bit. I do admire their survival skill.

I did these three in order to show that, even given a Formatted Structure, there is still a great deal of flexibility in a Sonnet.

Sonnet 77: Leaf Cascade

So often Mother Nature makes a spot
That paints a place in several shades of green,
In hidden glades whose shades create a scene
That whispers in its silence, "so serene".

These are the treasures valued quite a lot,
By those whose intuition really knows,
The beauty locked within those stately rows
Of trees that grow supreme where water flows.

But you may search forever, yet cannot,
Find solitude the likes that Nature made,
As here, this weeping willow's leaf cascade
Makes waterfalls of foliage furnish shade.

This tall tableau of trees, of which I'm fond,
Stands here beside this quiet little pond.

Sonnet 78: Oaken Arms

I see these mighty oaks in spring,
Before their leaves begin to bud,
When melting snow's turned earth to mud,
But prior to the springtime flood.

I see these mighty oaks in spring,
Stand tall, to spread majestic limbs
In grandest geometric whims,
That softly whisper wind-borne hymns.

So, see these mighty oaks in spring!
Their branches, feathered to fine lace,
Caress the sky with stunning grace,
In arching swirls their fingers trace

Delight their naked springtime charms
That frame the world with oaken arms.

Sonnet 79: OH Dandelion

Oh dandelion, golden harbinger of spring,
I keep my eye on thee! You populate my lawn
Your lion heads appeared so suddenly one dawn,
A yellow carpet, spread for bees to feast upon

I find thy presence here a most amazing thing
Eradication of thy growth has been my goal
I've poisoned, pulled, and used all kinds of weed control
Yet still, I find entire generations whole

And, there's a reproductive weapon that you bring
As if your stubborn stamina were not enough
That golden head becomes a whitened ball of fluff
That spreads its seeds, when blows a single windy puff.

Though there are many angry thoughts these weeds inspire,
It's their survival strategy I must admire.

J. Visser Sonnet (aka. Hidden Rhyme Sonnet)

It was created by Audrae Visser, Poet Laureate of S. Dakota, (1974-2001). It reads much like a Blank Verse Poem, in that it is done in iambic Meter (12 Syllables, or Hexameter, in this case), and has no End Rhymes. However, it does indeed have a Rhyme Scheme, but it is hidden in the middle of each Line, rather than at the end. So it becomes extremely subtle. In fact, it takes the Scheme of a Typical Petrarchan Sonnet, with its Rhyme Scheme of:

abbaabba cdecde.

The Volta also remains at Line 9.

It is so subtle that it can be easily missed. So I repeated the Poem here, revealing the Rhyme. I must say, that after having written one and reading several others, my reaction is "Why?" I see no real value in hiding the Rhyme, other than the pure challenge of writing one. Maybe each one should start with an introduction and challenge to the reader to find and define the Rhyme Scheme. Otherwise, I'm not very enamored.

In any case, my submission is *Exploring Cliff Cave*. I think you'll see what I mean. At least, once revealed, one does become amazed that it is there.

Sonnet 80: Exploring Cliff Cave

Exploring sandstone cave is dangerous, but seems
Beguiling and enthralls adventure smitten souls.
Watch out for ceiling falls, as frequently it does.
You need to be quite brave, but also very smart.
Initials you engrave, to prove that you've been there,
In those soft sandstone walls, remain a long long time.
As history recalls your presence, it may stay,
Or end up on your grave, if you're not careful then.

So when you climb so high, to see the hidden sights,
It's fine to peer inside, exploring what you've found,
But stop to catch the view that you've been climbing for,
And watch the clouds go by from awesome eagle's heights.
With common sense abide, when you're searching the cave.
All will go well with you, if you remain alert.

(Now here it is repeated with the rhyme revealed in bold)

Exploring sandstone **cave** is dangerous, but seems
Beguiling and **enthralls** adventure smitten souls.
Watch out for ceiling **falls**, as frequently it does.
You need to be quite **brave**, but also very smart.
Initials you **engrave**, to prove that you've been there,
In those soft sandstone **walls**, remain a long long time.
As history **recalls** your presence, it may stay,
Or end up on your **grave**, if you're not careful then.

So when you climb so **high**, to see the hidden sights.
It's fine to peer **inside**, exploring what you've found,
But stop to catch the **view** that you've been climbing for,
And watch the clouds go **by** from awesome eagle's heights.
With common sense **abide**, when you're searching the cave.
All will go well with **you**, if you remain alert.

K.   Welsh Sonnet

While writing my book of Sonnets, I realized that the Welsh weren't represented in the series of Sonnet Formats, so I created this one for it. Another one of my creations. I used three Awdl Gywydds with a Cyhydeddfer attached to the third one to give me the recognizable 14 Lines of a Sonnet.

So, what are those strange terms?

The Awdl Gywydd consists of a four Line Quatrain using a 7 Syllable Meter (a definite departure from most Sonnet's iambic Meter) with a unique Rhyme Structure as well, where the End Rhymes form a recognizable "abcb" pattern, but **line 2** carries an In-line Rhyme to match the **First Line's** End Rhyme (the "a" Rhyme) at either the second, third, fourth, or fifth Syllable, while the **Fourth Line** similarly carries the End Word of the **Third Line** (the "c" End Word) as an In-line Rhyme somewhere between the second and fifth Syllable. So the Awdl Gywydd's Rhyme Scheme can be represented as follows:

xxxxxxa
xXaXXxb
xxxxxxc
xXcXXxb,

where the large X represents the **Alternate Positions** of the In-line Rhymes. This is a very Welsh style, and is known as Cross Rhyming. The Variability of the location is also very Welsh.

I then closed the third Awdl Gywydd, with a Cyhydeddfer, which is simply an 8 Syllable Rhyming Couplet, often used as a Cauda (Tail) for one of the Welsh Forms, as I did here.

My example is *Ghost Ship - Lady Lovibond*. It is a Historical Poem about a Ghost Ship, and a dangerous part of the English Channel. I repeated the Poem a second time, to show how the Rhymes go. Although there is no Closing Couplet, per se, the last two Liines do Rhyme. That became necessary due to Enjambment between Lines twelve and thirteen. That is unique to this particular Poem's Poetic License.

Sonnet 81: Ghost Ship - Lady Lovibond

(With Rhyme revealed)

What debris lay on the shore
by the oar and wooden crate?
Who knows what the tide washed in,
or sins Goodwin Sands relate?

Was a woman's bad omen
wrought ship's men a timeless fate
on the Lady Lovibond,
where rages spawned in firstmate.

Killed the sailor at the wheel.
Forced ship to reel into shoals.
Everyone was lost at sea.
Now every fifty years, souls
see that ghost ship off Dover Straits,
after seventeen forty eight.

What debris lay on the **shore**
by the **oar** and wooden **crate**?
Who knows what the tide washed **in**,
or **sins** Goodwin Sands relate?

Was a woman's bad **omen**
wrought ship's **men** a timeless **fate**
on the Lady Lovi**bond**,
where rages **spawned** in first**mate**.

Killed the sailor at the **wheel**.
Forced ship to **reel** into **shoals**.
Everyone was lost at **sea**.
Now eve**ry** fifty years, **souls**
see that ghost ship off Dover **Straits**,
after seventeen forty **eight**.

CHAPTER 8. SONNETS WITH UNUSUAL LINE LENGTHS

Most readers of Poetry are familiar with, and used to, a Poem written in the Typical iambic Meter, the most common being Pentameter (10 Syllable Lines), followed by Tetrameter (8 Syllables), and possibly Hexameter (12 Syllables). Usually the Meter holds constant throughout the Poem. But does this need to be the case? The answer is a resounding – NO!

In fact, I am about to provide you with 14 examples of Formats that do not follow a Standard or Consistent Line Length at all. Yet they can still be classified as Sonnets. In this chapter you'll meet: the Cornish where the Poet can choose any Meter they like (mine varies between 7, 8 and 9); the Faux Free Verse Sonnet where the Line can be virtually Any Size; the Fusion with no specified Meter; the Hex Sonnetta having 6 Syllables per Line; the Japanese Sonnet having a 5, 7, or 3 Line Length (following Haiku and Tanka rules); the Limerick Sonnet with its Long, Short, Long Layout; the Lyricat's 7,5, 9 Sequences; the Sapphic Sonnet's shortened Fourth Line; the Saraband Sonnet's unspecified Meter; the Tory Hexatet's shift from 12 to 8 and back; the Tuckerman's unpredictably Variable Meter; The Welsh Sonnet's 7 Syllable Count; and finally, the Word Sonnet having each Line being one Word.

That's a lot to absorb in one chapter. Those 14 examples encompass 17 total Poems. They demonstrate how Rules can be stretched, yet Form still prevails.

A. Cornish Sonnet

The Cornish Sonnet is said to be influenced by Arab traders to the Cornish coast. This Verse Form is a merging of Arabic Meter and the Sonnet. Exactly when and how this came about is unknown. Early Cornish Verse is fragmented and stringy at best. The earliest literature in the Cornish language were fragments of religious plays. The language became all but extinct by the 18th century but what was preserved in some Verse are Octaves using 7 Syllable loose Trochaic Lines and Alternating Rhyme. Unlike Verse from other Celtic origins, deliberate use of Alliteration or other Devices of "Harmony of Sound" are not present. This Sonnet Form doesn't fit with these early findings, so it can only be assumed that it arrived on the scene much later than originally presumed.

The Defining Features of the Cornish Sonnet are:

2 Sestets made up of Linked Enclosed Tercets,

followed by a Refrain which is the Repeat of the **First Line** of each Sestet,

Metered at the discretion of the Poet,

Lines should be similar (not necessarily exact) Length.

The Rhyme Scheme is:

Abacbc Dedfef AD

The capital letters show that the **First Line** of each Sestet are repeated in

Refrain of the Closing Couplet.

My contribution is *Fountain with Fatsia*. Fatsia is the name of those very large leaves behind and around the fountain. The Meter changed from 8 to 9, and then to 7 in two Lines. I used some Feminine Rhyme also.

Sonnet 82: Fountain with Fatsia

The fountain in the garden flows
Surrounded by green Fatsia.
An oriental plant that grows
In such abundance in Japan,
Provides a pretty panacea
As any water fountain can.

Its overflow delights the eye,
Where spillings dribble from the top.
They sally forth to trickle by,
Cools a nearly naked nymph,
Who watches each and every drop.
He catches some in drenched triumph.

The fountain in the garden flows
Its overflow delights the eye

B. Faux Free Verse Sonnet

The word "Faux" means "Imitation." That's where this Format gets its name. It imitates a Free Verse Poem, but is, in fact, a Structured Sonnet. Another Format created from my imagination. Of course, it uses my favorite Triple Rhyme Scheme Layout. In a Faux Free Verse Sonnet, the Text is laid out just like any Free Verse poem, except it has a Rhyme Scheme and a Syllable Count. It is actually Structured, but in disguise. Each Stanza is really just a Single Line in the Sonnet, so there are 14 Stanzas (the Typical Sonnet's 14 Lines). They actually read as iambic Tetrameter. So the poem is pretending to be a Free Verse Poem, because it looks like one. The Rhyme Scheme is:

aaa bbb ccc ddd ee.

My poem is *The Spot*. Naturally, it looks much longer than any other Sonnet you may have seen. I added in some other Techniques that are Typical in a Free Verse poem too. I took that image at the Minnesota Arboretum in Chanhassen, Minnesota one beautiful October afternoon, while out capturing the Fall colors.

Sonnet 83: The Spot

Just
take me to
that hidden glade

with a carpet
of
leaves and shade,

where
thoughts
flow free
and dreams are made.

Released
right here
beside this brook

with Autumn
everywhere

you look.

A cloak
along the path you took,

and
hanging clusters
in the trees

that r u s t l e
in the gentle
b-r-e-e-z-e

are
things
that set
the mind
at
e-a-s-e.

Where Nature creates solitude,

and
make a most
ROMANTIC MOOD

where interuptions
won't
intrude.

It's there
I wish
to promise you

My heart
remains forever
TRUE.

C. Fusion Sonnet

I highlighted this Format back in Chapter 6 as one with Extra Lines. Here we focus on its extraordinary Line Construction. Which varies in the Free Verse and Coda segment. It was invented by the Greek Poet, Yannis Livadas (born in 1969), and popularized by Sonnet Modal. I was drawn to this one by the Triple Rhymes imbedded in it.

This falls under the auspices of the Modern Sonnet Genre. As such, it breaks several Sonnet Rules. Most notably, it has 21 Lines rather than the Typical 14. The Fusion comes from blending in 4 Lines of Free Verse at lines 11 through 14. It has a Strict Structure and Rhyme Scheme, but is more flexible in the area of Meter. Here are the complex rules:

14 Line Poem followed by a Half Sonnet of 7 Lines acting as a Coda or Tail to add additional stability to the Poem. No particular Meter is followed, Fusing it with the modern Free Verse style.

First Fourteen Lines:

  Same Rhyme in 1st,5th,9th & 10th Lines.

  Same Rhyme in 2nd,3rd & 4th Lines.

  Same Rhyme in 6th,7th & 8th Lines.

Rhetorical questions in 9th & 10th Lines.

Negative and pessimistic note in the first 10 Lines.

Free Verse carrying Optimistic Tone in 11th, 12th,13 & 14th Lines.

Volta gradually through 9th, 10th and 11th Lines.

Next Seven Lines:-The Half Sonnet acting as a Coda.

  Same Rhyme in 16th and 17th lines.

  Same Rhyme in 18th and 19th lines.

Volta in the 20th Line.

No set Meter.

I submit here the poem *Cash*, which is the name for my brother Richard's bulldog (pictured here). For this Poem the Rhymes Scheme, as laid out above is:

A1, b,b,b, A2, c,c,c,a,a (4 lines free verse)--- A1, d,d,e,e,a, A2,

where the capital letters indicate repeated lines.

The Syllable Count for this one is:

10,10,10,10,9,10,10,10,11,10 – 10,8,7,9 – 10,6,6,9,7,10,9.

Sonnet 84: Cash, My Brother's Dog

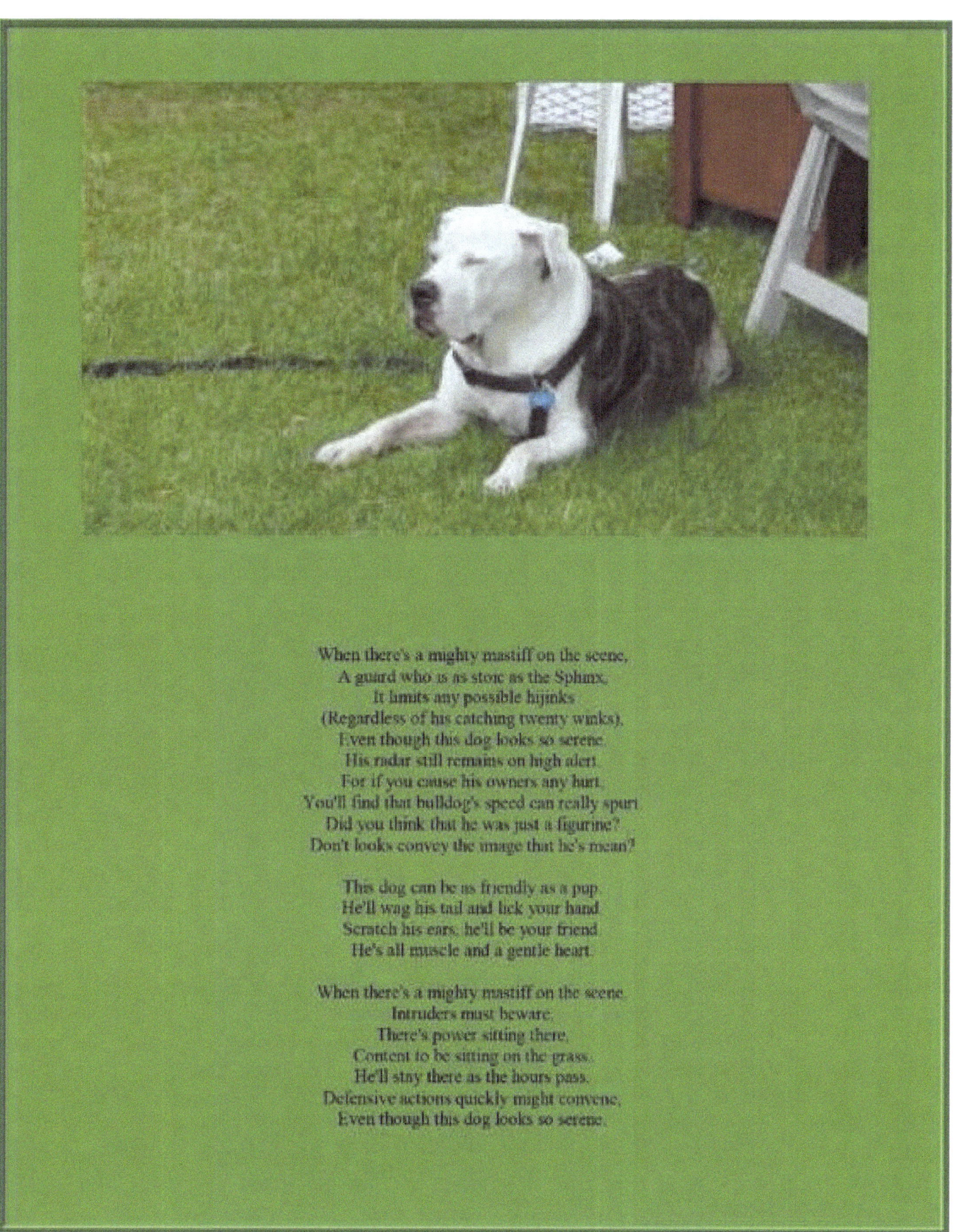

When there's a mighty mastiff on the scene,
A guard who is as stoic as the Sphinx,
It limits any possible hijinks
(Regardless of his catching twenty winks).
Even though this dog looks so serene,
His radar still remains on high alert.
For if you cause his owners any hurt,
You'll find that bulldog's speed can really spurt.
Did you think that he was just a figurine?
Don't looks convey the image that he's mean?

This dog can be as friendly as a pup.
He'll wag his tail and lick your hand.
Scratch his ears, he'll be your friend.
He's all muscle and a gentle heart.

When there's a mighty mastiff on the scene,
Intruders must beware.
There's power sitting there.
Content to be sitting on the grass.
He'll stay there as the hours pass.
Defensive actions quickly might convene,
Even though this dog looks so serene.

D. Hex Sonnetta

You originally met this Form back in Chapter 5 as a Stanzaic Variation. Now we focus on it as to its Line Lengths. It is a Poem having only six Syllables per Line. So it has a short peppy Cadence.

It consists of two Six-line Stanzas and a finishing Rhyming Couplet with the following Set of Rules:

Meter: Iambic Trimeter (6 Syllables)

Rhyme Scheme: abbaab cddccd ee.

This particular Form uses six Syllables of iambic Trimeter per Line. Thus, the name Hex Sonnetta, as it Keys off the number 6. The first part of the Form's name refers to the Syllable Count per Line, as well as Six Lines per Stanza. The second part of the name, Sonnetta, is to show this to be a Form similar to the Sonnet, yet with its Shorter Lines and different Rhyme Scheme, it is not the Typical Sonnet. Not only does this Poem have Six Syllables per Line, it also has a Set of two Six-line Stanzas, giving an extra "Hex" to the meaning of Hex Sonnetta. The Rhyme Scheme, with the two 6-line Stanzas has more of an Italian feel. The Rhyming Couplet completes the Classic 14 Line Format of the Sonnet.

The Sonnet I present here is *Wayward Wings*. One can't help but be impressed by the wingspan of the Great White Egret that I captured gliding over a pond in Battle Creek Park at Woodbury, Minnesota. It was my inspiration. I Deviated a bit by putting the Volta at Line 7.

Sonnet 85: Wayward Wings

These Wayward Wings of mine
get in the way sometimes.
Unfurling oftentimes
is frequently not fine,
when things just don't align
while seeking rapid climbs.

Yet still, they're fine to glide,
to surf the winds with ease.
They capture every breeze
with little toil applied,
when I decide to ride
long distance, overseas.

They're difficult to fold,
and slow to be unrolled.

E. Japanese Sonnet

Here is another Sonnet Format that I created. It Keys off a few Japanese Forms. This Japanese Sonnet actually blends several Japanese Formats into a 14 Line Structure that also contains other Sonnet Features, such as a Rhyme Scheme. The Format begins with a 5-7-5 Haiku followed by a 5-7-5-7-7 Tanka. It then executes a 3-5-3 Haiku and closes with a Rhymed 1-6-1. Because I want to emphasize the Japanese correlation, this Format must end with the word **"Hai"**, which is Japanese for "Yes".

A Sonnet usually carries a "Volta", so mine is in the 3-5-3 (Lines 9 - 11). Still the Haiku and Tanka require a similar Turning Point, called a "Kiru", in each of its Formats, so I tried to achieve that too. I think I got it in each Haiku. Not so well in the Tanka.

The total Rhyme Scheme Is:

aba bcbdd eec ddd.

The Syllable counts are:

5-7-5 5-7-5-7-7 3-5-3 1-6-1

My poem is: *Japanese sonnet (bright decoration*s). Because it is a Blend it carries some Japanese Elements, but not all, just as it carries many Sonnet Features, but varies greatly in others. The Japanese Features include: the Format of the Title in Parens, **without** Capital Letters (unless a Proper Name), and declaring the Format; no Capitalization or Punctuation in the Poem; Turns or Kigos; the word "Hai"; and, short Line Lengths. The Sonnet features are: Rhyme, Alliteration, 14 Lines, and Volta.

Sonnet 86: Japanese Sonnet (bright decoration)

bright decorations
multi-colored lilies grow
wondrous creations

stunning floral show
in homes or apartment flats
makes the garden glow
in colors that catch the eye
while observers tend to sigh

blossom's bloom
colors any room
poisons cats

try
to grow a few nearby
Hai

F. Jazz Sonnet

I couldn't define any one particular Poet that created this Genre. I think it rapidly evolved through several Poets. Wanda Coleman, Alan Ginsberg, and Carl Sandberg, are well known for them. Even Shakespeare has been put to Jazz.

Jazz Poetry is a Literary Genre defined as Poetry necessarily informed by Jazz Music—that is, Poetry in which the Poet responds to and writes about Jazz. Jazz Poetry, like the Music itself, encompasses a variety of Forms, Rhythms, and Sounds. Beginning with the birth of Blues and Jazz at the start of the twentieth century, Jazz Poetry can be seen as a thread that runs through the Harlem Renaissance, the Beat Movement, and the Black Arts Movement—and it is still vibrant today. Source: Poets.org.

A Jazz Sonnet has the familiar Layout of a Traditional Sonnet with its first 12 Lines separated into 3 Quatrains and a Closing Rhymed Couplet. However, none of the Lines in the Stanzas have an even Syllable Count, making iambic Verse difficult. This promotes Discordance (Blue Notes?). But there is Rhyme, it's just not what you'd typically find. You'll see Elements that play against each other, while others blend. After all, Jazz sought to be different. Each Jazz Sonnet is unique in Style, Meter, and Rhyme. So be creative when you write one.

My Jazz Sonnet is *Groovin'*. It does have three Quatrains and a Closing Rhymed Couplet. I created that image from a Power Point slide using some CD's, a guitar-shaped candle, and font. Then I let it loose with the Rhyme Scheme used, which is:

a,b,a,b - c,d,d,e - e,c,g,g - h,h.

Then really mixed it up with the Syllable Count:

11, 9, 11, 5 – 11, 14, 13, 7 – 11, 7, 9, 9 – 4, 4.

What fun!

Sonnet 87: Groovin'

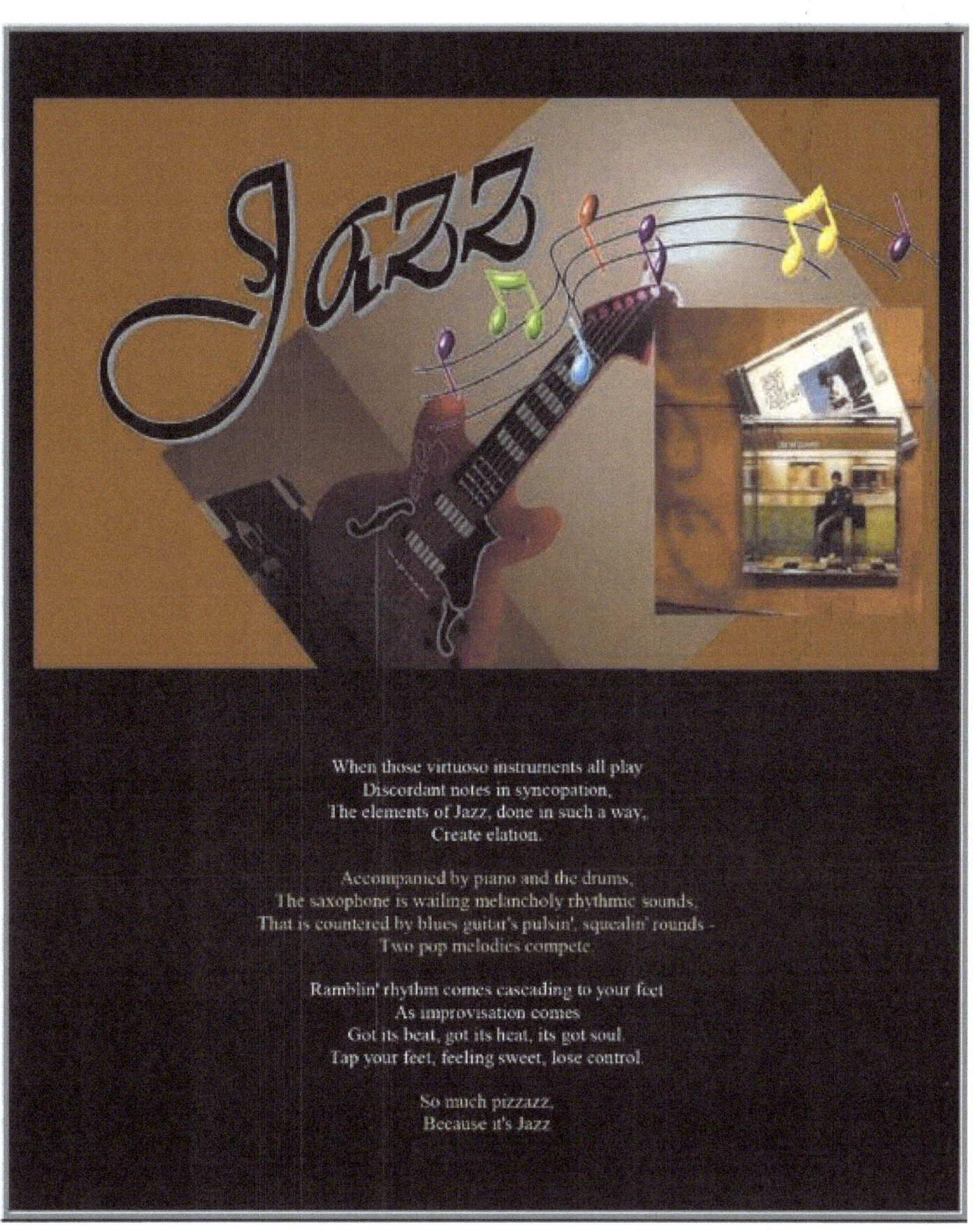

When those virtuoso instruments all play
Discordant notes in syncopation,
The elements of Jazz, done in such a way,
Create elation.

Accompanied by piano and the drums,
The saxophone is wailing melancholy rhythmic sounds,
That is countered by blues guitar's pulsin', squealin' rounds –
Two pop melodies compete.

Ramblin' rhythm comes cascading to your feet
As improvisation comes
Got its beat, got its heat, its got soul.
Tap your feet, feeling sweet, lose control.

So much pizzazz,
Because it's Jazz

G. Limerick Sonnet

I introduced you to this Form, which I created, back in Chapter 2, as a well-known Poetry Style that was Transitioned into a Sonnet. Here we have it due to the Line Lengths. The Format uses the signature Limerick Syllable Count and Rhyme Scheme.

According to the dictionary, a Limerick Form consists of 5 Lines (two Long, followed by two Short, and closed by 1 Long Line). The first, second and fifth Lines must have matching Lengths of seven to ten Syllables (8 or 9 is most typical). The third and fourth Lines only have between five and seven matching Syllables. So there is a bit of flexibility.

The long Cadence is either: da DUM da da DUM da da DuM da; or, da DUM da da DUM da da DUM.

The short Cadence is either: da DUM da da DUM; or, da DUM da da DUM da.

I modified the Standard Limerick to create a Sonnet. Since the Limerick uses a Quintet (5 Line) Structure, I elected to give it two Closing Couplets (or a Quatrain) rather than one, in order to achieve the Classic 14 Lines. For the first Stanza, I mixed 9 with 5 Syllables. In the second Stanza, I used 8 with 5. The Volta comes at the first Couplet (Lines 11 and 12).

The Rhyme Scheme is:

aabba ccddc ee ff.

The syllable count is:

9,9,5,5,9 – 8,8,5,5,8- 9,9 – 5,5.

My example here is *Crooked Trees*.

Sonnet 88: Crooked Trees

The trees on our block have grown crooked.
Their chance to be stately don't look it.
But is it too late
to make them grow straight?
To test each, we went up and shook it.

Each tree trunk was as solid as steel.
Their profile is something unreal.
But taking them out
ain't what I'm about.
I hope to restore their appeal.

Oh wait! I just read in a book,
that's how Japanese make them look.

Well, what do you know?
They don't have to go!

H. Lyricat Sonnet

I must give great credit to my good friend Pantygynt, a fellow Fanstorian, for creating a Sonnet Version of Catherine Ginn's (aka. I'm a Cat) new Lyricat Format. If you recall, he also created the Pantygonnet described in Chapter 7. Creative juices are really flowing on the Site these days. Catherine Ginn is also a Fellow Poet on FanStory. She was the "Number 1" Poet on the Site in 2016 for most of the year.

The LyriCat Sonnet creates three Quatrains with a Repeating Line, and a Couplet. It Mimics the 7-5-9 Meter of the standard LyriCat Format, with the following Meter Structure:

7/5/9/5 - 7/5/9/5 - 7/5/9/5 - 5/5.

The Rhyme Scheme a bit more complex, as it is:

abAb acAc adAd ee,

where the "A" represents the Repeated Line. Volta on Line 9.

My Version is *Baby News*. It is a Family Portrait of my daughter Jodi and her daughter Nicole, who recently had my great-grandchild. A girl named Bell Rose.

Sonnet 89: Baby News

Granddaughter Nicole,
makes me, I gather,
when she takes on mother role,
the great-grandfather

Putting a new living soul
on family tree,
when she takes on mother role,
related to me.

Let all the hilltops extoll,
a precious new life,
when she takes on mother role,
as Drew's happy wife.

I just heard the news.
Rejoicing ensues.

I. Sapphic Sonnet.

I came across a Sapphic Ode Sonnet in my Sonnet research, but I found that particular one to not truly follow the Sapphic Format, since it really was following an iambic Model with a short 4th Line. So, I wrote this one myself following the real guidelines of a Sapphic Verse. So this Sonnet has the Classic 14 Line Format of 3 Quatrains and a Rhyming Couplet, but the Meter follows the Sapphic Structure, as outlined below, for a Sapphic Verse.

The Sapphic Verse dates back to ancient Greece and is named for the Poet Sappho. Sapphics are made up of Four-lines Stanzas with three LongLlines, frequently of 11 Syllables, followed by a Short Line of typically 5 Syllables. The main Building Blocks of the Sapphic are Trochees and Dactyls. The Trochee is a Metrical Foot with one Stressed Syllable followed by an Unstressed one, while the Dactyl contains a Stressed Syllable followed by **two** Unstressed ones. The first three Lines of the Sapphic contain two Trochees, a Dactyl, and then two more Trochees (making 11 Syllables). The shorter fourth, and final, Line of the Stanza is called an "Adonic" and is composed of one Dactyl followed by a Trochee (making 5 Syllables). Hence the Syllable Count is:

11/11/11/5 -11/11/11/5 -11/11/11/5-11/11.

So, if you characterize a Stressed Syllable as "-", and Unstressed as "/", the Metric of a Sapphic Line would be:

-/-/-//-/-.

and the Adonic would be:

-//-.

However, there is some flexibility with the Form as when two Stressed Syllables replace both the second and last Foot of each Line.

While most Sapphic Lines are Unrhymed, because this is a Sonnet, I Rhymed this Poem in a Classic Scheme of:

abab cdcd efef gg.

My input is *Water Garden*. The picture is from the Japanese Garden area at Como Park in St. Paul, Minnesota. Remember while reading it, that this is not an iambic Meter. I did use a bit of In-line Rhyme here too.

Sonnet 90: Water Garden

Water falling is the most perfect setting
Anyone could ever appreciate, when
Walking through the forest without forgetting
Pathways where you've been.

Terraced gardens gently surround cascading
Rivulets, that fill the ravine with music,
Symphonies with rocks that are serenading.
Gently acoustic.

Such sights, such sounds, racing around the bubbling
Brook, where every nook has a look that's pleasing
Here in quiet park, it's a never troubling
Place for easing.

Go there when you need to resuscitate your
Energy within your poor Soul's unseen core.

J.   Saraband Sonnet

I hope you recall the Saraband Sonnet from Chapter 5 as a Stanzaic Format, which we see again here for its unusual Sonnet Line Lengths, as it allows virtually any Metrical Foot.

A Saraband Sonnet is a Form that consists of a Tercet + Quatrain + Tercet + Closing Quatrain. So here it Mimics the 3-4-3-4 character of the dance., but lacks a Couplet. It can be configured in Various Styles: English, Italian, Spanish or French, making it extremely flexible. Each Stanza can be unique, but here are the Basic Rules.

Stanza 1: a Tercet, Rhyme aba or aaa.

Stanza 2: a Quatrain, any Standard Quatrain Form or Rhyme.

The Stanza Forms may be mixed, taking on any of the Classic Forms as shown below.

English: abab or abcb.

Italian: baab.

Spanish: bcbc.

French/American: bbcc.

Stanza 3: a Tercet, but must be same Tercet Form as Stanza 1, and requires at least Line 2 of both Tercets to Rhyme.

Stanza 4: a Quatrain, any Quatrain Form and Rhyme.

Any Metrical Foot.

Any Metrical Line.

Some authorities insist on eight Syllables but this is not cut and dried.

Rhyme Scheme: depends on the Form chosen.

The Volta the First Line of the second Tercet.

For this chapter I wrote *Patterns*. The scene is along the Mississippi River, at the Upper Landing in St. Paul, Minnesota. My Muse cut loose upon viewing the patterns, and created a pattern of its own. I stayed basically with the desired 8 Syllables, but threw in a couple 7's and a 9 Syllable Line. So the complete Rhyme Scheme is:

aba cdcd ebe fgfg.

The Syllable Count is:

7,8,8 - 7,8,8,8 – 8,8,8 – 8,8,8,9.

Sonnet 91: Patterns

I love to watch patterns form
as sunlight, shade, and textures play,
when sky is clear and climate's warm.

Combinations form a scene
where straight lines meet those curved, or round.
Some contradictions may abound
when arch and rectangles convene.

And yet, the eye absorbs it all
presenting masterful display.
Oh, let the poet's mind recall!

Behold a sight in play with light,
at riverside bench-seating zone,
where one can sit, ideas ignite
emotions from patterned thoughts made known.

K. Tory Hexatet.

You saw this first in Chapter 4, because of its Couplet placement, the again in Chapter 5 as a Stanzaic Variation, and finally here for its Line Length.

It consists of an Octet (or Octave) + Couplet + Quatrain, with a Rhyme Scheme of:

ababcdcd ee ffgg.

The Format features the first eight Lines (the Octet) in 12 Syllable iambic Hexameter, but the Rhyming Couplet holds to eight Syllables (iambic Tetrameter), located at Line 9, rather than at the end. The last four Lines of the Closing Quatrain revert back to 12 Syllables. So the Poem retains the signature total 14 Lines of a Standard Sonnet, but the Hexameter is not Typical for most Sonnets, and the shift back and forth with Tetrameter certainly isn't.

The Couplet in the center provides the "Changing Point", or Volta. The shorter Meter provides a visual, as well as oral impact. Thus, it makes a direct statement and could be read by itself.

My example consists of the poem *The Passion of Pan (The Lilac Legend).* The long Line lengths lend themselves well to the use of In-line Rhyming, as I have done here. The Botanical name for the Lilac is Syringa. Actually "Lilac" is the French name for this fragrant, early Spring bloomer that flowers for only a couple of weeks, after which it provides a dense green bush. I have provided here the Greek legend of the Lilac. Pan was a Satyr and Syringa was a beautiful Woods Nymph. The wood of the lilac bush actually can be made into a flute, in the Spring while the sap is running strong. The bark can be made to slip off the stem, the wood notched, and then the bark holed and slipped back on.

Sonnet 92: The Passion of Pan (Lilac Legend)

The Greek god, Pan, a goat-like man, loves sylvan glens.
On flute he'd sport, dance and cavort, to much appeal,
while searching damsels in the local fields and fens.
This satyr found ideal, a maiden most surreal.
Syringa had created passion in his mind,
but she rejected Pan, and ran through woods to stream.
At edge, some spirits pledge to make her hard to find.
They turned her to a lilac. Pan had lost his dream.

But then, winds whispered through her wood.
Pan thought the music very good.

He found her to be, a very musical tree.
So he cleverly took her, trimmed her stems and tips,
creating fragrant flute. His passion meant to be.
Now she's a constant consort, often at his lips.

L. Tuckerman Sonnet

I introduced you to Tuckerman in Chapter 3 as a Variation by a Famous Poet. Now I focus on the unusual Lines Lengths. Tuckerman wrote Sonnets with free abandon and with virtually no regard for any kind of Pattern at all. His Sonnets burst from the gate in a flurry of Rhyme, without any Stanzas, then, after the first few Lines, Rhymes fall seemingly at random, as in his "*Sonnets, First Series*," which Rhymes:

a b b a b c a b a d e c e d, with a Volta at L10.

For this chapter I wrote *Anticipation*. It was inspired by a visit to the local lease-less Dog Park, where anticipation was clearly evident. The Syllable Counts are:

14, 7, 10, 10, 9, 8, 11, 8, 10, 7, 10, 12 – 10, 10.

Sonnet 93: Anticipation

What a marvelous thing to behold- ANTICIPATION!
Kenetic energy bound ,
just instants before that moment profound
is unleashed from the point of causation,
while participants quake and surround
the object they focus upon,
at the source of very intense fixation,
while anxiously waiting around
as the master performs the gyration
to launch an orb into space,
like a Titan with Olympian skill,
into an orbit that spreads out hither and yon.
Oh what expectation! Oh what a thrill,
for that eager group hoping to give chase!

M. Welsh Sonnet

From Chapter 7's Rhyme Variation, we now discuss the Welsh Sonnet for Line Length here in Chapter 8. . Another one of my creations. I used three Awdl Gywydds with a Cyhydeddfer attached to the third one to give me the recognizable 14 Lines of a Sonnet.

The Awdl Gywydd consists of a four Line Quatrain using a 7 Syllable Meter (a definite departure from most Sonnet's iambic Meter) with a unique Rhyme Structure as well, where the End Rhymes form a recognizable "abcb" Pattern, but **Line 2** carries an In-line Rhyme to match the **First Line's** End Rhyme (the "a" Rhyme) at either the second, third, fourth, or fifth Syllable, while the **Fourth Line** similarly carries the End Word of the **Third Line** (the "c" End Word) as an In-line Rhyme somewhere between the second and fifth Syllable. So the Awdl Gywydd's rhyme can be represented as follows:

xxxxxxa

xXaXXxb

xxxxxxc

xXcXXxb,

where the large X represents the **Alternate Positions** of the In-line Rhymes. This is a very Welsh style, and is known as Cross Rhyming. The Variability of the location is also very Welsh.

I then closed the third Awdl Gywydd, with a Cyhydeddfer, which is simply an 8 Syllable Rhyming Couplet, often used as a Cauda (Tail) for one of the many Welsh Forms, as I did here. For more information on Welsh Forms, Wikipedia has a very good treatise under "Traditional Welsh Poetic Metres."

For this Chapter, my example is *The Bond*, a Poem about a man and his dog. Once again, I wrote it twice. The second time is to reveal the Cross Rhymes.

Sonnet 94: The Bond

The bond between man and hound
is often found as they walk.
Both released to run and play,
the way kindred souls can lock.

What better team, man and dog,
to walk, to jog, be outside --
a healthy practice for each
as they reach their goal in stride.

Dogs are truly man's best friend,
and in the end, they're loyal.
They'll hunt. They'll fetch. They will herd,
without any word to spoil
the gift that comes additional --
a dog's love, unconditional.

(Poem with rhymes revealed)

The bond between man and **hound**
is often **found** as they **walk.**
Both released to run and **play,**
the **way** kindred souls can **lock.**

What better team, man and **dog,**
to walk, to **jog,** be out**side** --
a healthy practice for **each**
as they **reach** their goal in **stride.**

Dogs are truly man's best **friend,**
and in the **end,** they're **loyal.**
They'll hunt. They'll fetch. They will **herd,**
without any **word** to **spoil**
the gift that comes **additional** --
a dog's love, **unconditional.**

N. Word Sonnet

The Word Sonnet is a relatively new Variation of the Traditional Form that was championed by Seymour Mayne, a Canadian Poet who teaches at the University of Ottawa. This Format is Seymour Maynes's long-running project of what he calls and practices as "Word Sonnets." In their One-Word Structure there is a strong resemblance to the look and feel of Chinese Poetry. These Minimal Forms of Poetry and verbal composition go back to the 1960s. In essence, it is a Fourteen Line Poem, with **One Word** for each Line. Concise and usually visual in effect, this "Miniature" Version can contain one or more Sentences, as the articulation requires.

Word Sonnets attempt to be pithy and suggestive Poems in their own right. Many draw on the seasons and also aim for a Compact Resonance that may attract the reader to return to them again and again.

If you are interested in learning more about the Style, here are two very informative links that you may want to paste into your search line. The first is an overview by Seymour himself. The second is a hilarious, and very good, dissertation on how to make it into a 14 Word Shakespearian Sonnet.

http://poemsand poetics.com/2014/02/seymour-mayne-hail-15-word-sonnets.html

http;//stephenfrug.blogspot.com/frank-sidwicks-fourteen-word-sonnet.html

I find the Format very flexible and playful. Although there is only One Word per Line it is amazing what you can do with it. I'll demonstrate that here by providing 4 examples.

The first is *Meet*. This one should grab you immediately with its simple, yet stunning, Visual Impact. I tailored the Word Widths to give the Poem its shape. No Rhyme at all.

The second is *Obsessiions*. Here I used Sonnet Stanzas and a Rhyme Scheme of:

aabbccd – deeef – ff.

The third Sonnet is *Rescue*. Here I played with Long and Short Words to Mimic the impression of a ladder.

Finally, the fourth Poem is *Sore Loser*. Again I play with Stanzas to convey a very Free Verse feel to this image of my two grandchildren, Isaac and Skylah, interacting. I was noting here that the boy was trying hard to ignore his persistent sister.

I hope this Set, shows you just how versatile and powerful this Form can be. Especially when blended to an image.

Sonnet 95: Meet

I
go
out
when
desire
causes
needful
company
dearth.
Await
true
gal
to
X

Sonnet 96: Obsessions

Interaction
satisfaction
brings
things
about
throughout
sessions.

Obsessions
create
innate
mate
reactions.

Relations
complications.

Sonnet 97: Rescue

Sonnet 98: Sore Loser

I

Do
not
play
games
with
you.

Do
I ?

So
you
won't
anger
easily

CHAPTER 9. SONNETS WITH UNUSUAL METER

Another Variant characteristic of the Sonnet Form is to have an Atypical Meter, one that Deviates from strict iambic Pentameter or iambic Tetrameter. You've already met most of this group, with the exception of the Curtal Sonnet, but I felt the group is worth a closer examination.

Here we will look at the Curtal Sonnet for the first time. Then we will re-examine the Limerick Sonnet, the Pushkin Sonnet, the Sapphic Sonnet, and lastly the Word Sonnet. Each has their unique personality. The Curtal Sonnet has Sprung Rhyme. The Limerick Sonnet plays a Long/Short Cadence. The Pushkin comes in both English and Italian Versions that relay on Feminine Rhyming, which is worthy of note. The Sapphic Sonnet carries its Greek overtones. The Word Sonnet is most radical of all, yet so playful.

I hope you find this group as interesting as I do.

A. The Curtal Sonnet

There is a bit of controversy about this Format as to its True Structure, its Pedigree, and even if it can be called a Sonnet. Most sources identify it as a "Curtailed" Sonnet, and identify the creator of the Form as Gerard Manley Hopkins in 1877 using his radical "Sprung Rhythm." His format has 10.5 Lines that are arranged in two Stanzas. The first Stanza has Rhyme Scheme "abcabc," and the second is either "dbcdc" or "dcbdc." The very Last Line is Indented and Shorter. He described the Form as a contraction of the Petrarchan Sonnet, whereby the 8 Line Octave becomes 6, while the Sestet is reduced to 5. It should have a Pivot between the Sestet and Quintet.

However, *Poetry Through the Ages*, described it this way.

"The 10-line, two-Stanza Curtal Sonnet actually pre-dated the Petrarchan form,... A good example is embedded within the 29 movements of Dante's, *La Vita Nuova*."

Dante's Curtal Sonnet predates Hopkins by 400 years. It had a Rhyme Scheme of "aabbba cddc," in Pentameter. Hopkin's Format used a weird Meter he called "Sprung Rhythm." From what I can tell he paid no attention to Meter at all, but rather to Accent. In his poem "Pied Beauty", the Meter was Variable and the Syllable Counts were: 9,12,12,10,11,10, - 10,11,14,10,2.

This intrigued me, so I thought it appropriate to examine it closer here. I found that not all Lines necessarily start with a Stressed syllable, but most do. Here's an example of a Stanza from his poem Pied Beauty.
"**Glory** be to **God** for **dap**pled **things**—
For **skies** of **coup**le-**col**our as a **brind**led **cow**;
For **rose-moles** all in **stip**ple upon **trout** that **swim**;
Fresh-firecoal **chest**nut-**falls**; **finch**es' **wings**;
Landscape **plot**ted and **piec**ed—**fold**, **fal**low, and **plough**;
And áll **trádes**, their **gear** and **tack**le and **trim**."
I bolded the Accented Syllables in each Line to show what he was doing. Although the Syllable Count is:
9,12,12,10(or 9, depending whether you count "fire" as 1 or 2 Syllables), 11, 10,
if you only count the Accents, it becomes an organized Structure as:
5,5,5,6,6,6.

Sprung Rhythm is a Poetic Rhythm designed to imitate Natural Speech. It is constructed from Accents in which a Syllable is Stressed followed by a variable number of Unstressed Syllables. Some believe he merely coined a name for poems with Mixed, Irregular Feet, like Free Verse. However, Hopkins was very careful to keep the number of Accents per Line consistent across each individual work, a trait that Free Verse does not share. Sprung Rhythm may be classed as a Form of Accentual Verse, due to its being Stress-timed, rather than Syllable-timed. Hopkins's advocacy assisted in a revival of Accentual Verse.

My example here is *Dangled Art*. I wrote it twice; once in iambic Pentameter (with 2 Feminine Lines), then in Sprung Rhythm with Accents bolded. I hope this helps clarify the idea. The Sprung Rhythm required me to modify the Poem a bit. The Syllable Counts change from a consistent 10, in the first Version, to: 9,8,9,10,10,12, - 11,10, 8,11,3. I followed Shakespeare's Rhyme Scheme. The Accent Sequence becomes:

5,5,5,5,7,7 – 5,4,4,5,2.

Hopkin's Version required subtle modifications, and he places emphasis differently than the iambic.

Sonnet 99: Dangled Art

What art doth dangle here from ancient trees?
If art, indeed, these twisted visions be.
Or could they merely be some strange bird's nest,
providing airy comfort, at its best?
Nay, these proclaim a man's hand, I attest,
these wicker baskets hanging in the breeze.

Oh, subtle is the art's imagination,
adorning local riverside pathways.
They dwell in places that hold high our gaze,
and render these rare forms appreciation.
So Gaze!

(re-written I Sprung Rhythm)

Art doth **dan**gle **here** in **an**cient **trees**.
If **art**, **these twis**ted **vi**sions **be**!
Could they **mere**ly **be** some **strange bird's** nest,
Pro**vid**ing **ai**ry **com**fort at **its best**?
Nay, **these** pro**claim** a **man's hand**, I at**test**.
Man made these **wic**ker **bas**kets, **hang**ing **in** the **breeze**.

Oh, **sub**tle is the **Art's** i**mag**ination,
A**dorn**ing **lo**cal **riv**erside **path**ways
In **plac**es **hold**ing **high** our **gaze**,
And **ren**der these **rare forms** ap**pre**ciation.
Gaze, **Gaze** on!

B. Limerick Sonnet

I introduced you to this Sonnet Format twice before. The first time was in Chapter 2, as a modification of a well-known Poetic Style. Then it was noted again in Chapter 8, for its unusual Line Length. Now here, we have it for its Non-iambic Meter.

According to the dictionary, a Limerick form consists of 5 Lines (two Long, followed by two Short, and closed by 1 Long). The first, second and fifth Lines must have Matching Lengths of seven to ten Syllables (8 or 9 is most typical). The third and fourth Lines only have between five and seven Matching Syllables. So there is a bit of flexibility.

The Long Cadence is either: da DUM da da DUM da da DuM da; or, da DUM da da DUM da da DUM.

The Short Cadence is either: da DUM da da DUM; or, da DUM da da DUM da.

I modified the Standard Limerick to create a Sonnet. Since the Limerick uses a Quintet (5 Line) Structure, I elected to give it two Closing Couplets m(or a Qautrain) rather than one, in order to achieve the Classic 14 Lines. For the first Stanza, I mixed 9 with 5 Syllables. In the second Stanza, I used 8 with 5. The Volta comes at the first Couplet (Lines 11 and 12).

The Rhyme Scheme is:

aabba ccddc ee ff.

The Syllable Count is:

9,9,5,5,9 – 8,8,5,5,8- 9,9 – 5,5.

In this example, *When the Rain Stops*, I have my wife, Karen, posing for me. Since Limericks don't necessarily have to be ribald, or humorous, it isn't. Although it may be a bit silly. I added an Extra Line, because I couldn't resist, but that's not a requirement.

Sonnet 100: When the Rains Stop

For months there was nothing but showers,
then rains put the buds on the bowers.
For the wonder of spring
is, it grows everything,
resulting in fields full of flowers.

Now, fields will attract many kinds
of creatures, with blooms on their minds.
Like bees and butterflies,
and insects any size-
the kinds that a botanist finds.

There was an old lady who goes
with flowers held up to her nose.

That way she could tell
their wonderful smell.

And dream of lost loves, I suppose.

C. Pushkin Sonnets

Since Chapter 3, when you met Pushkin as being a Famous Poet who created both English and Italian Sonnet Formats, we've seen many Derivations of the Form. His weren't radical, as Tetrameter and Pentameter are quite Typical to the Genre, but he was the one who introduced the frequent use of the Feminine iambic Format to great effect.

The Pushkin Sonnet (aka: Onegin Sonnet), contains a couple of unique features. The first is in its Meter, and the second is in its Layout. It was popularized (or invented) by the Russian Poet, Alexander Pushkin, through his novel in Verse, *Eugene Onegin*. The English Format features iambic Pentameter, while the Italian is done in iambic Tetrameter, both with the Pushkin signature Rhyme Scheme:

aBaBccDDeFFeGG,

where the lowercase letters represent Feminine Endings (i.e., with an additional Unstressed 11th Syllable) and the uppercase representing the typical Masculine Ending (i.e. Stressed on the final 10th Syllable) in the English, and the Italian having Feminine Endings as well (i.e., with an additional Unstressed 9th Syllable) and the uppercase representing the typical Masculine Ending (i.e. stressed on the final 8th Syllable). So that is the first Feature mentioned; the English Version is written in **iambic Pentameter** and the Italian Version in **Iambic Tetrameter**).

The second unique Feature involves the lack of Stanzas. Unlike other Traditional Forms, such as the Petrarchan Sonnet or Shakespearean Sonnet, the Pushkin Sonnet **does not** divide into smaller Stanzas of four Lines or two in any obvious way.

For this chapter, I have provided an example of each.

The first is *Sleeps Silently in Snow*. It pictures downtown St. Paul, Minnesota in winter from across the river at Harriet Island. It is the English Version. The Syllable Count is:

11,10,11,10,10,10,10,10,11, 10,10,11,10,10.

So, the 11 Syllable Lines are feminine. Note their subtle impact on the Rhythm.

The second Pushkin Sonnet is *Such Souls are We,* is the Italian Version. It features an image of my daughter, Aisha, and son-in-law, Jeremy. They have since separated and are divorcing. Although, the sentiment was mine during a darker period of my life. The Syllable Count is:

9,8,9,8,9,9,8,8,9,8,8,9,8,8.

Note here that I added two additional Feminine Lines. This is acceptable. However, when adding Feminine End-Rhymes, it is customary to add not just one, but two, making a pair. I think that, with the shorter Line Length, the Feminine Lines become even more distinguishable.

Sonnet 101: Sleeps Silently in Snow

They say that there is nothing quite so quiet -
a city sleeping silently in snow.
Upon this observation, can't deny it,
For here before my eyes a mute tableau.
No children play, I hear no single cheer.
There's not a soul to swing or scamper here.
The whistles of the riverboats have ceased.
I see no evidence of man or beast.
And yet, inside the buildings, clothed in concrete,
the daily commerce bustle carries on,
the kind that families depend upon,
protected from what winter snowstorms excrete.
Old Winter bring your fury at its best,
and let this playground stay at silent rest.

Sonnet 102: Such Souls are We

It hurts my tender heart's devotion.
We always were in love and friends.
Now riddled with such split emotions
that come to cruel cathartic ends,
like ships windblown in two directions,
that drift without true course corrections,
we're doomed to miss our mark at sea.
Alas! Alas! Such souls are we!
To never know what came between us,
and leave what's better left unsaid,
to ponder in the days ahead.
It seems it all so superfluous.
Unmanly? Yes! But I shall cry,
that day when we must say goodbye.

D. Sapphic Sonnet

You've met this Sapphic Sonnet in Chapter 8, as a Format having a departure from the normal Line Length with its shortened fourth Line of each Stanza. Here we will investigate it for being of an unusual Meter.

The Sapphic Verse dates back to ancient Greece and is named for the Poet Sappho. Sapphics are made up of Four-line Stanzas with three Long Lines, frequently of 11 Syllables, followed by a Short Line of typically 5 Syllables. The main building blocks of the Sapphic are Trochees and Dactyls. The Trochee is a Metrical Foot with one Stressed Syllable followed by an Unstressed one, while the Dactyl contains a Stressed Syllable followed by **two** Unstressed ones. The first three Lines of the Sapphic contain two Trochees, a Dactyl, and then two more Trochees (making 11 Syllables). The shorter fourth, and final Line of the Stanza is called an "Adonic" and is composed of one Dactyl followed by a Trochee (making 5 Syllables). Hence the Syllable Count is:
11/11/11/5 -11/11/11/5 -11/11/11/5-11/11.

So, if you characterize a Stressed Syllable as "-", and Unstressed as "/", the Metric of a Sapphic Line would be:
-/-/-//-/-.
and the Adonic would be:
-//-.

However, there is some flexibility with the Form as when two Stressed Syllables replace both the second and last Foot of each Line.

My example here is *Glowing Buds*. I took the photograph in bright sunlight one afternoon when the buds were really lit up. I hope I captured that well. For those used to iambic Meter it feels awkward, but it has a charm of its own. While most Sapphic Lines are Unrhymed, because this is a Sonnet, I Rhymed this poem in a Classic Scheme of:
abab cdcd efef gg.

Sonnet 103: Glowing Buds

Sunlight shining over the buds of springtime,
glowing brightly, tiny as neon fireflies.
Green so tensely shining they pantomime lime,
greeting the sunrise.

Miss them if you hurry on by, so busy,
Pressure causing actions done in a tizzy.
People often, are surrounded by beauty,
only they don't see.

Stop awhile to notice such things on pathways,
where you'll find surprises down there to see them.
You may even find a chartreuse hued item
Glowing in sunrays.

Sunlight, spring time, new life is sprouting brightly.
Treasures growing, people shouldn't take lightly.

E. Word Sonnets

These are such fun, I'm happy to give more examples since I introduced them in the last Chapter as Sonnets with Atypical Line Lengths. Here we focus on their unusual Meter. Of course, even the word "Meter" is a stretch. Since, how can there be such a thing with only one word?

This Format is Seymour Maynes's long-running project of what he calls and practices as "Word Sonnets." In their One-Word Structure there is a strong resemblance to the look and feel of Chinese Poetry. These Minimal Forms of Poetry and Verbal Composition go back to the 1960s. In essence, it is a Fourteen Line Poem, with **one word** for each Line. Concise and usually visual in effect, this "Miniature" Version can contain one or more Sentences. It is prized for its flexibility, and really comes alive when paired with a strong image.

I've given you another 3 here to ponder.

The first is *Out House*. Forgive this touch of Potty Humor, but it lends itself well to this Style. Besides, it's a touch of historical reality.

The second Word Sonnet is *Moment*. That's my face there. I leave the reader to fill in the blanks. Note that I laid this one out in Rhymed Word Quatrains to provide a Classic Sonnet look. It even has a Rhyme Scheme of: a - a – b,b – cc.

The third one is *SO*! It is a sad social commentary on the sad state of affairs that comprises our professional baseball team here in Minnesota. That is my grandson, Jeremy (JT). Note here the use of a Sentence.

Sonnet 104: Out House

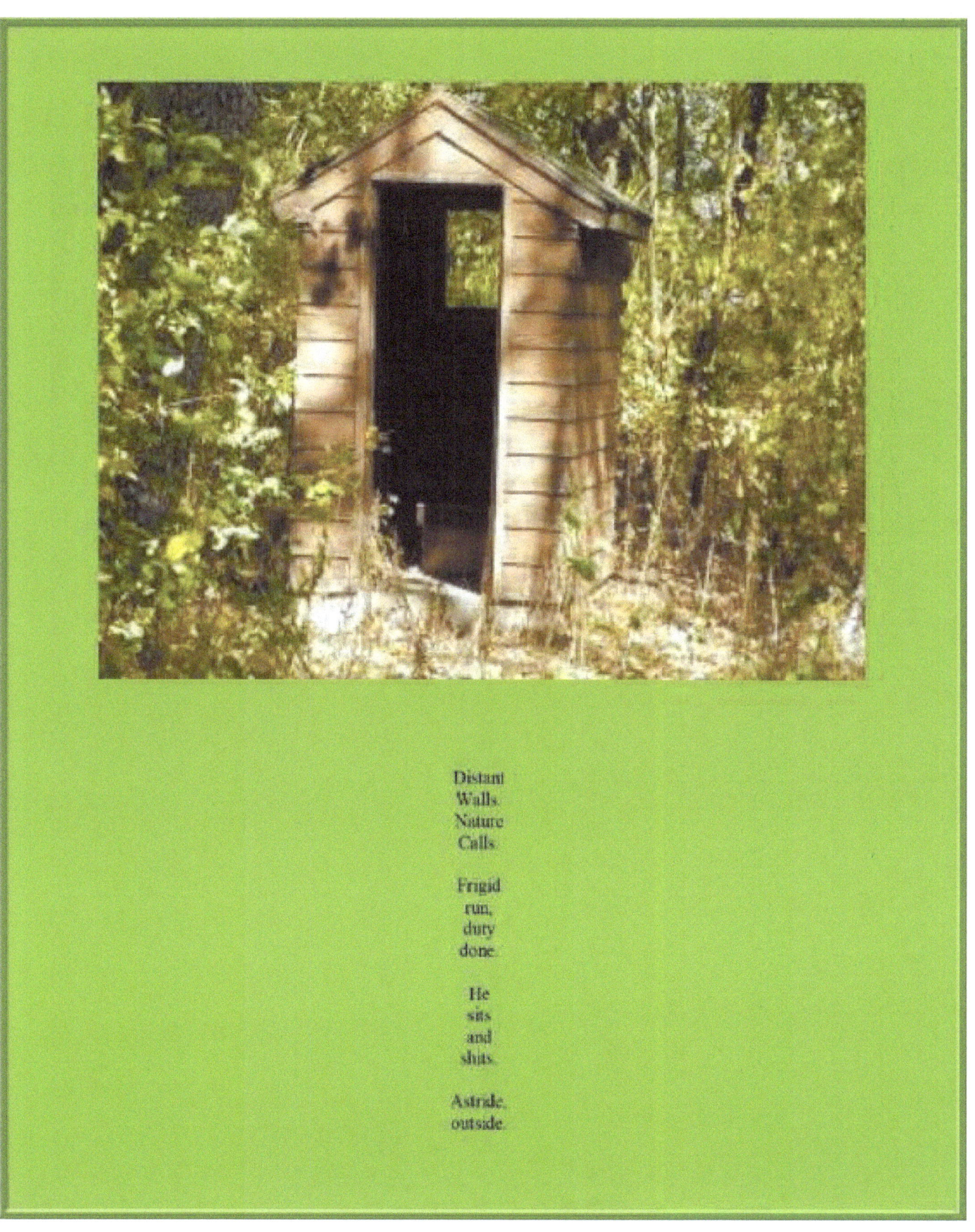

Distant
Walls.
Nature
Calls.

Frigid
run,
duty
done.

He
sits
and
shits.

Astride,
outside.

Sonnet 105: Moment

A
Moment
In
Time

A
Feeling
So
Sublime

Watched
Above
With
Love

Sweet
Complete

Sonnet 106: So!

CHAPTER 10. SHORTENED SONNETS

This is a very controversial Chapter in the book. After all, if nothing else, it seems that having 14 Lines is the Very Essence of a Sonnet. And yet, the great Dante Alighieri himself wrote a longer Variation with 20 Lines. He also wrote a shorter one with 10.5 Lines. In fact in Chapter 6, I introduced you to eight Sonnet Formats with more than the typical Fourteen Lines. So why not ones with fewer. It seems that the cat is already out of the bag, so to speak.

In this Chapter we'll take another look at the Curtal Sonnet, and then reveal a new entrant, the Sonnetino. It's a short Chapter, but may be worth some examination. You can look at the evidence yourself, and see if they truly measure up (no pun intended).

A. The Curtal Sonnet

You were first introduce to this Format just one Chapter ago in Chapter 9, Sonnets with Unusual Meter. Here attention is focused on it Shortened Stature. There is a bit of controversy about the Format as to its true Structure, its Pedigree, and even if it can be called a Sonnet at all. Most sources (including Wikipedia, Poetry Soup, The Poet's Garret, Sonnet Central, and even Webster's dictionary) identify it as a "Curtailed" Sonnet, and identify the creator of the Form as Gerard Manley Hopkins in 1877 using his radical "Sprung Rhythm." His Format has 10.5 lines that are arranged in two Stanzas. The first Stanza has Rhyme Scheme "abcabc," and the second is either "dbcdc" or "dcbdc." The very Last Line is Indented and Shorter. He described it as a contraction of the Petrarchan Sonnet, whereby the 8 Line Octave becomes 6, while the Sestet is reduced to 5. It should have a Pivot between the Sestet and Quintet.

However, history provides a significant Pedigree Precedent noted by a Site called Poetry Through the Ages that described it this way.

"The 10-Line, two-Stanza Curtal Sonnet actually pre-dated the Petrarchan Form, but was only used by the more masterful structural poets. A good example is embedded within the 29 movements of Dante's, *La Vita Nuova*."

Dante's Curtal Sonnet predates Hopkins by 400 years. It had a Rhyme Scheme of "aabbba cddc," in a more typical Pentameter. So, at the very least, the Curtal Format is a Precursor of the True Sonnet, or at best, the Original Form that later evolved. Very strong argument for inclusion in the Sonnet Family.

My contribution to this chapter is *Hidden in the Fog*. The image is of the dome of the St. Paul Cathedral, in St. Paul, Minnesota. In seeking an inspiration for a Poem, I came across this image once again. As I sought to see the cross mounted above it through mist, I was inspired to write this poem.

To be as true as possible to the Format, I wrote this one in variable Spondee. Spondee is a beat in a Poetic Line which consists of two consecutive (or more) Accented Syllables (Stressed/Stressed) or "DUM-DUM" Stress Pattern. It is a Poetic Device that is not very common, as other Metrical Feet, like iamb and Trochee. We rarely find Poems written in Spondee alone; however, Poets use Spondee by combining with other Metrical Feet, as I have done here.

Sonnet 107: Hidden in the Fog

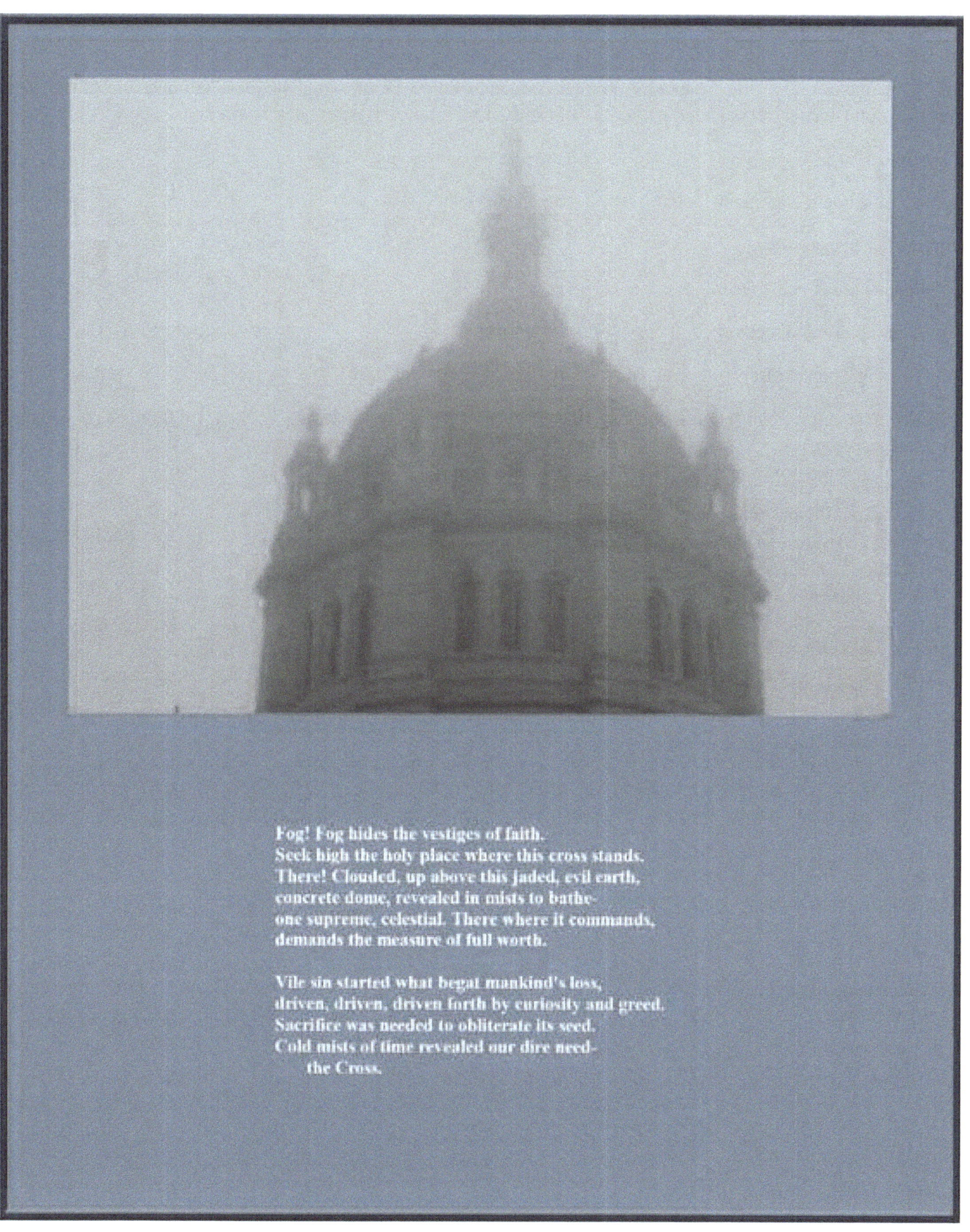

Fog! Fog hides the vestiges of faith.
Seek high the holy place where this cross stands.
There! Clouded, up above this jaded, evil earth,
concrete dome, revealed in mists to bathe-
one supreme, celestial. There where it commands,
demands the measure of full worth.

Vile sin started what begat mankind's loss,
driven, driven, driven forth by curiosity and greed.
Sacrifice was needed to obliterate its seed.
Cold mists of time revealed our dire need-
    the Cross.

B. The Sonnetino

The Sonnetino is a very short, Sonnet-like Format, created by fellow Fanstorian, Jyoti (aka. lightink). In fact, the name means **Sonnet-like**. Jyoti modeled it after the 10 Line Curtal Sonnet. Here are her instructions.

Sonnetino:

-A Five Line Poem (Quintrain), comprising a Tercet and Couplet

-Rhyme Scheme, aaabb

-Written in iambic Pentameter.

-The Tercet presents a scene or conflict,

- the Closing Couplet offers conclusion or resolution (with an optional turn).

In favor of it being a Sonnet, it has so many of the elements that a Sonnet requires. The Standard Elements of a Sonnet are these:

1. A Structured Poem, usually of 14 Lines
2. A formalized Rhyme Scheme.
3. A Structured Meter, usually iambic Pentameter
4. A structured Stanza Scheme
    a. The English Version with 3 Quatrains and Closing Couplet
    b. The Italian with an Octave and Sestet (or, 2 Quatrains with 2 Tercets)
5. A Turn, or Volta
6. A developed Theme Progression (Main Theme, extended Metaphor, a Twist or Conflict, Closing Summary).

It can be, and has been argued that, changing one or more of the Elements, does not change the Essence of a Sonnet. If you can retain some, or most of the Elements, it is still a Sonnet.

The Sonnetino is Structured, has formalized Rhyme Scheme, requires iambic Pentameter, has a Stanza Scheme, a Volta, and a Theme. Mostly it lacks 14 Lines. Otherwise, it has quite a few Sonnet Elements.

I provide two examples here.

The first is *Bus Stop*. The picture is actually of a bus stop in downtown St. Paul, Minnesota.

The second is *Eagle Perch*, a Duo Sonnetino (two Sonnetinos).

After reviewing them, I have to conclude, that they are not Sonnets. To me, they just read like any other 5 Line Stanza (Quintrain). Making it Duo, is even more so. MAYBE MY EXAMPLES ARE POOR. Otherwise, sorry Jyoti.

Sonnet 108: Bus Stop

Oh see! Such opulent display is thus!
A cupola in stone, to catch a bus?
A simple shelter from the rain for us.
That's all a touring traveler should need.
Although, impressive structure, it's agreed.

Sonnet 109: Eagle Perch

Stand tall upon thy perch of gnarled limbs.
Iconic freedom, spark of battle hymns.
Ignite our thoughts of flight, those soaring whims.
You graced the heavens, as you chased the wind,
While man was once to earthbound surface pinned.

Today, though we may sail to higher heights,
And dare to dream of interstellar flights,
The visage of an eagle still excites.
As symbol of our nation's civic pride.
Your true majestic stance can't be denied.

CHAPTER 11. SONNETS WITH REPEATING REFRAINS

The French are very enamored with Poems that have Lines or Phrases that Repeat in the Poem, and as I have shown, many well-known Styles have been modified into Sonnets. It is this feature that we will examine here in this Chapter. These Types of Poems, whether Sonnet or not, require a Strict Structure, so as to be able to manipulate the desired Effect. Often the first Stanzas and/or first Lines of a Stanza, then the Couplet, play a Key Role in this activity. Many, as I do, consider the Forms to carry a unique beauty in the Repetition, requiring Creative Skill to instigate the necessary Transitions and Impacts. Others find the Repetition to be boring. The choice is yours.

We'll start with the Cornish Sonnet that takes the First Line of two Stanzas to create the Couplet. Next will be the Couplet Sonnet that uses the First Two Lines of the Poem to do the same. Then there is the Echo Sonnet that intricately plays with First and Fourth Lines for an Inverted Rhyming Couplet. The Kyrielle does a similar activity using First and Fourth Lines with a firm Staccato of the Fourth Line and a Standard Rhyming Couplet, as opposed to an Inverted one. The Pantoum intricately weaves all four Lines of the first Stanza into a hop-scotch type pattern. We'll look at the Lyricat Sonnet, Quatern Sonnet, Rondel Prime Sonnet, Swanette, Tirell Sonnet, and the Triolet Sonnet. These will reveal Waterfall Effects, Ripple Effects, Peek-a-boo Effects, and more. It is a very intriguing group that warrants a close look. When I'm done, I hope you'll have a fond appreciation of them too.

A. The Cornish Sonnet

I first introduced you to this Format back in Chapter 8, due to its Deviation from the iambic into a Variable Meter. Now we'll take a look at its Refrain usage.

The Cornish Sonnet is said to be influenced by Arab traders to the Cornish coast. This Verse Form is a merging of Arabic Meter and the Sonnet. The defining features of the Cornish Sonnet are:

2 Sestets made up of Linked Enclosed Tercets,
followed by a Refrain which is the repeat of the **First Line** of each Sestet,
Metered at the discretion of the Poet,
Lines should be similar (not necessarily exact) Length.
The Rhyme Scheme is:
Abacbc Dedfef AD

The capital letters show that the **First Line** of each Sestet are Repeated in the Refrain of the Closing Couplet. Again, the **First Lines** of the two Stanzas create the Closing Couplet.

My example here is *Water's Edge*. It is a social commentary on the historical presence of a prior civilization overshadowed by another. For an interesting history, Google "Kaposia." In this one, I kept to a uniform 7 Syllable Count, but could have chosen to have a Line with 6 or 8 Syllables interspersed.

Sonnet 110: Water's Edge

City raised by water's edge,
drawing people to its shore,
where historians allege
flatboats and canoes once roamed,
detailed in the local lore
shamans vocally intoned.

Concrete bonds your vistas now.
River flow still dominates.
Crafts much bigger now somehow
ghost Kaposia's landfall --
echoes from its final fate,
time's transition to St. Paul.

City raised by water's edge,
concrete bonds your vistas now.

B. Couplet Sonnet

A Couplet is a Pair of Lines of Meter in Poetry. A Couplet usually consists of two Lines that Rhyme and have the same Meter. The term "Couplet" was first used to describe Successive Lines of Verse in Sir P. Sidney's *Arcadia* in 1590:

"In singing some short coplets, whereto the one halfe beginning, the other halfe should answere."

Couplets in iambic Pentameter are called *Heroic Couplets*. John Dryden in the 16–17th century and Alexander Pope in the 18th century were both well known for their writing in Heroic Couplets. Couplets also appear as part of more complex Rhyme Schemes, such as Sonnets, usually as a Closing Couplet.

A Couplet Sonnet is made up of all Couplets. In fact there are 7 Rhyming Couplets to make up the typical 14 Lines. The unique feature is that the First Two Lines are **also** the Last Two Lines, so the Rhyme Scheme is:

AAbbccddeeff AA,

where the capital letters indicate the Repeated Lines.

My example is *Rain Filled Culverts*. This poem actually pre-dated this book by a number of years, and I hadn't noticed that I had made an additional modifications, until I added it here. It still is a Couplet Sonnet. There are definitely 7 Couplets, but I complicated the Refrain by Echoing the Second Line throughout the Stanzas. So for this poem, the Rhyme Scheme actually became:

A,A1, b,b – a,A1,c,c – a,A1,d,d – A,A1. That reduced the number of Rhymes, but maintained the Coupled Nature. It was written as Heroic Couplets as well. This shows how Poets can frequently take a Format and embellish it more, as I have done here.

To Compensate, I also included a more typical Couplet Sonnet in *Yellow Lilies*. It is done in iambic Tetrameter. The picture was taken of some Lilies growing in my brother Richard's back yard.

Sonnet 111: Rain Filled Culverts

The rain filled culverts now have waterfalls
When raging torrents turn between stone walls,
That splash and crash and dash about the pond,
A sight of strength and charm of which I'm fond.

A loud cascading cacophony calls,
When raging torrents turn between stone walls,
Cold water rushes freely over rocks,
While tossing stones about like tumbling blocks.

A vortex wave exists that spins and sprawls,
When raging torrents turn between stone walls,
As worldly troubles leave me feeling raw,
It lifts my soul aloft in stunning awe.

The rain filled culverts now have waterfalls
When raging torrents turn between stone walls.

Sonnet 112: Yellow Lilies

These lilies add their golden glow
Wherever their bright petals show.
Their stamens lift to taste the air
as petals open wide to share
The pollen with the bugs and bees.
Their bulbous roots can help appense
The culinary Asian taste.
They look delightful in a vase.
But, lily colors we most prize,
Delighting visions in our eyes.
That's why we love to cultivate
Them, for the mood that they create.

These lilies add their golden glow
Wherever their bright petals show.

C. Echo Sonnet

I was introduced to it by Gungalo, a wonderful woman who became my Poetic Mentor, and taught me that there were so many lovely Formats.

The Echo Sonnet is a relatively new Form devised by the well-respected English Poet, Jeff Green. It takes its shape from three Envelope Quatrains and a Couplet, the Last Line of each Stanza is a Refrain that links the Quatrains and gives us a Rhyme Scheme of:

A, b, b, A1, a, c, c, A1, a, d, d, A1, A, A1

Where the first "A" sets the A Rhyme and Repeats once in Line 13. The "A1" of Line 4 matches the Rhyme established in "A", but is a distinct Repeating Line that Echoes 3 more times in lines 8, 12 and 14. This Type of Poem, then, has 4 Rhyme Sets of "A, b, c, and d." The Rhyming Couplet uses both the "A" and "A1" Rhymes. So, here, we have an interplay derived from Line 1 and 4 of the First Quatrain.

The Echo Sonnet is based on French Repeating Forms, but unlike those Forms which are normally Syllabic, the preferred Meter is Iambic Pentameter, or similar, and being a Typical Sonnet, it should be presented as a 14 line Poem.

My example is *Sweet Music*. The picture is of my wife's guitar and music stand.

Sonnet 113: Sweet Music

Sweet music makes a world-redeeming whole.
Without it, can't imagine how we'd be,
But life would lose delightful symmetry.
It echoes through the fibers of my soul,

With rhythms that fulfill life's gaping hole,
Of melodies that sooth the savage beast,
Or keep the couples dancing at the feast.
It echoes through the fibers of my soul,

It plays a temperament relaxing role.
The sounds bring background beauty to the world,
As soft symphonic soundbites are unfurled,
It echoes through the fibers of my soul.

Sweet music makes a world-redeeming whole,
It echoes through the fibers of my soul.

D. Kyrielle Sonnet

You first met this Format back in Chapter 2 as a well-known Form that was transitioned into a Sonnet. Now we'll look at its Refrains. Very much like the Echo Sonnet, this Variant also uses Lines 1 and 4 of the First Stanza, but instead of a double use of the "A" Rhyme, it uses both the "A and B" Rhymes to be the Repeated Refrains. So that necessitates either a Coupled or Alternating Rhyme Scheme, rather than an Enveloping Rhyme.

The Kyrielle is a Poetic Form that originated in Troubadour Poetry. The name "Kyrielle" derives from the *"Kýrie,"* which is part of many Christian Liturgies. The original Kyrielles were written in Rhyming Couplets (or Quatrains), where the Repeated Refrain was religious, using the Phrase "Lord, have mercy", or a Variant on it, as the Second Line of the Couplet or Last Line of the Quatrain. In less strict usage, other Phrases, and sometimes single Words, developed to be used as the Refrain. Each Line within the Poem consists of only eight Syllables (Tetrameter). There is no limit to the number of Stanzas a Kyrielle may have, but three is considered the accepted minimum. Now-a-days, the Religious Aspect has been lost. The Format has evolved into a pure Poetic Expression.

This Sonnet is made up of three Rhyming Quatrains and a Non-rhyming Couplet. Just like the traditional Kyrielle Poem, the Kyrielle Sonnet also has the Repeating Line or Phrase as a Refrain (usually appearing as the Last Line of each Stanza).

While each Line within the Kyrielle Sonnet consists of only 8 Syllables, French Forms have a tendency to link back to the beginning of the Poem. So common practice is to use the First and Last Line of the First Quatrain as the Ending Couplet. This would also reinforce the Refrain within the Poem.

Therefore, a good Rhyming Scheme for a Kyrielle Sonnet would be:

AabB, ccbB, ddbB, AB, or

AbaB, CbcB, dbdB, AB,

 where the capital letters indicate the Repeated Lines.

My sample here is *Majestic Mountain Goat.* I took this photograph in a local Cabella's Sporting Goods Store in Woodbury, Minnesota. Note how the Refrain powerfully reinforces the Main Theme of the commentary.

Sonnet 114: Majestic Mountain Goat

Majestic is the mountain goat,
on rocky craig, in pure white coat.
Alert and standing proud and tall.
Now stuffed and mounted on a wall.

Its balance always strong and sure.
On stones, footholds remain secure,
to stand aloof, above it all.
Now stuffed and mounted on a wall.

What fate befell this graceful beast,
when once its lifelong journey ceased?
What tragic fortunes to recall?
Now stuffed and mounted on a wall.

Majestic is the mountain goat,
now stuffed and mounted on a wall.

E.   The Lyricat Sonnet

I introduced you to the Lyricat Sonnet back in Chapter 8, due to its unusual Line Lengths, but here we focus on the Form as to its use of the Refrain.

The LyriCat Sonnet creates three Quatrains with a Repeating Line, and a Couplet. It Mimics the 7-5-9 Meter of the standard LyriCat Format, with the following Meter structure:

7/5/9/5 - 7/5/9/5 - 7/5/9/5 - 5/5.

The Rhyme Scheme is a bit more complex, as it is:

abAb acAc adAd ee,

where the A represents the Repeated Line. Volta on line 9.

Note that the Repeated Line is not the first, second or fourth Line of the Stanza, as we have previously seen. Here it keys off the third Line of the first Stanza, and remains so, for the next two Stanzas, but is not involved in the Closing Couplet at all.

My version is *Gathering Gloom*. It definitely was a threatening sky I photographed that day. The Refrain helped to strongly reinforce my concern. I thought the use of a Question would also add to the drama, and draw the reader in.

Sonnet 115: Gathering Gloom

See the sky, as storm clouds bloom
that darken the day!
What threat invests this gathering gloom,
to chase us away?

See them in the distance loom,
pledging violence.
What threat invests this gathering gloom,
for dry audience?

Heed warnings of pending doom
as fire flashes bright.
What threat invests this gathering gloom,
turning day to night?

Actions may abort.
Pray the stay is short.

F. Pantoum Sonnet

The Pantoum is another well-known Poem Format that was transformed into a Sonnet, as I identified in Chapter 2. Since it uses several Repeated Refrains, it is also highlighted here.

The Pantoum is a Poetic Form derived from the "pantun," a Malay Verse Form: specifically from the *pantun berkait*, a series of interwoven Quatrains. It is composed of a series of Quatrains; the second and fourth Lines of each Stanza are Repeated as the first and third Lines of the next Stanza. The Pattern continues for any number of Stanzas, except for the Final Stanza, which differs in the Repeating Pattern. The first and third Lines of the Last Stanza are the second and fourth of the penultimate; the First Line of the Poem is the Last Line of the Final Stanza, and the third Line of the First Stanza is the second of the final. Ideally, the meaning of Lines shifts when they are Repeated although the Words remain exactly the same: this can be done by shifting punctuation, punning, or simply recontextualizing.

The Sonnet Variation is a 14 Line Poem with 12 continuous Lines of "abab" Alternate Rhyming Lines linked to a closing Rhymed Couplet. It can also be formed in the contemporary manner of three separate Quatrains with Closing Couplet, of the Traditional way with 14 Lines together (as done here). In either case, the Rhyme Scheme for this Pantoum Sonnet is:

A1/B1/A2/B2/ B1/C1/B2/C2/ C1/D1/C2/D2/ A2/A, or

A1/B1/A2/B2 – B1/C1/B2/C2 – C1/D1/C2/D2 – A2/A

where the capital letters indicate Repeating Lines, and the numbers differentiates between two or more Repeated Lines.

So what we see here is an intricate Interweaving of Refrains that starts by using **ALL** the Lines of the First Stanza, then proceeds to play a game of Rippling Rhyme, until it reverts to a Couplet of Reversed "A" Rhymes.

I provided two examples here. I did one of each Layout.

The first is *Pink Ladies*, showing some more flowers from my brother, Richard's, yard. It is done in the Compressed Format. In this Format, when the transitions are done smoothly, a reader almost doesn't notice the frequency of the Repeats right away.

The second Sonnet is *A Day by the Lake*. It shows a photograph of fishermen that I took on a lake in Woodbury, Minnesota. It is done in the more Conventional Manner. In this Format, the Refrain Pattern is more distinguishable.

Sonnet 116: Pink Ladies

These lilies grace the hedge in luscious pink.
Their petals open like a mother's arms.
Inviting butterflies to take a drink
Of nectar, adding to their floral charms.
Their petals open like a mother's arms,
Pink ladies fill the air with lovely scent
Of nectar, adding to their floral charms.
We savor them to maximum extent
Pink ladies fill the air with lovely scent.
And lend their vibrant color to the scene
We savor them to maximum extent
They look so beautiful against the green
Inviting butterflies to take a drink.
These lilies grace the hedge in luscious pink.

Sonnet 117: A Day by the Lake

There is no better way to spend a day.
I love to spend it here upon a lake,
While tucked away in fav'rite private bay,
With all its many pleasures to partake.

I love to spend it here upon a lake,
I'm ready when the weather fin'ly clears,
With all its many pleasures to partake,
Where Nature's sound is music to my ears.

I'm ready when the weather fin'ly clears,
When I might choose to take a quiet walk,
Where Nature's sound is music to my ears,
And I might spot an Eagle or a Hawk.

While tucked away in fav'rite private bay,
There is no better way to spend a day.

G. Quatern Sonnet

Yet another well-known Poetic Form transformed to a Sonnet from Chapter 2 is the Quatern Sonnet. Its use of the Repeated Refrain places it here in this chapter as well.

The Quatern (Latin meaning "4 each") is a French Verse form, possibly from the Middle Ages since it is so close to the Retourne and Kyrielle which also came from that period. The Quatern like so many other French Forms employs a Refrain. The Defining Feature is the movement of the Refrain within the Quatrain from Stanza to Stanza.

A Quatern is a Poem consisting of four Quatrains, where the First Line of the poem Ripples through each Stanza. It becomes the Second Line of the Second Stanza, the Third Line of the Third Stanza, and the Last of the fourth. So it is a Progression that makes for a very lovely Waterfall Effect as the Line "Ripples" from beginning to end of the Poem. This creates a Rhyme Scheme of:

Abab bAba abAb babA, or

Abab cAca adAd eaeA,

where the capital letter signifies the Repeated Line. The first choice uses only two Rhymes, while the second uses five. See where the "A" Refrain falls in each Stanza.

Written in Tetrameter.

Therefore, to make a Quatern Sonnet, you merely turn the last Quatrain into a Rhymed Couplet, using the Repeated Line as the Last Line of the poem, but retaining the Waterfall Effect. The trick is to use the Repeated Line in various ways, changing its Aspect, while still being a Repeated Refrain. The Rhyme Scheme becomes:

Abab bAba abAb aA.

For this chapter, I wrote *Landing Loon*. I captured an action shot of the bird that is the Minnesota State Bird. Note how lovely the Transitions of the Waterfall Effect are.

Sonnet 118: Landing Loon

Behold, the landing of the Loon
upon the waters of the lake!
His feathers flapping, splashes strewn,
while leaving ripples in its wake.

A magic moment shared when I
behold the landing of the Loon,
to frame within my camera's eye,
completing perfect afternoon.

Then I and nature both commune
within the eco-element.
Behold, the landing of the Loon!
Imagine my astonishment.

I won't forget this time too soon
Behold, the landing of the Loon!

H. Rondel Sonnet

Still another friend from Chapter 2, the Rondel Sonnet also does Interactions with the Refrain. A Rondel Poem is a Verse Form originating in French Lyrical poetry of the 14th century. It was later used in the Verse of other languages as well, such as English and Romanian. It is a Variation of the Rondeau.

A Rondel is a Poem with two Quatrains followed by a Sestet where the First Two Lines of the Poem become Repeated as the Last Two Lines of the next two Stanzas (the second Quatrain and the Sestet). Sometimes the Second Line is dropped in the Last Stanza. It is usually in Tetrameter, but is always iambic.

So, the Rhyme Scheme would be:

ABba abAB abbaAB (Prime),

or

ABba abAB abbaA (Classic).

The conversion to a Sonnet is quite simple. Change the Meter to Pentameter and separate the last two Lines of the Sestet to make it a Couplet. In actuality the Rondel, as introduced in France about 1544 by Clermont Marot, was a Sonnet. But the Classic Form became more popular. The Rhyme Scheme then for the Sonnet becomes:

ABba abAB abba AB.

So here we have use of the First Two Lines of the First Stanza, rather than the First and Fourth Lines that we have seen earlier, that holds the Couplet in the same Sequence.

My example is *Pincers Probe*. It contains my social commentary on abortion. You can see how the use of the Double Refrain makes a powerful point. The picture is a photo of my great granddaughter, Belle Rose, an example of what those lives thrown away in abortions could have been.

Sonnet 119: Pincers Probe

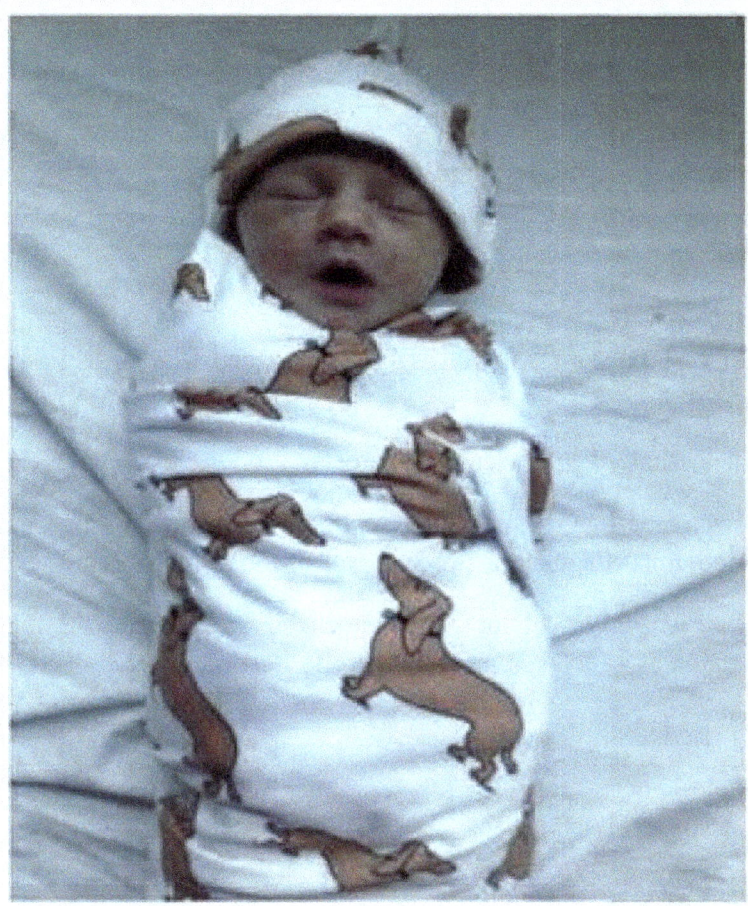

The pincers probe the nether parts,
while demons watch with glee and smile.
We rip apart the baby's hearts.
Those innocents that we defile.

To deaf ears, silent screaming starts,
ignoring an internal trial.
The pincers probe the nether parts
while demons watch with glee and smile.

The tissues now on sterile carts,
were once a child, a life worthwhile.
In millions, discards reconcile
with women's right to choose, cruel farce.

The pincers probe the nether parts
while demons watch with glee and smile.

I. Swannet Sonnet (or just Swannet)

The Swannet Sonnet whilst not the creation of the Canadian poet, Gloria Carpenter, has become her trademark being used in conjunction with her elemental and avian photo studies in British Columbia.

It is a straight forward Form comprised of 14 Lines with 3 Quatrain Stanzas of Enveloping Rhyme (abba) and a Rhyming Couplet. The Key Feature is the Repeat of Line 1 and 4 to also become the Closing Couplet.

The Rhyme Scheme is:

(A1)bb(A2) cddc effe (A1)(A2),

where "A1" is the First Line of the First Stanza, as well as the Couplet, and "A2" is the Last Line of the First Stanza, and the Last Line of the Poem.

The Meter is not specified but is usually Tetrameter or Pentameter.

Here is another Form that utilizes Line 1 and 4 of the First Stanza, to create the Closing Couplet, making it very similar to the Echo Sonnet, except for not impacting Stanza 2 or 3; as well as the Kyrielle Sonnet, except for its Rhyme Scheme.

My example here is *Turning Two*. The little devil looking so angelic in the photograph is my grandson Isaac. I wrote this in iambic Tetrameter. Just wrote it as a social commentary on the "terrible twos."

Sonnet 120: Turning Two

When little angels turn to two,
They often change their halo rings
To Devil's horns and other things.
They make us wonder what to do.

We pray it's just a passing phase,
As mischief is their major joy.
Will time improve that naughty boy,
And bring about much better days?

When spanking, parents must avoid,
Our skills are pushed beyond all hope.
We dangle at the end of rope,
When antics make us most annoyed.

When little angels turn to two,
They make us wonder what to do.

J.   Tirell Sonnet

I identified the Tirell Sonnet as one created by Famous Poets in Chapter 3. Now let's investigate the use of the Refrain. It uses the First Two Lines of the Poem **reversed** as the Closing Couplet.

The Tirell Sonnet was created by Robert Tirrell Leonard, a Poet from Woburn, MA. who is also a Politician and Author of several Poetry Collections.

The Tirrell Sonnet (an American Model), is quite different and has a unique feel to it. It starts with a Couplet followed by a Tercet, followed by a Quatrain, adding the Volta with a following Tercet and then **reversing** the order of the Repeated Couplet as a Refrain.

So it is: Couplet + Tercet + Quatrain + Tercet + Reversed Couplet.

It features only 3 Rhymes (a,b,and c). It is written in iambic Pentameter.

This can create an Introspective Feel to the whole Poem.

The Rhyme Scheme is:

A1, A2 - b,c,b - c,b,b,c - b,c,b - A2, A1,

where the capital letters indicate the Repeated Lines and the numbers provide identification.

Here I provide the example *Dances in the Ferns*. The image was taken in the Fern Room of the Como Park Conservatory in St. Paul, Minnesota. The statue is part of a water fountain. The Mystical Feeling of that image was the inspiration of the Poem.

Sonnet 121: Dances in the Ferns

A female form, she dances in the ferns.
Such grace displayed there, singing as she turns.

A captivating, undulating voice,
Appealing sound, with impact most profound.
My heartbeats joined the rhythm of her choice.

A stunning sight, this vision spun around
in wild abandon. Made my eyes rejoice!
Imagining the goddess Eurydice,
unclothed and free upon this fern-filled ground.

I must be dreaming. Visions oft' entice.
The mind unravels and becomes unsound.
And yet, I see her without prejudice.

Such grace displayed there, singing as she turns.
A female form, she dances in the ferns.

K.   Triolet Sonnet (aka. Sonn Triolet)

I first informed you about this creation of mine back in Chapter 2 for being an adaptation of a well-known Poetic Format. It shows up here as a Format that uses Refrains. It keys off the First Two Lines of the First Stanza in an intense way.

A Triolet is a French Form with a Double Refrain. It consists of 8 Lines (an Octave) with a Rhyme Scheme of:

ABaAabAB,

where the capital letters represent the Repeated Lines. It can be written in any Meter, but being French in origin, iambic Tetrameter is the favorite, while iambic Pentameter is a favorite of the Sonnet Form. So I propose that it should be either one or the other.

To convert to a Sonnn Triolet, requires three Triolets followed by a Rhymed Couplet. In this format, instead of three Quatrains and a Couplet, I have 3 Octaves and a Couplet. It still is 3 Stanzas followed by a Closing Couplet (blending English with Italian). Still has a formal Rhyme Scheme - that of the Triolet.

My example for this chapter is *Juxtaposed Elements*. I took this photograph of a family out walking and identified some Key Elements of the Composition – outdoor activity together, the vitality of the sun, and shadows. I did this one in iambic Tetrameter. I use a touch of Elision on the word "family" to keep the Rhythm. With such a Tight Compression of the Refrains in each Stanza, Punctuation become critical in order to provide the proper meanings throughout the Transitions.

Sonnet 122: Juxtaposed Elements

A lovely fam'ly on a stroll,
together in a happy group,
with baby in device they roll.
A lovely fam'ly on a stroll,
Fresh air and walk, a healthy goal
that lets their energy recoup.
A lovely fam'ly on a stroll,
together in a happy group.

That sunshine falling down on them,
on such a warm and special day,
is like an effervescent gem.
That sunshine falling down on them,
sends from sky's glowing diadem
vitality in each array.
That sunshine falling down on them,
on such a warm and special day.

Embraced, they are, in silhouette.
Wherever the long shadows grow,
they dangle like marionettes.
Embraced, they are, in silhouette.
dark replicas the sunlight gets,
that follows them, both to and fro.
Embraced, they are, in silhouette,
wherever the long shadows grow.

Three elements that juxtapose:
the family, the sun, and shadows.

CHAPTER 12. EXPANDED SEQUENCE SONNETS

This chapter may very well be the most intriguing, and certainly the largest one of the book. All the Sonnets here are long and larger than life, so to speak. These are the ones that are meant to tell stories, to paint history, and to weave a tale. Some include multiple Sonnets. Some are interlinked in fascinating ways.

In this chapter you'll be introduce to the Heroic Sonnet, a Building Block to other Formats; to the Super Sonnet, that proudly displays the four main Rhyme Schemes; the Super Sonnet that adds more Quatrains; the Sonnet Trilogy with three separate Non-interlinked Sonnets; the Tiara of Sonnets that presents three Sonnets, one in English, one in Petrarchan, and the third in Spenserian Format; the Coronet of Sonnets having four Formats – the English, Petrarchan, Spenserian, and the Rubaiyat Forms; the Crown of Heroic Sonnets, having 7 Interlinked Sonnets; the Wreath with 15 Sonnets having an Acrostic Sonnet that holds the First Lines of all the other Sonnets; the Sonnet Cycle, with 20 or more Sonnets; and the Sonnet Sequence, with 50+ Thematic Sonnets.

Plan to spend some time here. I hope you find it as rewarding as I do.

A. Heroic Sonnet

The Heroic Sonnet is the Cornerstone Format of the Crown of Heroic Sonnets, which links a string of seven of them together. Unlike other Sonnets this Format does not require a Volta (or Turn), in that it is meant to convey large amounts of information, or a story. It consists of four Quatrains typically in iambic Pentameter, using one of two classic Rhyme Schemes throughout, either "aabb" (Coupled) or "abab" (Alternating). It is closed with the usual Rhyming Couplet. So it contains 18 Lines, rather than the usual 14 Lines of a Standard Sonnet, in order for it to tell a longer story. That's where the "Heroic" designation comes from - that extra Quatrain.

My example here is *Lush Lagoon.* This picture is of the lagoon at Lake Phalen, in St. Paul, Minnesota. I thought it makes the perfect backdrop for this Idyll Poem. I hope I captured the essence of a day spent laying in the grass, and enjoying the environment. I went with here a Coupled Rhyme Scheme of:

aabb ccdd eeff gghh ii.

Normally this format is used for a large Sequence of Poems to tell a story, but since it stands alone here, I thought I'd make it an Idyll Poem, which is a simple Descriptive Work in Poetry or Prose that deals with rustic life, or pastoral scenes, or suggests a mood of peace and contentment.

Sonnet 123: Lush Lagoon

When I seek out a place of solitude,
there's always water in the interlude,
a place where I and nature oft' commune.
I look for something like a lush lagoon.

Where lovely weeping willows line the shore,
I'll watch the sky-borne raptors swoop and soar,
or contemplate, as clouds go drifting by,
the mysteries of when, or how, or why.

It's magic with the feel and smell of grass,
that cradles me as idle moments pass.
I'll dip my toes into a languid pool,
allowing me to keep my body cool.

I long to feel the touch of gentle breeze,
and watch the flowers with the honey bees.
Such colors are the vibrant greens and blues,
the ones that nature often gives in hues.

Now, given all I've said, I have to say,
I'd love to do it each and every day.

B.   Super Sonnet

A Super Sonnet is composed of several Quatrains closed by a Rhyming Couplet. It generally utilizes all four of the Primary Rhyme Schemes:

Alternate Rhyming - abab

Coupled Rhyming - aabb

Enveloping Rhyme - abba

Skipping Rhyme - abcb

So, the poem writes a Set of the Four Types, and then Repeats them as many times as the Author wishes. The Four Sets are necessary in every four Stanza Series, but not necessarily in the same Sequence. One required feature though, relates to the very Last Stanza, which is **always** the "abcb" Skipping Rhyme Type. That Unrhymed Third Line of that Stanza sets the Rhyme for the final Rhyming Couplet, thereby **linking** the last Quatrain to the Couplet. The creator of this format in unknown, but there are many examples of this Form around. There is no specified Meter.

My example is *Homeless Halloween*. For this poem I used only two Sets of the Four Types (eight Stanzas) plus a Rhyming Couplet. In the first four Stanzas, I used - Alternating, Coupled, Skipping, then Enveloping. For the second Set, I went with – Coupled, Enveloping, Alternating and then Skipping. This Poem has a bit of Social Commentary. Meter was Variable.

Sonnet 124: Homeless Halloween

The biggest trick is finding shelter.
The treat is something sweet to eat.
In City heat they often swelter,
They need shoes when they have cold feet.

Halloween amongst the homeless
Where people couldn't care much less,
Should surely open up your eyes.
As they survive the open skies.

Will your children even see them,
Chasing treats in their cute costumes?
See people living in the street,
Within their makeshift cardboard rooms?

Your homes are warm and so comfy,
And full of scattered unused toys.
Any yet, those needy girls and boys
Could also use some playful glee .

They go to sleep with hunger pains
Exposed to chilling winds and rains,
Possessions all in paper bags,
For clothes, they're mostly wearing rags.

Your parents sing you lullabies
And cater to your needs and wants.
You often eat in restaurants
And have the finest school supplies.

On Halloween the things to fear,
Are not the ghosts or being haunted
Its losing all those gifts you have,
Becoming homeless and unwanted

After gorging on sweet candy,
Can you spare some unwanted clothes?
Your old coat may come in handy,
To a kid with a runny nose.

Don't forget the homeless on Halloween.
Acts of kindness improve a dreary scene.

C. Sonnet Trilogy

This is another Sonnet Format that I created. It is really quite simple. There are three consecutive Sonnets, **not** Interlinked, all of which have the same Rhyme Scheme and Meter, but tell a continuing story.

I provide the example of *Be Careful What You Ask For*. This poem is a Set of three Modern Sonnets. I show here that a Sonnet can be Humorous too. The Rhyme Scheme is "aabb" (Coupled). The Meter is Tetrameter, but not iambic. This is a joke I once was told. I just Paraphrased it here and put it in Poetic Form.

Sonnet 125: Be Careful What You Ask For

1.
So, three men arrived at the Pearly Gates.
Each one quite apprehensive 'bout their fates.
St. Peter anxiously began to swoon,
Because their sudden deaths had come too soon.

"You were expected 'bout a month from now.
Your places aren't quite ready, anyhow."
So flustered, didn't know just what to do.
He went to ask God for an interview.

And God said, "We'll just have to let them choose
What they'd like to be, while our working crews
Prepare for them a proper Heaven's place.
It just must not be of the Human Race."

Because they'd already left human kind,
Another species form they'd have to find.

2.
Instructions given for a month of time,
To take a form that each would think sublime,
Would give the three relief and bits of glee
Unique to their own personality.

The first one said. "It wouldn't be too boring
To be an Eagle, over mountains soaring."
Although his attitude was deemed aloof,
His spirit was lifted aloft. Then - POOF.

The second said. "I know, I'd like to be
A Dolphin out cavorting in the sea."
The last one said. "I think that I'd be lucky
To be a Stud in beautiful Kentucky".

Each got their new experience to try,
And so it was to be, as time went by.

3.
Then came the day their places were now done.
So Peter asked to retrieve everyone.
The angel wondered where they might be found.
The Gate Saint was required to expound.

"You'll find the first one o'er the Grand Canyon.
He's flyin' free and soarin' 'neath the sun."
"The second's swimin' in the Southern Sea.
He's flippin', floatin', happy as can be."

"I thought that last guy's wish was rather strange,
But still, it was my pleasure to arrange."
"He's in Kentucky by that new church door.
Per his request, he is a two-by-four."

So, if you're given a selection task,
Make sure you're careful how and what you ask.

D. Tiara of Sonnets

Fellow Fanstorian, Catherine Ginn (aka. I Am Cat) came up with this brilliant concept and should be commended for it. It is based on the concept of the Crown of Sonnets, which has a Sequence of seven Sonnets, Interlinked by Last-to-First Lines, and concluding with the Final Line being the same as the First Line of the First Sonnet. Thus creating a Circle that is similar to the Crown, but smaller. The Tiara of Sonnets, then, has the same concept, but with only three Sonnets. Thus a much smaller Tiara, rather than a Crown. An option is to write each Sonnet in a different Format, but that is not a requirement.

For this Chapter, I wrote three Tiaras, just because I liked this Form. They all have a similar Theme. I guess I was overwhelmed by Spring Fever. For each Tiara, to show the three Primary Sonnet Formats (the Petrarchan, the English, and the Spenserian), I thought I'd write them using the option of one Stanza in each Format here.

The First Tiara is *Crabapple Bloom*. It is written in iambic Pentameter. It captures three phases of a Crabapple Tree's transition from winter gloom, to bloom and then to fallen petals. Each Sonnet used a different hue of red to describe it – claret, ruby, carnelian, and crimson. It touches on the Winter Myths of Boreas and the Zephyrs, and the Spring Myth of Gaiia and the Anemoi. Each Style is clearly on display.

The second Sonnet is *Rosebud in Springtime*, done in iambic Pentameter. Its theme is about a Rose's Bloom Sequence; first the promise, then the emergence, and finally full bloom. I did it with a touch of Elizabethan. I weave in the legend of Chloris and her springtime songs.

The third is *Spring Buds*, another Ode to Spring. It's actually a repeat of the second Sonnet, just reproduced with a different image and slight word changes. Enough to make it a different Poem. I did this just to show the impact that the image and overall Composition has on the Poetry. You don't have to re-read it if you don't desire to, just feel the image and composition Transition Impact. If you do read it, see if you can tell what was changed in the text.

Sonnet 126: Crabapple Bloom

1. A Petrarchan Sonnet - Transition

What sheer delights blaze, when Crabapples bloom,
where claret buds soon fill the bluest skies.
A stunning treat to soothe our winter eyes
accustomed to the cold and leaden gloom,
when Boreas blew winds where Winter looms.
Now Zephyr's west winds yield this bright surprise
that carries Spring whose fruits will soon arise
to fill the sky with blossom's sweet perfume.

The Anemoi have fought for Gaia's hand,
as seasons change from dim to bright display.
Mere mortals live within its constant sway,
while greater forces soon transform the land.
Where growth and rebirth stage a springtime stand,
a poet's dreams are made on such a day.

2. An English Sonnet -- Charm

A Poet's dreams are made on such a day,
when ruby shoots adorn its wooded arms.
The Crabapple displays its winning ways.
In early Spring it shows its greatest charms.

With glowing shades of dark carnelian red,
its petals swathe broad limbs in Nature's jewels,
to grace the azure sky, as branches spread,
declaring now, that brilliant color rules.

Oh Spring, so long awaited, has arrived!
These buds proclaim it so, without a doubt.
Another year these fruit trees have survived
to spread their charm and fragrances about.

What lovely sentinels of pure delight!
A Crabapple in bloom is quite a sight.

3. A Spenserian Sonnet -- Disbursal

A Crabapple in bloom is quite a sight.
Its buds explode in beautiful arrays,
where whorls and swirls of elegance unite,
creating lovely, natural bouquets
upon a tree in colorful displays
of floral patterns, like a garden show.
They flutter in the breeze on windy days,
and ripple like the waves that come and go.
But then, the stronger winds begin to blow
and loosen flower's grip from writhing tops.
Soon crimson petals fall to earth like snow.
Upon a rose strewn trail each flower drops.
    Such wonders in the yards and forests loom.
     What sheer delights blaze, when Crabapples bloom.

Sonnet 127: Rosebud in Springtime

1. The Promise -- A Petrarchan Sonnet

A rosebud in the springtime, tiny sprout,
A promise that adorns those naked thorns,
as yesterday's lost brilliance Winter mourns,
thy latent beauty hides 'til coming out.
Contained within cruel seasonal redoubt,
thou burst in colors that thy past forewarns.
Content to wait the signals thus reborn,
shall wait to see such loveliness you flout.

For then, thy day will come, when all is right,
as heat and moisture beckon when to grow.
Within a rush, as messages unite,
thy pod erupts, revealing all to show
its coded colors, beautiful and bright --
the sweetest blossoms souls could ever know.

2. The Emergence -- An English Sonnet

The sweetest blossoms souls could ever know,
begin within the stir of Nature's song.
Each petal swirls, unfurls, to Maestro's bow --
a movement meant to bring its force along.

Unwrapping with the grace of dance ballet,
corollas sway to tunes that Chloris sings,
as springtime's balladeers often portray
this goddess as the one who blesses Spring.

For, is a rose in spring not Nature's gift
of colors bright and scents of sweet perfume?
Indeed, its purest beauty can uplift,
while balm of rose aromas richly loom.

Such attributes of roses soon attest,
when roses bloom in springtime, we are blessed.

3. Full Bloom -- A Spenserian Sonnet

When roses bloom in springtime, we are blessed.
Thou kissed by sun to flash in morning dew,
on hues that painter's pallets once possessed,
by masters on Parisian's famous rue,
bring swirls of pink, or yellow, red or blue.
Once Spring releases messages to blush,
thy resins rise in petals, to shine through,
and grace yon gardens with good Nature's brush,
upon thy flowers brandishing their bush.
Let's not forget that first portent of Spring,
when sap formed buds within its fluent rush,
and promised real delights that springtime brings.
      There's no surprise there's happiness to tout -
      A Rosebud in the springtime, tiny sprout.

Sonnet 128: Spring Buds

1. The Promise -- A Petrarchan Sonnet

A bud that grows in springtime, tiny sprout,
with promise that adorns those naked thorns,
where yesterday's lost brilliance Winter mourns,
thy latent beauty hides 'til coming out.
Contained within cruel seasonal redoubt,
soon bursts the colors that thy past forewarns.
Content to wait the signals thus reborn,
thy stay shall see such loveliness thou flouts.

For then, thy day will come, when all is right,
as heat and moisture beckon when to grow.
Within a rush, as messages unite,
thy pod erupts, revealing all to show
its coded colors, beautiful and bright --
the sweetest blossoms souls could ever know.

2. The Emergence – An English Sonnet

The sweetest blossoms souls could ever know,
begin within the stir of Nature's song.
Each petal swirls, unfurls, to Maestro's bow –
said movement meant to bring its force along.

Unwrapping with the grace of dance ballet,
corollas sway to tunes that Chloris sings,
as springtime's balladeers oft' may portray
this goddess as the one who blesses Spring.

For, is a rose in spring not Nature's gift
of colors bright and scents of sweet perfume?
Indeed, its purest beauty shall uplift,
while balm of rose aromas richly loom.

Such attributes of roses soon attest,
when roses bloom in springtime, we are blessed.

3. Full Bloom – A Spenserian Sonnet

When roses bloom in springtime, we are blessed.
Thou, kissed by sun to flash in morning dew,
hast hues that painters' pallets once possessed,
by masters on Parisian's famous rue,
to bring swirls pink, and yellow, red or blue.
Once Spring releases messages to blush,
thy resins rise in petals, to shine through,
and grace yon gardens with good Nature's brush,
upon thy flowers brandishing their bush.
Let's not forget that first portent of Spring,
when sap formed buds within its fluent rush,
and promised real delights that springtime brings.
    There's no surprise there's happiness to tout –
    a bud that grows in springtime, tiny sprout

E. Coronet of Sonnets

Yours truly came up with this Configuration as well, but it was named by my good friend Jim Bartlett (aka. Pantygynt) of FanStory. This poem has 4 Interlinked Sonnet Formats - The English, Petrarchan, Spenserian, and Rubaiyat. Each is written in iambic Pentameter. Each carries its own signature Rhyme Scheme, as follows:

English: ..... abab cdcd efef gg

Petrarchan: abbaabba cddcdd

Spenserian: ababcbccdcd ee

Rubaiyat: .... aaba bbcb ccdc dd

My example is *Revealed and Concealed*. I used the four Formats to present the changes in Scenic Depth that a forest undergoes in each season. One season for each Format. The picture was taken in a pine forest near my home in St. Paul, Minnesota. I tried to capture the Fall foliage showing through the trees. I love how each Poetic Form has its own Distinct Flavor.

Sonnet 129: Revealed and Concealed

English Sonnet

So, note the scenery as seasons flow.
The density and depth wanes with the time,
created as the leaves that come and go,
when winter, summer, spring, and fall align.

In summer, leaves are thick and colored green.
They limit what pedestrians can see.
The leaves leave little space left in between,
while grass and bushes grow below each tree.

When all the vivid vistas are concealed,
the paths and byways tend to be compressed.
The foliage hides the beauty, not revealed,
because the blended shades have coalesced.

In summer, sights arise around each bend,
but summer yields the season in the end.

Petrarchan Sonnet

But summer yields the season in the end,
as fall puts pretty pigments on display
in wondrous color canopy arrays
that mix the foliage in artistic blends -
the painted palette Nature's touch extends.
Each hillside soon becomes a rich bouquet --
the reds, resplendent treats in every way,
while yellows, rusts, and green hues all contend.

However, trees soon drop some early leaves.
So sights, that once were hidden, now are seen,
as woods reveal their secrets 'hind the screen -
a tangled brush and opaque branch reprieve,
revealing vistas hiker's eyes perceive
as cold winds blow where winter's whims convene.

Spenserian Sonnet

As cold winds blow where winter's whims convene,
the leaves get stripped from twisted, woody limbs,
to blanket paths of forested ravines.
The coverings are dropped and color dims.
The lack of leaves, leaves landscapes looking grim.
Then, suddenly, the sky is filled with snow.
The stillness soon creates a silent hymn,
while woods become a crystal white tableau.
Lament the lack of color, but don't go
without appreciation of brisk air,
and fresh flocked foliage flashing sunny glow,
in winter wonderland beyond compare.
    The snow provides a vast pearlescent hue.
    As winter wanes, the green is overdue.

Rubiat Sonnet

As winter wanes, the green is overdue.
Then springtime rains come swiftly passing through.
They wash the ground and set the season's turn,
 to bring the things that help the earth renew.

The seeds and trees begin renewal's churn,
producing leaves and buds, for which we yearn.
Then, once more, colors dominate the scene,
and we will celebrate their rich return.

Yet there's a price to pay in growth's routine,
when sights will yet again become unseen,
as leaves and thickets tend to quickly grow
into a dense and denigrating screen.

 It's all a part of nature's changing show.
So, note the scenery as seasons flow.

F.   Crown of Heroic Sonnets

The Crown of Heroic Sonnets is a Sequence Poem consisting of seven Heroic Sonnets usually addressed to one person. It is concerned with a single Theme as each Sonnet explores a different Aspect of the Theme and is Interlinked to the Preceding and Succeeding Sonnets by Repeating the Final Line of the Preceding Sonnet as its First Line and by having its Final Line become the First Line of the next Sonnet.

Also, the First Line of the First Sonnet is repeated as the Final Line of the Final Sonnet thereby bringing the Sequence to a close; a Circle uniting the Beginning and End of the entire Poem. Thus, the name Crown.

Each Sonnet uses a Heroic Sonnet Format to provide for a long story. I love the Form for historic presentations. A Heroic Sonnet is an iambic Pentameter based Poem that adds a Heroic Couplet to either two Sicilian Octave Stanzas, or four Sicilian Quatrain Stanzas. In other words, it's eighteen Lines of iambic Pentameter broken into three or five Parts with the last Part being a Couplet. The Rhyme Scheme has usually been;

a,b,a,b,a,b,a,b - c,d,c,d,c,d,c,d - e,e (Octaves), or

a,b,a,b - c,d,c,d - e,f,e,f - g,h,g,h - i,I (Quatrains).

In this segment, I present 6 examples. I know that is quite a few, but I include here all I have written to date. They take a lot of time and energy to write, and I wanted to ensure that they are published somewhere. So, I have included them all here.

The first is *A Pirate's Tale*. It is the first one I ever wrote, and tells the Fictional Story of a remorseful Pirate about to be hanged. Yes that is me with one of my knives that I collect. I used a bite of Dialect.

The second one is *Buffalo – The Great Slaughter* that tells the story of the loss of the great Buffalo Herds in North America, from the perspective of a Buffalo Hunter.

The Third is *Minnesota Early Explorers – 1600's*. It highlights the early History of Minnesota Explorers, it covers possible Viking excursions, Brule, De LaSalle, Father Marquette, Father Hennepin, Daniel Graysolon, and the Voyageurs.

The fourth is *Robbing Paul to Pay Peter*, and intentionally plays on a well-known Phrase. It tells the story of how the Capitol of Minnesota got stolen from St. Peter and ended up in St. Paul.

The Fifth is *Scientific Inquisition*. It relates a dark period of history where Science was Repressed by the Church. The Renaissance and the Inquisition occurred at the same time. In this story, I tried to imagine what it must have been like to live at this time of Massive Contradiction as Columbus' discovery of the New World challenged Old Concepts that the world was Flat. It was a time when the Greek Philosophies were rediscovered and new ideas of Science, Engineering, and Art exploded, while the Church continued to attempt to Suppress these new ideas. A Fictional Character relays how it was for Gallileo, Guordano, Da Vinci, and the burning at the stake of Bruno.

The last one is *Shetek Massacre at Slaughter Slough*. It relates a piece (one Battle) of the Sioux Uprising in 1862.

Although the reads are long, I hope you'll find the effort worthwhile\

Sonnet 130: A Pirate's Tale

I.

And now the gibbet and the rope are mine,
A pirate's plight 'twas oh so aptly earned.
Much misdirection wrapped me in this twine,
Turned from a better life that I have spurned.

It weren't all roses on those Dublin docks.
In fact, there be a lot of crime and grime,
Street urchins stealin' bread and throwin' rocks.
They counted me among them at the time.

Me dad was always drunk when na at sea.
At least the man me mum said was me pop.
'Course couldn't trust her claim's veracity,
Her visits by strange men would never stop.

So at those times mama was occupied,
Well, I was free ta do what'ere I pleased,
And hung with those ta whom few rules applied.
Who'd snatch and grab the things that could be seized.

So, nurtured in a school of crime and strife,
This course I started on became me life.

II.

This course I started on became me life.
Amongst the seamen and tough privateers.
As tales of looted gold were runnin' rife,
I grew ta hang about along the piers.

Soon I was lost ta dreams of gloried fame,
An stole away on ship bound for the sea.
I found dark hold ta play me hid'n game.
Two days from land the crew discovered me.

The Bosun tossed me overboard at first,
But then the Cap'n had them throw a ring.
'Twas hauled upon the poop deck , where I cursed
Me fate in parley that changed everything.

Impressed ta be a member of ship's crew,
Ta carry grog and holy stone the deck,
A boy whose age 'twere only ten plus two,
Soon learned ta be a hardened ship's roughneck.

Ahoy me hearties, thus me tale began
So listen well, I'll tell it best I can.

III.

So listen well, I'll tell it best I can.
For life aboard a ship is na all joy.
As oft' 'tis just adrift without a plan,
Thar's only work or boredom for a boy.

It takes adjustment time ta live at sea,
Ta acclimate ta movement of the ship.
Me guts took weeks ta git all nausea free
I hugged the rail for most first sailin' trip.

Had ta avoid the grasp of dirty men,
Divertin' them with food an hearty drink.
Our officers were blind ta much mayhem,
And then there was the filth, the grime and stink.

But soon I was accepted one of them.
I learned all aspects of the seaman's craft.
As skills grew, found far less things ta condemn,
And at me prior squeamishness, I laughed.

So now, approved as member of the clan,
I grew ta be an ocean-huggin man.

IV.

I grew ta be an ocean-huggin man,
Which means I love the sea 'fore anything.
Ashore I'll take a woman when I can
But they were left when 'ere the sea would sing.

I sailed with crew who knew a thing or two
'Bout how ta make our true intentions clear.
When Jolly Roger flew forth inta view
Our quarry knew they's chased by buccaneer.

We'd fire a warnin' shot across its bow
Ta force the prize ta slowly swing about.
We'd fix a grapplin' hook upon her prow,
Then jump aboard ta clear defenses out.

With blazin' pistols and sharp cutlass blades,
Inflicted deadly wounds and broken bones.
We killed the crew and ravished any maids.
Then sent them off ta visit Davy Jones.

I found this bloody carnage such a thrill,
I learned just how much fun it was ta kill.

V.

I learned just much how fun it was ta kill,
And spend the loot in pure debauchery
At ports that would support the pirate's will,
Ta ransom booty that we took at sea.

We terrorized the Caribbean ports
And captured helpless ships upon the main.
Bloodlust and murder were our cruel cohorts.
We held all civil laws in pure disdain.

We coveted all Spanish gold doubloons,
And planned ta find as many as we could.
We stayed at sea most sunny afternoons.
Against all stormy nights we even stood.

The risks were very high, as were rewards.
So, many fools were drawn into the fire.
A life that's ruled by musket and the sword
Is much too temptin' object of desire.

When fate has fickled ways ta comprehend,
The lesson's learned too often at the end.

VI.

The lesson's learned too often at the end,
And I was no exception ta the rule,
Expectin' evil actions ta transcend,
When comes the judgment for a life that's cruel.

That lesson came on sailin' ta the fore
One foggy mornin' moored in our home port.
Surprised by one large British Man-of-War
There was no hid'n place we could resort.

It came downwind with blazin' eighty guns,
And put our prize corsair ta sudden shame.
Caught in their berths each bloody mother's son
Jumped overboard when ship was set aflame.

The red coats fished us out like we were cod,
Then trussed us as the criminals we were.
For once, there were a few sent prayers ta God.
The news our capture really caused a stir.

At London twere all hauled out from the brig,
Then sentenced by the court ta "Dance the Jig".

VII.

Then sentenced by the court ta "Dance the Jig",
I spent me days caged like an animal,
While friends and family didn't care a fig,
For who'd defend a jaded criminal.

It all began for glory and romance,
Now I concede that here me time is done.
Calamity concludes this circumstance
Ta reach the end at only twenty one.

Hindsight regrets the choices that I made.
I can't escape the fiend that I became.
While misbegotten fame and fortune fade,
There really is nobody else ta blame.

I should have acted differently somehow.
Like, maybe should've gone ta Sunday school,
And stayed far from the docks. It's too late now.
I understand quite well, I was a fool.

I must admit 'twas all me own design,
And now the gibbet and the rope are mine.

Sonnet 131: Buffalo - The Great Slaughter

I. How it was.

The buffalo, once princes of the plains,
a shadow now, where mighty herds had reigned.
As destiny conspired 'gainst their domains,
'til only few survivors have remained.

Back then they roamed in thund'rous, dusty clouds,
where sixty million strong owned middle earth,
on open prairie grass, 'twas never plowed,
and Indians all knew their sacred worth.

The bison's meat was very low on fat,
but full of protein's life-sustaining force.
Their furry hides made blankets, belts, fur hats,
plus coats, warm boots, and mittens too, of course.

In fact, for natives, nothing went unused:
the organs, brains, all bones, and even guts.
They made nomadic life richly infused,
with buffalo trail ruts among their huts.

It's here where tragic destiny may show,
I've lived a life of hunting buffalo.

◇

II. My story

I've lived a life of hunting buffalo,
and later I became ashamed of that,
but early on in life it wasn't so.
I couldn't see the future, were I sat.

My given name is simply Matt Montana,
whose family crossed through the famous GAP,
then settled Tuscaloosa, Alabama,
to farm the land, but also hunt and trap.

'Twas eighteen forty three when trouble struck.
My Pa was out there sweatin' in the field,
mosquito ridden lowland full of muck,
when backache, headache, fever was revealed.

It went away, but then came back instead.
It caught my Ma, my sister, brother too.
Within a month, my family was dead,
and I was left there, wond'rin' what to do.

I figured that, to leave there was the best.
With Pa's Kentucy rifle, headed West.

◇

III. Going West, the Sighting

With Pa's Kentucky rifle, headed West.
I also had his trusty Bowie Knife.
These things would guide my life, I can attest.
For fickle are the winds that rule a life.

I walked all day, found shelter every night.
Then met a friend named Alan on the way.
We followed wagon trails in easy sight.
Saw most majestic scene on one fine day.

From top of hill, we spotted endless herd
of buffalo, that ran in thund'rous roar.
From South to North, their bovine bodies blurred.
For day and night they passed by, by the score.

I never seen such numbers here before.
They left a great impression on my mind,
a dazed amazement, at my very core,
a stirrin' in my soul, yet undefined.

I shot one at the back of the stampede,
An action that forever set the seed.

IV. Gettin' to Kansas

An action that forever set the seed,
a taste of something barely known to me.
Unwary as to where that taste may lead,
we traveled on, 'til we reached St. Louie.

From there we worked a paddleboat to Kansas,
as stokers, shoveling coal into the fire.
Fort Leavenworth had promised some bonanzas,
for those who shoot the buffalo for hire.

They needed meat to feed the hungry troops.
So with a borrowed wagon and my gun,
we found a herd, and shot a couple groups,
providin' bison food for everyone.

That gave me a good living for a while.
I sold my gun, but won one playin' cards.
now I hunt buffalo in frontier style,
My Sharpes can shoot them from three hundred yards.

In sixty two, the railroad barons came.
Then wholesale slaughter soon became the game.

V. The Railroads

Then wholesale slaughter soon became the game.
Oh sure, they needed meat to feed the crew,
but endless herds on tracks were most to blame.
We started killin' thousands, not a few.

The railroads made a carnival of it,
where train cars left their windows down to shoot
at herds, while leavin' carcasses to sit,
and rot there in the sun, along the route.

Now I became a well-paid hunting guide,
who takes large groups to shoot with wanton care.
They only want the skull, the horns, and hide.
They leave the rest decayin' everywhere.

In sixty five, the Civil War would end.
Now Sherman, Grant and Sheridan would act.
Without the bison herds, the tribes would bend.
Make buffalo extinction now a fact.

From here, the prior death toll number pales.
They authorized the kill on greater scales.

◇

VI. The Great Slaughter for Fun and Profit

They authorized the kill on greater scales.
I found myself enamored by the pitch.
At twenty five gold bucks for hides, in sales,
and seventy five cents per tongue, I'm rich!

See, Bison have a quirk, when one is shot,
the others stand, not knowing what to do,
so in a day, I can shoot quite a lot,
about two fifty with my skinnin' crew.

That's sixty five cool hundred dollars cash,
a fortune in this certain century.
Enough to make too many marksmen dash,
to earn a wage at this activity.

And there were even betting contests held,
to see which hunter could kill off the most.
They'd shoot until their barrels nearly melt.
The plains became a place of bison ghosts.

The natives lost what tribes depended on,
By eighty five, the buffalo were gone.

◇

VII. Aftermath
By eighty five, the buffalo were gone.
I lost my source of livin' once again.
The plains were now a charnel field of bones,
and filled with bored and idle riflemen.

But then, redemption came through from the East,
as fertilizer came to great demand,
while lying there were sundried bones of beast,
to gather free, as plentiful as sand.

We shot the bison, tamed the indians,
shipped trains of bones out eastward by the ton,
a blow to beasts and Homo Sapiens.
I'm sad to say, that's how the West was won.

So, write about the slaughter, misery.
I'm Matt Montana, that's my given name.
Remember, when you give my history,
our nation, whole, bares both the blame and shame.

Of those vast herds, a tiny few remain
The buffalo, once princes of the plains.

◇

Sonnet 132: Minnesota Early Explorers -1600s

Father Marquette and his symbol of peace

1. Pre-European

Land known for all its lakes, river defined,
In wilderness by paddle broached, and oar,
New land is now revealed to most mankind,
Broad waterways get opened to explore.

Beginning to the end, 'twas land much blessed
With forests where wild animals could roam
And fish-filled waters anglers put to test.
Indigenous peoples called this their home.

The Black Duck, makers of effigy mounds,
Have lived and prospered for nine thousand years.
Their sacred lands and tribal hunting grounds
Contain their ancient arrowheads and spears.

Then came Ojibwa, Cherokee, and Sioux,
To gather moose, the beaver, hare, and bear,
The turtles, wolves, and all the Bison too,
Where there for taking as food, use, or care.

These various cultures waged their wars, yet thrived,
Before the Europeans first arrived.

2. Great Lakes Exploration

Before the Europeans first arrived
The natives lived by custom, wits and chance.
In legends contact rumors have survived -
Of maybe Vikings, certainly of France.

The French were by this time in Canada,
St. Lawrence River helped to founded Quebec;
And brave explorers with much stamina,
Were willing for an advent'rous trek.

Among the first, Etienne Brule,
Who followed the St. Lawrence River trace.
He sailed the Great Lakes, where Indians say
The sacred Spirit had founded their race.

Then De LaSalle sailed 'long the shoreline banks
With Hennepin, to seek a passage north.
They built a boat of stoutest wooden planks.
The "Griffon", named, as it was sallied forth.

They soon encountered huge Niagara Falls.
As Hennepin's diary note recalls.

3. Northern Mississippi River Discovery

As Hennepin's diary note recalls.
Just one of many to appear in book.
Sent ahead, while De LaSalle built walls,
In hopes to have a Mississippi look.

With two companions in birch-bark canoe,
The three set off into the vast unknown
Down Illinois River. They found it too!
That mighty river finally had shown.

He claims he sailed to Gulf of Mexico,
Then all the way went back to Minnesota.
Historians argue, "Where did he go?"
Detained for years by band of the Dakota.

A Sioux group captive, traveled far with them.
He saw it, and named St. Anthony falls.
Today it's a Minneapolis gem.
Back then, an item his memoir recalls.

The famous facts that historians draw --
Two North American falls that he saw.

4. Duluth Makes Way for Fur Traders

Two North American falls that he saw
Became his most historic legacy.
Remember, he was under captive's paw
With need for a released captivity?

Well, that fact's this tale's most noteworthy truth.
As from the garrison at Montreal
Came Daniel Graysolon, Sieur Du Lhut
Negotiating Hennepin's recall.

He was intrepid, an interpreter,
Negotiated many noted truce,
Superior's best fortress outfitter,
Wrote treaties setting north fur traders loose.

They settled regions, married oft' within
Chief's blessings, women of the local tribes.
A brand new culture, Meti, woiuld begin
To live among them, as record describes.

And so we find a cultured unity,
A French and Indian community.

5. The French Claim

A French and Indian community
That lasted until other nations came.
'Twas culture blended with impunity,
Without a bit self-consciousness or shame.

The upper river was mapped by Marquette,
La Salle, for France, declared a large land claim.
The Mississippi basin was soon set,
becoming part of French King's vast domain.

"New France" was what this area was called,
But map creators named it for the King,
So Louis XIV's name was soon installed.
"Louisiana" had a better ring.

Now, while this claiming was all going on,
The priest explorers mapped, wrote, taught and held
Their services, in spots they came upon.
Their knowledge of the region soon was swelled.

The priests had now transcribed America
Within its vast uncharted area.

7. The Voyageurs

Within its vast uncharted area
Was land that Minnesota hence became.
Where waterways with wet criteria
Have beavers that brought voyageur acclaim.

Through woods, and streams, and lakes, paddling all day,
They portaged, large canoes upon their backs,
Within pristine BWCA.
Their legends live in hist'ry's written tracts.

The Sixteen Hundreds were the eras when
The Frenchman thrived in forests and on lakes.
There were not many towns or forts back then.
They lived upon wild paths that nature takes.

Respecting people and environment,
Fur-traders and those bold French voyageurs,
Had opened ways for future settlement
Who followed leads of those who hunter furs. .

That type of person was never content
To live in anything but open tent.

8. Legacy

To live in anything but open tent,
Where wind rules waves upon the bays.
They traveled rivers, and the lakes, these men'
They left their marks. Their influence still stays.

Along with others who much later came
To Minnesota's vast interior,
A Wisconsin river bears Brule's name.
Its rapids flow into Superior.

You will see Hennepin in many places
Nearby St. Anthony's falls, that he named,
And Father Marquette's name frequently graces
Those charts in parts that his trip maps proclaimed.

Old Daniel Greysolon, don't forsooth
For role exploring the unknown Great Lakes.
Has name recalled in Port Town of Duluth,
A fit reward for journey's highest stakes.

So brave are men who traveled out to find
Land known for all its lakes, river defined.

Minnesota.

Sonnet 133: Robbing Paul to Pay Peter

I.
Chicanery and greed played primal roles
With Minnesota forming as a state;
The story most intriguingly unrolls
With greed as they proceed to legislate.

The politicians ultimately prove
How perfidy provided utter gall,
Mischievous machinations planned to move
The capital away from far St. Paul.

This tale has mystery and true intrigue,
Of dealing with corrupted governor,
Political patronage and fatigue;
A drunken gambler, prostitutes, and more.

With land in hand just begging to be sold
So, grab a seat, get yourself a brew
Allow some time to let this tale unfold
About when boundaries were thrown askew,

As "Paul is robbed to pay St. Peter's" fee,
A page of Minnesota history.

II.
A page of Minnesota history,
When Franklin Pierce looked for a governor,
He picked Mexican war hero to be.
Who captured Haumantla, in that war.

A chosen leader for the future state.
A powerful man with plans of his own,
To highest potentate, as fate dictates.
In eighteen fifty three - a true unknown.

Was sworn in by the US President.
He had some thorny problems in his soul
Of larceny, that some come to resent,
When greed would breed bad blood, through his control.

For in the early days, on which we teeter,
Most representatives lived to the south.
Much easier to gather in St. Peter,
Than travel to St. Paul, much further north.

The situation rose among the clan
That laid the groundwork for a profit plan.

III.
That laid the groundwork for a profit plan,
Since Willis Gorman was the man in charge
Who thought his best investment was to pan
His holdings in St. Peter, which were large.

So, he convinced his crony legislators
To pass a bill to move the capital.
Began construction using huge road graders.
And building things around St. Peter's mall.

He laid out nicely functional foundations
With roads for heavy traffic, double-wide.
And found an architect for his creations-
A capital to fill the town with pride.

A perfect plan to denigrate St. Paul.
He hoped he'd be real rich once things aligned,
To his plots, in St. Peter, boons would fall.
The problem was the bill – he hadn't signed.

The law requires Gov's to sign the bill,
But Willis stayed put in St. Peter still.

IV.
But Willis stayed put in St. Peter still,
To oversee the plans he put in place.
He needed trusty patron now to fill
The role of courier to quickly race,
A legate lacking scruples in the senate.
With proven loyalty, on whom to bet,
A lackey to be used as loose lieutenant,
And such a man was Joseph J. Rolette.

Furtrader, gambler, and a politician,
Controled enrollment bills within the house,
A natural to grab the proposition,
Though many men considered him a louse.

So, Gorman thought that Rolette was his man,
Entrusting Joe to find him right away.
While he himself laid out his full town plan,
Expecting harvest of a huge payday.

This bill of eighteen fifty seven passed.
Just need signing by the Gov'nor fast.

V.
Just need signing by the Gov'nor fast.
Here's what readers need to understand.
The legislative session wouldn't last,
Expiring the possession of the land.

Now, Joe Rolette should not have been so trusted.
Nobody had considered how he felt --
The capital's location readjusted,
Just wasn't how he thought things should be dealt.

This gambler's inclination was to hide.
He found a perfect hide-a-way hotel.
Ok, it had a brothel too, inside,
Where he could drink and gamble for a spell.

He'd hide there while the clock was ticking down,
While knowing, all he had to do was wait.
He dallied with the damsels until dawn,
And drank into a catatonic state.

But none of that was much of his concern,
With time that leads the senate to adjourn.

VI.
With time that leads the senate to adjourn,
While frantic politicians were distressed,
Police were called to find and overturn
The rocks, achieving poor Joe's quick arrest.

With all the constables in hot pursuit,
The ladies of the night had hid him well.
The hotel manager was in cahoots,
And all his gambling friends would never tell.

And so, our Joe stayed hidden for a week,
Enjoying all the pleasures one could want:
Rich hands of cards, hot ladies on each cheek,
And even fine chef's fare from restaurant.

Our fine French friend was hero of the city.
For his dynamic actions, tip a brew.
Had he not taken steps, would be a pity.
He taught the governor a thing or two.

While dock of legislative session closed,
Joe entered meeting hall quite unopposed.

VII
Joe entered meeting hall quite unopposed,
And all there present knew it was too late.
With unsigned bill in hand, the cheering rose
From those opposed, who knew it met its fate.

The capital, St. Paul now would remain,
While anger from the governor and friends
Would fall forgotten, dusty lost refrains
Along St. Peter's newly formed dead ends.

While Willis Gorman to this very day
Will curse the name of Joseph J Rolette,
Whose gamble with the world came into play,
And caused a crooked plan to be upset.

'Til eighteen fifty seven Gorman ruled,
But never made the fortune he had sought.
It vanished like the wind, when he was fooled,
Thus proving loyalty cannot be bought.

Where power and high profits were the goals,
Chicanery and greed played primal roles.

Sonnet 134: Scientific Inquisition

I.

I'm just a simple lad from Italy
Was born in early fifteen forty eight
In Padua. Its university
Renowned by many, thought to be first rate.

This was before the trouble all began,
When total fear had soon consumed my life.
But first, there's too much history to span,
So I'll begin this tale before that strife.

A nobleman of high regard was dad,
And I was blessed with lovely loving mom.
They raised me up with all the best they had,
Provided finest schools without a qualm.

So I grew fast into the smartest lad,
Was sent off to the University,
Where all the finest knowledge could be had,
And men of stature filled the gallery.

When asked, I'd say, to coin a simple phrase,
For me, these were the most exciting days.

II.

For me, these were the most exciting days,
The world was changing most significantly,
Courageous men had challenged old beliefs,
Columbus' voyage loosed pent up energy.

What once thought flat was actually round,
Ideas, new views were breaking old taboos,
Conjectures proved mathematically sound,
It seemed each day brought more exciting news.

For now, a full-scaled Renaissance was on
And irrepressible ideas released.
The lore of ancient Greece relied upon,
While scientific method soon increased.

Was here that I first met with Galileo,
Became acquainted with his telescope,
Apprenticed to one Giordano Bruno,
Began my slide down very slip'ry slope.

Still unaware of what was yet to be,
In heady times of pure discovery.

III.

In heady times of pure discovery,
I learned from extraordinary men,
As Galileo once had mentored me,
And Bruno showed the heavens, now and then.

The lure of science had ensnared my soul,
As research took us to revealed unknown.
DaVinci's talent had sublime control,
His curiosity was not alone.

With Bruno's thoughts about the cosmic states,
I plotted seven planet's orbit paths,
The frequency of their celestial rates,
And light emitted in the aftermath.

Then Giordano from his social peak
Bequeathed to me degrees of high estate.
These happy moments, those of which I speak,
Were prior to events that set his fate.

When church's doctrines start to call the tune,
Our days of freedom numbered all too soon.

IV

Our days of freedom numbered all too soon,
It came so unexpectedly because
From Inquisition, thought we were immune,
Our work condemned as fundamental flaws.

My own eyes saw through telescopic lens,
The path of planets, moon, and other stars,
Supporting the conclusions of my friends,
Relationships of Earth to Sun and Mars.

Moon craters, Neptune, Venus, Saturn's rings,
Revealed to eager eyes of learned men.
Enlightened concepts that such knowledge brings
Condemned by God these facts, by papal pen.

This information that upsets the church
Has contradicted deep false dignity,
Soon those involved were left out in the lurch
To Inquisition's board of Inquery.

Our spiritual wills were soon to be tested
As I observed, when great men were arrested.

V

As I observed, when great men were arrested,
False doctrine played a very vital role,
Allowed by clerical force, uncontested,
I felt deep darkness would invade my soul.

What could such a courageous fellow do,
Confronted by outrageous accusations,
But state what they had found out to be true,
Endorsed by their scholarly reputations.

For these were not just ordinary men,
Great Galileo, and our Bruno too,
Were men with powerful connections then,
From Kings and noblemen friends that they knew.

This matter should be solved in rapid time,
Resolved once all the evidence is known.
The stated facts can't constitute a crime,
Once the empirical data's been shown.

The outcome found should be perfectly clear,
Unless dogma happens to interfere.

VI.

Unless dogma happens to interfere,
Where prejudiced minds are piously closed,
Then innocent men find no justice here,
Results have been already presupposed.

So Galileo lived imprisoned life,
And all his works declared a heresy,
While causing family much legal strife,
Its repercussions mattered much to me.

Priests hauled my other friend right off to Rome,
Where Bruno faced Cardinal Belarmino
Spent seven lonely years under its dome,
Defending honor with proud quid pro quo.

Intolerance crushed reason and all truth!
For his beliefs he wouldn't dare forsake,
In scene so barbarously most uncouth,
For science, Bruno burned alive at stake.

Events of such, shook deep into my bone.
My courage now is spent, I sit alone.

VII.

My courage now is spent, I sit alone,
I can't believe the damage that's been done,
Initiative of science has been blown,
Instilling total fear for everyone.

I'll hide my own work and then leave this place,
There's nowhere safe at all for careful thought
With profile low, I'll have to hide my face,
Seek refuge somewhere else, before I'm caught.

I thought that there was hope with latest pope,
But Paul the Fifth, just like Clement the Eight
Decided just to let the cardinals cope
With Inquisition's mad doctrine of faith.

Dark times coincide with intolerance,
Our golden Renaissance could now be stifled
We thought that honest proof would give a chance,
Before the bigoted church fathers trifled.

Been disillusioned now quite terribly,
I'm just a simple lad from Italy.

Sonnet 135: Shetek Massacre at Slaughter Slough

I.
A tragic case of misery and woe,
When cultures clashed and heated tempers flared
In places graced by lakes and buffalo,
When guns and blood was how the grievance aired.

Now consciously this tragedy unplanned,
Had viciousness of which you'd never think.
For eons past the natives loved this land,
Where bison by the millions came to drink.

Oasis cultures found a fall retreat
Where nature made an ancient hunting ground,
A place where pelicans and bison meet,
The shores were dotted with their funeral mounds.

A place to raise the children in their midst
Became home for Ojibwa and Dakota
Where peacefully the tribes could co-exist,
The corner of southwestern Minnesota.

This sacred land of hospitality
Soon known for its blood-hot hostility.

II.

Soon known for its blood-hot hostility,
When white men came and found this lovely place
About the year of eighteen fifty three.
At first the mood of hate was not the case.

For treaty land was purchased free and clear.
The Indians were promised aid and food.
So settlers could move in without a fear,
But greed and prejudice soon changed that mood

As threats and promises flowed off the tongues
Of Ramsey, Henry Sibley, and Luke Lea
'Bout pots and pans, food, blankets and some guns.
The tribes assigned their place and sacred area.

But promises were hardly ever filled,
And tribal customs soon were dispossessed.
So, many starved and others hardships killed.
The chiefs and warrior braves were not impressed.

It mounted to a passion-heated brew,
The August days of eighteen sixty two.

III.

The August days of eighteen sixty two,
It started 'round the lake they named Shetek.
When Grizzly Bear's war party wandered through,
The Koch's cabin was a total wreck.

John Voigt escaped, the others were forewarned.
They gathered at Wrights cabin for defense.
Old Pawn with warriors were all badly scorned.
Surrounded now, the cabin mood intense.

Inside the settlers pondered what to do.
Old Pawn had always been a friendly sort,
But joined by Grizzly Bear's large hostile crew
The pressure left him nowhere to resort.

So now he found his tribe was in between.
A likely choice to help negotiate.
White Lodge's warriors soon came on the scene,
A situation made to complicate.

These chiefs just added way too much commotion,
So soon the fatal deeds were set in motion.

IV.

So soon the fatal deeds were set in motion.
A truce between the whites and Indians
Was offered up to quell the hot emotions,
If they just trust the red Samaritans.

Old Pawn presents the peace truce as a friend.
He guaranteed safe passage with his clan.
Could friendships finally sway them in the end?
At least that's how the chief laid out the plan.

The redskins promised they would be unharmed.
If they just left and let them loot and take.
The settlers thought it best. They were well armed.
They left their things, set off along the lake.

The men, the women, and the children too,
On foot and wagon headed for New Ulm.
Six families on the Prairie, trekking through,
When arrow shots and bullets broke the calm.

Exposed the settlers only had one chance.
In grasses by the slough, they made their stance.

V.

In grasses by the slough, they made their stance,
Where blades grew tall and heavy fletch was thick.
Somewhat protected from both bow and lance,
It couldn't shield them from a bullet nick.

The battle hotly raged beyond four hours
As deadly bullets whistled back and forth.
Lean Grizzly Bear was killed beside the flowers,
But homestead blood flowed free and soaked the earth.

Fifteen had died, a dozen more were caught,
While some lay wounded, others made escape.
The captive women, sadly overwrought,
Were faced by wanton cruelty and rape.

Tom Ireland was wounded, lay dead, cold,
Still walked for miles, five days of foodless trials.
Young Merton Eastlick, just eleven old,
Hand carried baby brother fifty miles.

The warriors left, and once the smoke had cleared,
The victim's fate was worse than most had feared.

VI.

The victim's fate was worse than most had feared.
The dead were left for days, exposed to rot.
The captive kids and women disappeared,
Survivors grieving hard assessed their lot.

A friendly tribe paid ransom for the slaves.
Returned them back to their society,
But that meant little to the white enclaves
Who blamed all red men for atrocities.

Gov' Ramsey stated all Dakota "Go",
So Henry Sibley gathered up the troops,
Revenge for fight known as the "Slaughter Slough",
Defeated all the warring native groups.

Three Hundred injuns were condemned to hang,
Mankato's prison filled with sentenced souls.
Their families were grouped in marching gangs
To pens along the Mississippi shoals.

And so the war's resulting contribution,
A mass of warriors waiting execution.

VI.

A mass of warriors waiting execution.
Were closed up in Mankato's prison cells.
The local people seeking retribution
Would heap harsh treatment where the warriors dwell.

But Bishop Whipple thought poor precedent
Of hanging some who never shot their guns.
He wrote a letter to the president
To beg he please forgive less guilty ones.

So Lincoln finally heard this fervent plea,
And had his legal men review the case,
To give an ample opportunity
For justice to prevail in time and place.

Eyewitness testimony duly heard,
With written statements from the families,
Determined that the numbers were absurd,
Some qualified as brutal nominees.

With expectations high all over town,
Came tensions as the verdict handed down.

VII.
Came tensions as the verdict handed down,
With only thirty nine sentenced to death.
The hot-head whites could only curse and frown,
While Indians were given second breath.

Since it was seen that they had been provoked,
The numbers were reduced by quite a few.
Those known for murder/rape would be those choked,
Condemned to hang December, sixty two.

Four thousand people came to see them fall.
It turned out to be only thirty eight.
They climbed the scaffold stately, one and all,
Then sang their death songs, certain of their fate.

As they held hands, bags placed upon their heads,
Bill Duley, wounded at the slough, presides
To pull the lever, cut them down when dead.
He gained as much as justice done provides.

Thus ends a tale as true as stories go,
A tragic case of misery and woe.

G. Wreath of Sonnets

A Wreath of Sonnets sometimes also called a Garland of Sonnets, created as a Crown of Sonnets that was written by France Preseren in 1833. It was published for the first time in the German-language newspaper, on 22 February 1834.

It consists of 15 Sonnets and is enriched with an Acrostic in the Concluding Sonnet. Besides the complex and sophisticated content, A Wreath of Sonnets has an interesting Format as the Last Line of one Sonnet becomes the First Line of the next one, making all fourteen Sonnets of the an intertwining "Garland" of Lyric Poetry; one Sonnet cannot exist without the other. The First Lines of all the single fourteen Sonnets form in turn another Sonnet, called the "Master Theme" or the Magistrate, linking all the Sonnets together. In the more Modern Versions, this Master Poem becomes the First Sonnet.

I participated in a Group Activity where 15 Poets each provided one of the Sonnets. Mine was the Seventh Sonnet in the Wreath. First the Magistrate was written, so each Poet was provided with the First and Last Lines to their Poem from that Magistrate. The Theme was Global Warming. I didn't write the Master.

The following Poems and Poets from FanStory belonged to the Wreath:

Mater Sonnet by Kiwisteveh , Sonnet 1 by Ciliverde, Sonnet 2 by Tfawcus, Sonnet 3 by Mfowler, Sonnet 4 by Gloria, Sonnet 5 by Just2write, Sonnet 6 by The Death, Sonnet 7 by Treischel, Sonnet 8 by Domino2, Sonnet 9 by Kiwisteveh, Sonnet 10 by Lightink, Sonnet 11 Dorothy Fennell, Sonnet 12 by Mountainwriter49, Sonnet 13 by Pantygynt, and Sonnet 14 by Debbie Noland. This Poem below was the Acrostic Master Sonnet, where the Acrostic spells out the Phrase, "Mans Great Folly":

Majestic planet, bathed by oceans blue,

Adrift in space, enriched with beauty rare,

No other world we know is blessed like you

So long as we, your children, keep you fair.

Great wonders have we built, all at your cost;

Rapacious plunder drains the sweetest well.

Each generation takes, now all seems lost.

As climate alters, land and sea rebel.

The air grows thick, polluted by our waste.

For every tree we plant, a forest falls.

Our oceans choke on filth; man stands disgraced.

Like fools we bicker while your future palls.

Let's make a change right now, repair the rift;

You gave us life - we must return your gift.

I bolded the two Lines that I was given. My contribution, presented here, is simply called *Sonnet 7*.

Sonnet 136: Wreath Sonnet 7

Each generation takes, now all seems lost.
Resources dwindle, not to be replaced.
Without regard or reference to the cost,
We burn, we dig, we throw away the waste.

And as we do, our detritus pollutes
The land and sea and air that we must use.
Oh Mother Earth, you're spoiled by human brutes!
The damage that is wrought, you can't excuse.

But soon you'll find a way to compensate,
For if you don't, then everything will die,
And as it stands, it may just be too late!
Bad weather, earthquakes, flare-ups now apply

Oh Earth, your patience, only time can tell,
As climate alters, land and sea rebel.

H. Sonnet Cycle

A Sonnet Cycle is a **group** of Sonnets, **arranged** to address a particular person or **Theme**, and designed to be read both as a **Collection** of fully realized **individual** Poems and as a single Poetic Work comprising **all** the individual Sonnets.

A Sonnet Cycle may have any Theme, but unrequited love is the most common. The Arrangement of the Sonnets generally reflects Thematic Concerns, with Chronological Arrangements (whether Linear, like a Progression, or Cyclical, like the Seasons) being the most common. A Sonnet Cycle may also have Allegorical or Argumentative Structures which replace or complement chronology.

While the Thematic Arrangement may reflect the unfolding of real or fictional events, the Sonnet Cycle is very rarely narrative; the Narrative Elements may be inferred, but provide Background Structure, and are never the Primary Concern of the Poet's Art. They typically are a Collection of 20 or more Sonnets.

I contend that this Entire Book is a Sonnet Cycle. Its Theme is Sonnets and their Variations. The 170 Sonnets this book contains can each be read as individual Poems, but they are definitely Arranged in Specific Order, by their Style Variations. My Narrative Elements are more than inferred, out of necessity. However the Definition does say ''rarely'' as opposed to "never."

So there are no further examples in this Chapter. If you've read this far, you see my point.

I. Sonnet Sequence

A Sonnet Sequence is a group of Sonnets Thematically Unified to create a Long Work, although generally, each Sonnet so connected can also be read as a meaningful Separate Unit.

The Sonnet Sequence was a very popular Genre during the Renaissance, following the Pattern of Petrarch. But English Models also emerged. They typically include 50+ Sonnets.

The subject was usually the speaker's unhappy love for a distant beloved, following the courtly love tradition of the Troubadours, from whom the Genre ultimately derived. An exception is Edmund Spenser's Amoretti, where the wooing is successful, and the Sequence ends with an "Epithalamion", a marriage song.

Some notable Sonnet Sequences are:

Petrarch's *Canzoniere* (mid-14th-century, 227 sonnets to Laura, as well as 89 sonnets to Laura in death)

Sir Philip Sidney's *Astrophel and Stella* (1591, 108 sonnets and 11 songs to Penelope Rich).

Edmund Spenser's *Amoretti* (1594, 88 sonnets and an Epithalamion to Elizabeth Boyle)

Michael Drayton's *Idea's Mirror* (1594, 64 sonnets to Phoebe),

William Drummond's *Poems* (1616, 68 sonnets)

Elizabeth Barrett Browning's *Sonnets from the Portuguese* (1850, 44 sonnets to Robert Browning)

I have yet to write a Sonnet Sequence. This book is already large enough, and when I do, it will be its own book. So I provide no example here other than refer the reader to the list above.

CHAPTER 13. SPECIAL COMPLEX SONNETS

In this Chapter, the imagination has run wild with things to do with Sonnets, much like it can be done with any other Poetic Forms. What more can there possibly be beyond those places we have already explored, you say? Much more. Although I'll just give you a Sample Taste here.

It is here that we will examine ways to Combine several Forms, utilize other Meters, and borrow Rhymes from Famous Works. I'll introduce you to a Cleaved Sonnet incorporating the Petrarchan and Rondeau Formats; we'll examine an Anapestic Meter; we'll borrow the Rhymes from one of Shakespeare's Sonnets to write our own; and finally we'll incorporate two Forms (the Nonet and the Cinquain) into a single Sonnet. I think you see by now, that the things that a Poet can do to a Sonnet are virtually unlimited.

So turn the page and let's have some fun!

A. A Double Acrostic Cleaved Petrarchan/Rondeau Sonnet

How's that for a concept?

Written as inspired by Pantygynt's Poem, The Sirelei Songs.

There are actually five different Poetic Formats amalgamated in this Poem: an Acrostic, a Cleave, a Petrarchan Sonnet, a Rondeau, and an If/Then Poem.

An Acrostic poem is one where the First Letter of every Line spells out a Word or Phrase vertically down the front of the Poem. This is a Double Acrostic, because there are two separate Poems, each with their own Phrase. The two Poems are Color-coded so that the reader can see them more easily. The Acrostic Phrases have been **bolded** with letters enlarged, for the same reason.

The red side is a Petrarchan or Italian Sonnet with the Rhyme Scheme of:

abbaabba, cdccdc

in mixed Tetrameter. The red Acrostic reads: IF MEN WERE WITTY. The blue Acrostic reads: THEN WOMEN WOULD. The right hand blue poem is a Rondeau in mixed Tetrameter, save for the Repeated Line which is in Dimeter. The Rhyme Scheme here is:

aabba, aabR, aabbaR.

A Cleaved poem is a poem that is read in **Two Halves**, each being a Poem in itself, **then** read as one Complete Poem.

An If/Then Poem is one that poses an If-Then Hypothesis of cause and effect.

Punctuation is Limited as it would differ depending on which Poem is being read. I necessarily took some License with the Meter. Read intelligently, it will all make sense eventually.

My example is *The Power of Song*.

Sonnet 137: The Power of Song

The Power of Song
(A Double Acrostic Cleaved Petrarchan Sonnet/Rondeau)
(Also an If/Then Poem)

Read the red poem first, then the blue, and then finally, the whole thing from left to right

If	Then
Petrarchan Sonnet	Rondeau

If men were witty Troubadours	**T**hen women would listen 'til dawn
From music they'd soothe any soul	**H**eld as if magically drawn
Mastered, they could really control	**E**ach note as it hung in the air
Ethereal charms at its core	**N**ew, delivered with nimble flair
Nothing like it, ever before	**W**ith words reflected seldom on
Would seem to caress and cajole	**O**ver themes that Angels could spawn
Even though there's a simple goal	**M**oving gracefully as a swan
Released as the syllables soar	**E**very movement beyond compare
Eliciting wanton desires	**N**ow women would
Will women respond to a man	**W**ith only the words put upon
In ways that ignite carnal fires	**O**ver flames considered long gone
To swoon as the music inspires	**U**ndone by the light and the glare
That captures their attention span	**L**ike a pigeon trapped in his snare
Yielding to whom she now admires	**D**rawn forth by the lure of his song

                                            Then women would.

B. An 11-9 Metered Anapestic Heroic Sonnet

Anapests are a less common variety of Metrical Foot. The Anapest has Three Syllables - Unstressed, Unstressed, Stressed, like "da da DUM." Because of its Length and the fact that it ends with a Stressed Syllable, and so allows for strong Rhymes, an Anapaest can produce a very Rolling Verse, and allows for Long Lines with a great deal of Internal Complexity. The Rhythm is like a Waltz, rather than a March.

A Heroic Sonnet is one with 18 Lines and no Volta, but it closes with a Rhyming Couplet. . Here I have 4 Quatrains and a closing Rhyming Couplet. I used an uneven 11-9 Meter to emphasize Discordance. An Anapestic Rhythm also has a more Racing Cadence.

So this Format is a Combination of a Heroic Sonnet with Anapestic Meter.

My contribution to this Scheme is *Satan's Rage*. The 11 Syllable Lines include an Iamb. The Theme of this poem is Satan's Rage after Christ's Resurrection. Of course he takes it out on his minions. I use the Technique of Capitalization on some words to enforce how MAD he was. Satan is a sore loser.

Sonnet 138: Satan's Rage

I will DANCE on your tomb under silvered moon
at the edge of the darkened abyss.
Let the demons howl LOUD in the fires of doom
Their damned souls shall enflame by my kiss.

While this writhing mass SQUIRMs on my pointed fork
I will stir bubbling MIX to a BREW
All the noxious fumes SPREAD when the vials uncork
'Til the SMELL, holy HELL breaks on through.

With a banshee's SCREAM, I will REND empty air
Fill the sultry silence with my DIN.
'Til their eardrums BLEED from oaths I will swear,
So their heads will all SWELL from within.

Then my black BURNING EYES hypnotize in GLARE
As my smoking RAGE fully unfolds,
But this carnage unleashed really CAN'T compare
To the damage THIS DAY I behold.

For the sacrifice HE made on Calvary
Means that JESUS has unseated ME.

C. Modeled End-Line Sonnet

This Format takes the End-Line Rhymes from a Famous Poem and uses them to create a New Poem of the same Style and Meter. This was inspired by Gunaglo's poem, *Was the Bard Mistaken*, who took up a challenge to write a Sonnet using the End Rhyming words from Shakespeare's 73rd sonnet.

That time of year thou mayst in me behold,
When yellow leaves, or none, or few, do hang
Upon those boughs which shake against the cold,
Bare ruined choirs, where late the sweet birds sang.
In me thou seest the twilight of such day,
As after sunset fadeth in the west,
Which by and by black night doth take away,
Death's second self, that seals up all in rest.
In me thou seest the glowing of such fire,
That on the ashes of his youth doth lie,
As the death-bed whereon it must expire,
Consumed with that which it was nourished by.
This thou perceiv'st, which makes thy love more strong,
To love that well, which thou must leave ere long.

William Shakespeare

The fourteen End-Line Rhymes being those that Shakespeare used: behold, hang, cold, sang, day, west, away, rest, fire, lie, expire, by, strong, and long. Of course it must also be in iambic Pentameter.

Here's my attempt. My Sonnet is *Sunset Passion*. It is a Romance, Inspired by a sunset that I captured up on Lake Superior.

Sonnet 139: Sunset Passion

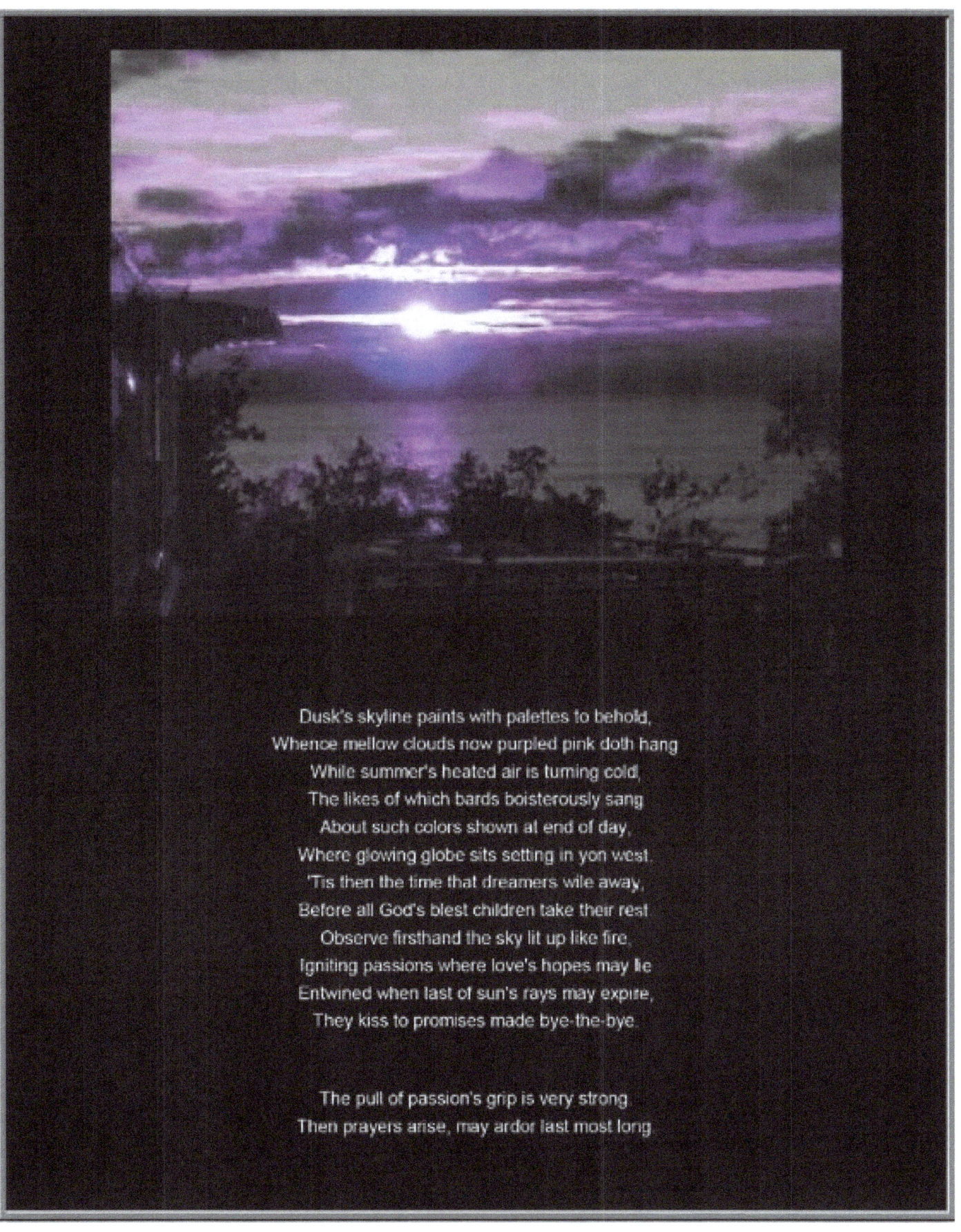

Dusk's skyline paints with palettes to behold,
Whence mellow clouds now purpled pink doth hang
While summer's heated air is turning cold,
The likes of which bards boisterously sang
About such colors shown at end of day,
Where glowing globe sits setting in yon west.
'Tis then the time that dreamers wile away,
Before all God's blest children take their rest
Observe firsthand the sky lit up like fire,
Igniting passions where love's hopes may lie
Entwined when last of sun's rays may expire,
They kiss to promises made bye-the-bye.

The pull of passion's grip is very strong,
Then prayers arise, may ardor last most long.

D. Nonet/Cinquain Sonnet

The Nonet/Cinquain is a Sonnet. I created the Form. It falls under the Category of Unusual and Complex Sonnets. So it is a Blend of Two Formats creating a whole. The top half is a Nonet, while the bottom is a Cinquain. Together they Blend to give a Sonnet's signature 14 Lines.

A Nonet is a Nine Line Poem. The First Line containing nine Syllables, the next Line has eight Syllables, the next Line has seven Syllables. That continues until the Last Line (the ninth Line) which has one Syllable. Nonets can be written about any subject. Rhyming is optional. There is no limitation to the number of Words per Line, only Syllables per Line. This provides a great deal of flexibility. Ideally, when centered, the work will form a nice Reverse-Triangle. A perfect Nonet has a nice set of nearly Straight Lines on each side.

A Cinquain is a Five Line Poem. The Format, inspired by Adelaide Crapsey in 1915, has a Fixed Syllable Count of: 2,4,6,8,2. Rhyming is also optional.

So, what makes this a Sonnet?

It is a Poem with 14 Lines, like most Sonnets. It has a Structure that defines an Issue and then resolves it. It has a Turn, or Volta (in this case at Line 10). Much like the Italian Format, this Form also has two Stanzas. But instead of being and Octave (8 Lines) plus a Sestet (6 Lines), this one has a Nanotet (9 Lines) and a Quintrain (5 Lines). Similar, but slightly different, yet recognizable. So who says it must be an Octave and Sestet? Still, you decide whether it should be given the Sonnet designation After all I've shown before.

Complex? Oh, yes. For starters, most Nonets are **not** Rhymed, but I not only Rhymed, I did it in a Pattern of:

abcabcabc,

even as the Syllable Counts declined.

The Pattern in the Cinquain is:

ddeed,

much like a Limerick. So the total Rhyme Sequence is:

abcabcabc ddeed.

My example is *Where Go the Flow*. It is the last Poem in this group. It blends two well-known Formats into a Sonnet – the Nonet and the Cinquain. This Verse was inspired on a winter's walk, when I saw the creek frozen over with ice and snow, but could hear the water still flowing underneath. The sun was right that day to capture the wonderful color of the ice. I also paid attention to Word Length in order to create the lovely Pattern that resulted.

Sonnet 140: Where go the Flow

Winter's not a surprising outcome,
as season's forces start seizing,
that thermal themes suffice,
when rapid waters thrumb,
to find forms pleasing,
meant to entice,
that become
freezing
ice.

Where go
the rippling flow
as surface disappears?
It's down below, just focus ears
to know.

CHAPTER 14. GRAB BAG.

This Chapter is just a Conglomeration of several Sonnets I've written. Their Format is Unidentified. I hope you'll will be able to identify them yourself. They are not in any particular Order, but in this Chapter, you'll find nine different Formats. Most will be English, Modern, or American Sonnets. Also interspersed are: Blank Verse, Byron's, Carrett, Rosarian, Rubaiyat, Shakespearian, Spenserian, and Triptic Sonnets. Will you be able to tell them apart? Turn the page and let's find out.

A. A Mix of Various Sonnets

As you read this Chapter, you'll find the Sonnets coming at you Unidentified. That's how many Poetry Books are. You just read and enjoy them. The main thing these all have in common is that, they are all Sonnets.

Think of this Chapter as a Treasure Hunt. I'll identify the Formats in the Book's Conclusion. Beyond recognizing the Blank Verse, Byron's, Carrett, Rosarian, Rubaiyat, Shakespearian, Spenserian, and Triptic Sonnets buried with all the English, Modern, or American Sonnets, are the Themes, Images, and Portraits. Don't overlook them.

I hope you feel the richness of the Thematic Diversity. You'll find a plethora of Topics, Moods, and Images. This Collection has animals cavorting, Animated Stills, social commentary, corporate insights, historical drama, holiday anecdotes, idyllic reveries, the joy of a beautiful day, grief from the loss of a loved one, myth and fantasy, reminiscences, romance, and winter tableaus.

Then there are my Personal Portraits of me and my family buried throughout this section. There's me sleeping in my bed, dressed in Renaissance garb, and at my keyboard. I included some Biographical Stories, as well as Family Portraits.

I love to convey the loveliness and character of my home State, Minnesota. All my Photographs in this Book are taken Here. This Chapter also includes local images such as Minnehaha Falls in both frozen and unfrozen states. There are flowers, landscapes, backgrounds, and people displayed here, even the Washburn Water Tower.

So, I hope you find these all interesting. Turn the page, and off we go!

Sonnet 141: A Good Day - Fishing

A water lily drinks the morning sun,
On floating leaves and stems of darkened green.
A perfect place for frogs and dragonflies,
A trout or bass might lie beneath the scene.

So dip a paddle into waters cool,
Upon sun silvered surface silently.
Then drift and cast a line towards wispy reeds,
'Til something really big strikes suddenly.

Now set hook firmly in the fishes mouth,
And feel the thrill of pull and jump about.
As fight for freedom quickly soon ensues,
With skill and patience, soon you land a trout.

At last, display with pride your catch today
And then release it, watch it swim away.

Sonnet 142: Angry Ancient Oaks

The ancient oaks that guard this glen
Are jealous of the folks who come,
Suspicious of the where and when,
Of stranger's past, who they've come from.

'Fore they've been fooled by cheats before,
Of forest treasures come to steal,
To strip the wood and leave the floor
So barren, it took years to heal.

So, let them know that you're a friend;
Despoil not any sacred ground!
Leave only footprints in the end
All else, leave as it was first found.

Then angry looks will turn to smiles,
And nature will rejoice for miles.

Sonnet 143: All Hallows Night

The tale's been often told in ancient scripts,
That unknown evil rots inside the grave,
Quite far beneath cold filth besotted crypts,
Where even sacred ground, it could not save.

As Satan's pact with God provides relief,
One single night of fright is to be seen,
Enhancing evil versus good's belief,
A night that's since denoted Halloween.

And so, this night some sick soul may arise,
Engaged in ghoulish games of fear and dread.
To cause some trick-or-treater great surprise,
When finding they are dabbling with the dead.

For some may find there's more than playful fright,
In darkened shadows on All Hallow

Sonnet 144: Cockled Whilst Away

What fiend doth steal mine true love's heart away?
Comes sneaking through dark shadows of the night
With liquored kiss that sets pure thoughts astray,
Oblivious of caring, wrong from right?

Whilst I am occupied with noble work,
For King and country faithfully I toil.
No duty, fight, or favor shall I shirk,
No Lady or fair maiden didst I spoil.

So mind ye, very soon will come the day
When I'll be granted leave to find my home.
Then twice, for dirty deeds, thy knave shall pay
No longer from my Lady whilst I roam.

Mine faith needs gathering from deep within,
May God help me forgive her for such sin!

Sonnet 145: Determination

Determination often wins the day;
No problem can't be solved, when it's applied.
Once one decides, desires won't be denied
when tasks are viewed in any different way.

Investigative skills are on display,
as problem resolution acts are tried.
Unique attempts may often coincide
when tasks are viewed in any different way.

Though some solutions seem a bit risque,
or acrobatic feats of some renown,
they'll win, while even hanging upside down,
when tasks are viewed in any different way.

Determination often wins the day,
when tasks are viewed in any different way.

Sonnet 146: Farewell 2015

Let's wish this Twenty Fifteen fair goodbye!
Wife's mother's death, and several health concerns
Created many months of twists and turns.
I'll shed no tender tear when it adjourns.

Such circumstance to ponder — laugh or cry,
As things broke down, investments did decline.
So many prayers sought miracles divine —
The best resort, when it won't help to whine.

Don't get me wrong, not all has gone awry.
There's published works, some parties, and awards,
Successful surgery, and move towards
New home with all its unforeseen rewards.

So toast the new and wish the old farewell.
A Happy New Year, all the Best as well.

Sonnet 147: Ford's Fate

Rest in Peace Ford Assembly line!
It's so sad that you had to close.
The thousands that once worked within,
Through actions that their bosses chose,
Now face economic decline,
True hardships and personal woes.

Faceless men in power's tower,
With careless stroke of fortune's pen,
Can change the fate of everyone,
Regardless of the "where" or "when".
As fruitless hopes in final hour
Don't stop its happening again.

Submersed in such a short-term view,
There's nothing to stay loyal to.

Sonnet 148: Forest Fantasy

I hold aloft a swirling candy cane.
'Twas on a tree, assume it was a gift.
It nestled there twixt needles of a pine
All shriveled and abandoned by a brook.

I pondered here just how this came about,
This morsel of some past and happy time.
A now forgotten trinket that I find
Amongst the grizzled needles of that pine.

And soon I stripped it of its meager shell,
To slip a languid swipe across my tongue.
A minty flavor met my favored taste,
With that small test, too soon the rest was gone.

Then suddenly I swooned, and as I fell,
I heard a lilting laughter from the knell.

Sonnet 149: Frozen Falls

The frosty touch of Old Man Winter's hand
Has placed his grip upon this frozen vale,
And holds in sway all aspects of the land
With just a puff of his most freezing gale.

For even water flowing swift and strong,
Cascading over precipice so great,
Cannot escape the season's touch for long,
Least even change the outcome of its fate.

For Boreas has turned the world to ice,
And loosed his children known as Wind and Snow,
Then clamped his chilly grip, just like a vice.
So mighty torrents are the last to go.

Yes, even waterfalls are frozen stiff,
To be transformed into an icy cliff.

Sonnet 150: God's Gift

My love, such joy I find in thee each day.
It lingers on my lips each time we kiss.
I feel it as you please me every way.
I must be dreaming passion such as this.
That sends me into spasms of pure bliss,
A fuel upon the fires of desire,
That burns so hot a lover can't dismiss
The smoking tendrils drifting ever higher
To reach love's levels, where we both aspire,
Amongst the cosmic clouds to sweetly drift,
While serenaded by angelic choir.
You're nothing short of God's most perfect gift.

Oh heaven, hear my prayer where I implore,
This love we have will last forever more.

Sonnet 151: Little People

These little people live here in the wood,
So simple and sincere among the trees,
In setting natural for such as these.
They live there where they know that life is good.
Some think that they are magic'ly possessed,
Because that's what the legends have foretold.
Along with a huge hidden pot of gold,
They'll disappear whenever they're distressed.

But if you win their trust with winsome ways,
They'll bless you with whatever you may wish,
And then you know you're in for better days.
They'll lift their hands and wave a magic swish,
Then "poof", it will delight you and amaze.
You'll never be again impoverished.

Sonnet 152: Marksman

Have you ever heard the story how William Tell
Was forced to shoot an apple off his own son's head?
With stellar marksmanship, it came out well.
His faith and steady aim was true, it can be said.

As I considered self of equal mastery,
His skill at hitting targets, meant to emulate.
For what young man's ego doesn't believe he's great?
I only lacked a target up against a tree.

Conveniently I had a willing brother, Joe,
Who was a trusting, fearless little 5 year old.
Put apple on his head to catch the dart I'd throw.
Unfortunately low aim was a bit too bold.

With dart in forehead stuck, I didn't try another.
I never again made target of my brother

Sonnet 153 : My Temperature is Rising

We know the earth's been warm and cold before
The Ice Age was ten thousand years ago.
While tropics ruled the age of dinosaur
Geology shows: cycles come and go

Does mankind make a difference to the blend?
Do waste emissions twist our climate's air?
Or, does the cycle tumble end-to-end
Regardless what the human race might do?

Despite what drives the pundits to despair
We overstate our true capacity.
The changes that our world is going through
Are natural swings of earth's geology

So you believe in global warming, huh!
Today the temperature is only three
To that idea, I'll have to say — ta-ta!

Sonnet 154: Proud Battle Lines

What princely prancing greets proud battle lines,
In gleaming armor and fine feath'red lace,
Convinced in heart and soul of cause divine,
Held steady, ready, firm, in ordered place.

Then oft' came bugle's shrill clarion call.
Hark knights, on horse alerted to its sound,
who pounded forth with fierce voice, one and all,
'Midst thund'rous sounds of hooves each churning ground.

In wild abandon, flew into the fray,
Where death stalked fields of woeful blood and gore.
Here panic-plagued fate ruled the daunting day.
Hence, many died on sands of foreign shore.

Both victor and foe wrought what blood was shed.
Yet outcome meant but naught to quaking dead.

Sonnet 155: Push and Pull

I stood transfixed upon the rocky shore
As brooding waves did dare to draw me in.
It seemed life had no meaning anymore.
I felt I couldn't stand this pain again.

Was this condition cruelly caused by sin?
Or, was it just a consequence of luck?
Well, either way, I thought I couldn't win
Or find relief from fate, where I was stuck.

These deadly thoughts were those I couldn't shuck.
The ocean pulled me on to be consumed.
As all my hurt emotions ran amuck
The crashing waves sang Siren songs of doom.

And yet, a seed still stirred there to survive,
A speck of hope caused me to stay alive.

Sonnet 156. Raindrops on Flowers

When the raindrops on the flowers
In summer early morning hours
Have moistened both petal and leaf
In suddenly sodden motif

Soon a kiss from heated sunlight
That will undoubtedly alight
Shall dazzle glistening dewdrops
As they linger on blossom tops

Then will the vegetation dance
Draped in ornamental romance
Within their green garden domains
On feeling gentle summer rains

'Tis just the way of nature's things
The joyousness renewal brings

Sonnet 157: Richard and Renie

When two hearts have come together as one,
Heavenly sparked by Colorado sun,
Nuptial bells proclaim husband and wife.
Together, forever, life's journey begun.

Richard and Renie's adventurous life
Was not without storms and perilous strife,
But love for each other has dampened their fears.
It cuts through the problems, sharp as a knife.

And now they have made it for forty years,
A life full of their love, laughter, and tears,
Their child and grand kids now take up their time -
An affectionate task that sweetly endears.

Now, lets acknowledge their glorious climb,
So cheeer! And here's to their love so sublime!

Contratulations Richard and Reenie!

Sonnet 158: Season's Sight

The season's sights are in the air
With spirits roaming everywhere.
As summer wanes and crops are in,
The Pumpkin Wraith rises here again.

So friendly in the daylight hours,
The night reveals his evil powers.
His wooden hand provides no fright
Until it grabs you in the night.

Don't be fooled by friendly welcomes,
They may yield some nasty outcomes.
Jagged smiles hide sharper teeth,
Beware the real fiend underneath!

He's our town friend to be seen,
But evil stalks on Halloween.

Sonnet 159: Simple Decorations

Granny's decorations were so simple,
With something like a common china plate
Garnering emotions they would kindle,
Of welcome that such simple things create.

She'd frame it with a hand-embroidered towel
A cloth that she's spent hours on to make,
Creating her own cozy cover cowl
That blends to form a beautiful keepsake.

Oh, how I miss my grandma's gentle touch,
Her smiles and all her warm embracing hugs.
These days I seem to miss her very much,
With simple things providing memory tugs

When china plates are placed upon a wall,
My grandma's home is what my thoughts recall.

Sonnet 160: Sorrow

I feel the sorrow deep within my veins,
That flows so slow with stresses and the strains.
I worry that the pain may never heal,
So I must kneel, to God make an appeal.

The loss of someone meaningful to me,
Can sap the soul of all vitality,
To spread a dreadful darkness deep within.
Such bitterness must surely be a sin.

But I shall carry on with all my might,
And hope someday that I will see the light.
I feel an angel near, holding my hand.
Although I find it hard, I understand.

So I shall shed all my tart tears today.
I'll find my happiness another way.

Sonnet 161: Such a Day

Delight in such a lovely autumn day!
It's wonderful to go and be outside.
Decide to walk, or jog, or just to sit,
Absorbing classic color on the trees.

Where gentle breezes blow, and birds do sing,
Content amongst the foliage, so serene
We dream to come and sit on benches there,
And calmly watch the world go drifting by

For here a cyclist stops to take a rest,
While avid jogger finds a ready path.
Two lovers sit and chat adoringly
As filtered sunlight dapples leaves on grass.

It's swell, and all is well on such a day,
When autumn leaves have turned where people dwell

Sonnet 162: Sweet Sleep

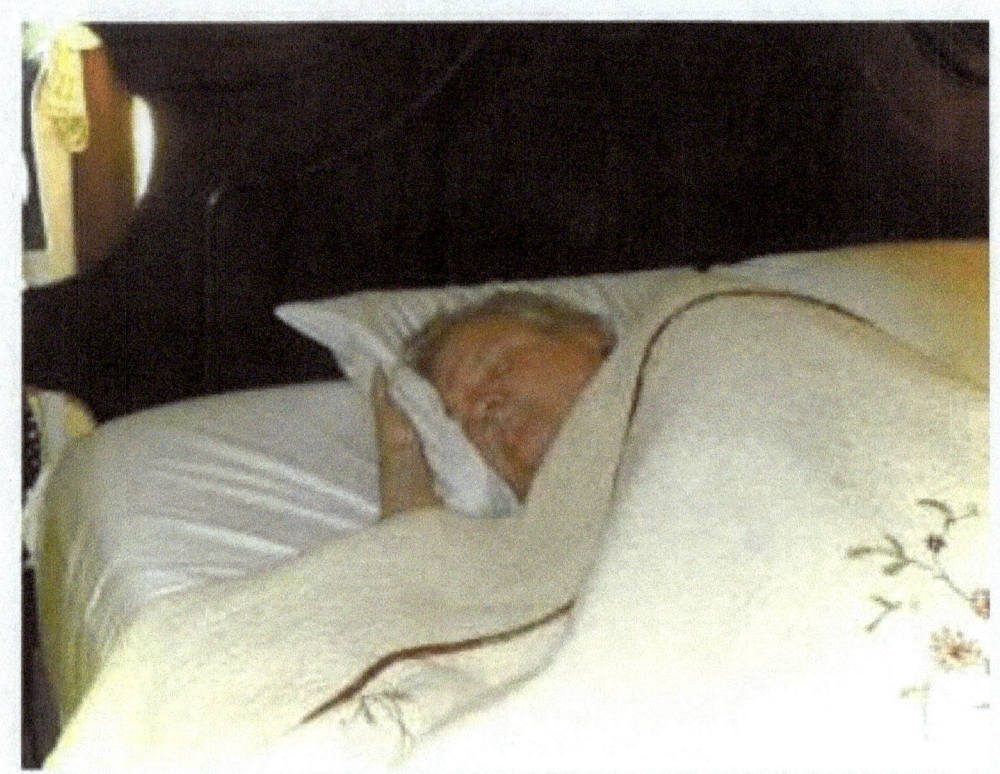

While tucked within the creases of my dreams,
With pillow gently to caress my head,
I tossed within the soft and silken seams
Of comfort from the covers of my bed.

My eyes were tightly closed on peaceful face,
My body prone, serene, and quite relaxed,
My mind adrift away to far off place,
I smiled while possibilities climaxed.

This place I rest is too good to believe.
I want to stay as long as possible,
Prolonging all these joys that I perceive.
I loath to leave a spot so beautiful.

So let me sleep a little more, I pray.
It's yet too soon to greet another day.

Sonnet 163: Stumped

Within dark Forest deep they blithely walked
Surrounded by fine beauty, most Divine!
Two Troubadours ambled along and talked
With mellow cheer, time passed, imbibing wine.

When strange stark silhouettes so clearly come.
Just Lurking! Bent in low bush near the path,
with open maws and stance of beasts untame.
Would teeth unleash and rend with fearsome wrath?

They stopped! They Looked! Uncertain of their plan.
Do alligators live in yonder park?
Brave fellows that they were, well-armed – they Ran!
Such terrors seem much worse there in the Dark.

Two Troubadours turned into craven chumps!
So terrorized. Left quaking! by some stumps!

Sonnet 164: The Dance

They danced in fields as yellow flowers bloom,
Still touched by gentle kiss of morning dew.
They twirled about, while spreading rich perfume,
With each spin love filled tender hearts anew.

As sparks flew in between each other's eyes,
Their touches burned with every sweet caress.
While wind was filled with soft sounds of their sighs,
He gently bent and lifted off her dress.

As early sun spawned tiny mist rainbows,
The two lay down on fragrant flowered ground.
Near babbling brook where gentle water flows,
An everlasting bond of love was found.

Now, since that day they've never been apart.
Their love remains within each other's heart.

Sonnet 165: The Falls

As people gather at the park,
Where water falling leaves its mark,
Its sight definitely enthralls,
At Minnehaha waterfalls.

It pours profusely off the cliff,
Cascading in a rippling riff,
That fills the valley with its sound.
Its fame is known for miles around.

In spring, snow melting makes it grow
'Til narrow banks might overflow.
Crowds love to watch it from the bridge,
Observing it below the ridge.

So in conclusion, may I say,
I'd love to go there every day.

Sonnet 166: The Signs

The ice is melting fast along the rivers,
As open waters now are peeking through.
So say "Goodbye" to season of the shivers
The warmth of spring is somewhat overdue.

The buds on trees, with promises of leaves,
Are showing now on branches that were bare.
It won't be long that springtime rain achieves
The fullness flowered fragrances can bear.

The eagle nests on trees upon the shore
Will soon bequeath brief glimpses of their young.
While male and female eagles have the chore
Of feeding hungry youth, once life's begun.

These signs are some the bards of spring have sung,
That herald home the news that spring has sprung.

Sonnet 167: Van Gogh

When Vincent Van Gogh, the painter renowned,
Was one of the finest artists around,
His vivid color and his broad brush stroke
Created a style that has never broke,
As still his popular paintings abound
To yet amaze, to delight and astound.
Artistic visions were brilliantly clear.
Until that day that he cut off his ear.
Then driven by bouts of desperate madness,
His mind was infused with devious sadness,
That caused his death in thirty seventh year.
The utter genius of his works remain dear.

Befitting acclaimed artistic endeavor,
His noble spirit shall remain forever.

Sonnet 168: War Weary Budgets

Our weary nation is so sick of war
In foreign places dubious of help
For people unattuned to ways of peace.
Ungrateful for our aid and sacrifice.

Political reactions countermand
The need to stay the course, to meet the wants
Of leaders with the backbone to succeed.
Instead they gut the budgets and withdraw.

Oh no! That's not the way it's meant to be!
Our legacy of freedom borne in blood
Must not be squandered, scattered to the wind.
Ignoring sacrifices of our dead.

The world remains a very dang'rous place,
And we should not relinquish diligence.

Sonnet 169: Washburn Watertower

The shoreline with this forest scene
Is blanketed in verdant green.
A water tower peeking through
Is in the Washburn neighborhood
Near where the fam'ly homestead stood.

It's plainly seen across the lake,
Where strolling walkers oft' partake
To glimpse this portion of the view,
When near the place her ashes rest,
As truly fits a last behest.

Her brood all grew near tower's site
This lake, her favorite place to be
She's near where she raised family
At rest in waters day and night

Sonnet 170: The Sonnets

So, are there fourteen lines in every Sonnet,
and with iambic pentameter on it?
Do all the Sonnets have a structured rhyme?
And are the stanzas quatrains all the time?

The English may have Shakespearean styles.
Italians also have their own profiles,
with eight line octaves and six line sestets,
that's really not as complex as it gets.

For I have found that there are many more.
In fact, there's variations quite galore,
of meter, length, and of stanzaic form.
Amazing how some poets stretch the norm.

I searched the network under every nook.
From all my findings, then, I wrote this book.

CONCLUSION

Well, that was quite the Journey. We traveled far through the terrain of the Sonnet, starting with the Standard Formats. Even there, there were surprises as we differentiated the Shakespearean from the English, and the Petrarchan from the Italian. The English Model took on even further parsing into the American and the Modern, while the Italian Form saw the Spenserian. Most people forget the Blank Verse Sonnet category all together,

Once grounded, we saw how many other well-known Poetry Formats were converted into Sonnets. We saw how some Famous Poets took liberties with the Structure. That opened the door to the whole concept of Sonnet Variation, such as: moving the Couplet, changing the Type of Stanzas, adding more Lines, adopting creative Rhyme Schemes, examining the Line Length, and Meter. We looked at Shorter Sonnets. We examined the impact of Sonnet Refrains. Then we moved into the domain of Sonnet Sequences, and finished with the Complex Variations. For me, I was amazed at the diversity and flexibility.

> The last Chapter was a Grab Bag of several Sonnets. Here is what their Formats were:
> American Sonnets - 142, 160, 165, and 167.
> Blank Verse Sonnets - 148, 161, and 168.
> Byron's Sonnet – 151.
> Carrett Sonnet – 153.
> Echo Sonnet – 145.
> English Sonnets – 141, 143, 149, 154, 159, 162, 163, 164, and 166.
> Modern Sonnets – 152, 156, 158, and 170.
> Rosarian Sonnet – 169.
> Rubaiyat Sonnet – 157
> Shakespearean Sonnet – 144.
> Spenserian Sonnets – 147, 150, and 155.
> Triptic Sonnet – 146

If you learned something new in this book, I am happy.

If you were amazed and entertained by the Poetry, I am glad.

If you liked the Synergy between the Image and Verse, I am delighted.

If you were convinced that Sonnets are more than previously thought, I am elated.

DESCRIPTIONS OF SONNETS.

1. **Acrostic Sonnet**

   An Acrostic Sonnet takes all the standard features of a regular Sonnet's 14 lines of three Quatrains and Closing Couplet, along with any of the typical Sonnet Rhyme Schemes. What makes it unique is that the First Letter of each line contributes to spell out the Words that make up the Title of the poem (either a word, words, or phrase).

2. **Alfred Dorn Sonnet.**

   An Alfred Dorn Sonnet is named after its creator and is distinguished by two Sestets bridged by a Couplet. The first one is an Italian Sestet, having a Rhyme Scheme of: abcabc. The second one is a Sicilian Sestet, taking the Scheme of: aeaeae. So the entire Rhyme Scheme becomes:
   abcabc dd aeaeae.

   Note that the "a" Rhyme is a Linking Rhyme between the 2 Sestets. Written in iambic Pentameter. The turn (or Volta) is at line 9, as in most Sonnets.

3. **American Sonnet**

   The American Sonnet is a derivation of the English Sonnet. It takes the typical 14 line configuration with three Quatrains and a Closing Couplet. The difference, much like the Spenserian, is in the Rhyme Scheme. Here, instead of using the Alternating Rhyme abab cdcd efef in the Quatrains, it uses Coupled Rhyme of aabb ccdd eeff. Besides that, an American Sonnet may break with traditional Iambic Pentameter, going with other Meters, such as: Hexameter, or Tetrameter.

4. **An 11-9 Anapestic Heroic Sonnet**

   Anapests are a less common variety of Metrical Foot. The Anapest has Three Syllables - Unstressed, Unstressed, Stressed, like da da DUM. Because of its length, and the fact that it ends with a Stressed Syllable, and so allows for strong Rhymes, an Anapaest can produce a very Rolling Verse, and allows for long lines with a great deal of internal complexity. The Rhythm is like a waltz, rather than a march.

   A Heroic Sonnet is one with 18 lines and no Volta, but it closes with a Rhyming Couplet. The Heroic Sonnet has 4 Quatrains and a closing Rhyming Couplet. It uses an uneven 11-9 meter to emphasize discordance. An Anapestic Rhythm also has a more Racing Cadence.

   So this Format is a combination of a Heroic Sonnet with Anapestic Meter.

5. **Arabian Onegin Sonnet.**

   An Arabian Sonnet is simply one that is comprised of two Quatrains followed by two Tercets, where each Stanza is Mono-Rhymed. Written in iambic Pentameter. The Onegin aspect adds a touch of complexity to the Rhyme Scheme by repeating End Rhymes (rather than Refrain Lines) in the following Rhyme Scheme:
   A,a,A,a - B,B,b,b - C,c,C - D,D,d.

   The Capital letters indicate the Rhymes that are repeated. The trick here is to write the repeats so that they sound unique and the Theme flows smoothly. Not sure why it was named that or who named it, as it doesn't resemble the Pushkin Sonnet in any manner.

   I am not particularly enamored with the format, as without the author notes, a reader could assume the poet is a Sloppy Rhymer.

6. **Asean Sonnet.**

   The Asean Sonnet was created by Jose Rizal M. Reyes. Its two unique features are: that it contains a Structure of an Octave (8 lines), plus a Quatrain (4 lines), closed by a Couplet (2 lines); and it is completely Mono-Rhymed for all 14 lines. This makes for a poem where a single Rhyme throughout requires a very careful choice of Rhyme Words and subject matter. Volta begins at line 9.

7. **Beymorlin Sonnet**

   The Beymorlin Sonnet is unique in its Mirrored Rhyming. It is structured within the conventional 14 line Format of a Sonnet, but it requires the Second Syllable of each line to Rhyme with the End-Rhyme of each line, in addition to carrying an overall Rhyme Scheme of the author's choosing.

8. **Blank Verse Sonnet**

   A Blank Verse poem is written without Rhymes. It does have a set Metrical Pattern, usually iambic Pentameter. But it is a Flexible Form that is often used in narrative and dramatic poetry. It was popularized by William Shakespeare. This also takes the Format of a Standard Sonnet (only Unrhymed) having 3 Quatrains with a Closing Couplet totaling 14 lines.

9. **Byron's Sonnet.**

   Lord Bryon wrote several Sonnets. Byron's Sonnets are obviously influenced by the Italian Form rather than the English and possess an Octave with a Sestet. The eight lines of the Octave comprises of a Progression of three in an Enveloping Rhyme of:
   a, b. b. a... a. c. c. a.,

   but it's the six lines of the Sestet that makes it unique, with its pattern of:
   d. e. d...e. d. e.

   This was his favorite and signature Rhyme Scheme. The total Interweaving Rhyme Scheme is:
   abba acca ded ede.

   It is written in iambic Pentameter. Volta at line 9.

10. **Carrett Sonnet.**

    The Carrett Sonnet was created by Stephen A Carter (Carter + Sonnet). It is a 15 line Sonnet consisting of 3 Quatrains with a Closing Tercet. It has an Inter-Twining Rhyme

Scheme, as follows:
abab cdce dfef fef

It requires a meter of 10 beats per line in iambic Pentameter.

11. Caudate Sonnet.

A Caudate Sonnet is another Expanded Version of the Sonnet. It consists of the 14 lines of the Standard Sonnet Forms followed by a Coda (Latin cauda meaning "tail", from which the name is derived). It starts with the Petrarchan Sonnet and adds a three-foot Tail, then adds a Heroic Couplet, then another Tail, then another Heroic Couplet. The origin is Italian. The Rhyme Scheme is:
abbaabba cdecde e ff f gg

The Tail echoes the Rhyme of the previous line (thus a Tail) with a 6 syllable Meter. The rest of the lines are in iambic Pentameter.

12. Compound Sonnet.

A Compound Sonnet is basically a Sonnet with everything Doubled or compounded. Compound Sonnets have: 28 lines of iambic Pentameter composed of three Octaves and a concluding Quatrain. Rhyme pattern is: aabbaabb for the first Octave, ccddccdd for the second, eeffeeff for the third and gggg for the Quatrain.

13. Cornish Sonnet.

The Cornish Sonnet is said to be influenced by Arab traders to the Cornish coast. This Verse Form is a merging of Arabic Meter and the Sonnet. The language became all but extinct by the 18th century but what was preserved in some Verse are Octaves using 7 syllable loose Trochaic lines and Alternating Rhyme. Deliberate use of Alliteration or other devices of "Harmony of Sound" are not present. This Sonnet Form doesn't fit with these early findings, so it can only be assumed that it arrived on the scene much later than originally presumed.

The defining features of the Cornish Sonnet are:
2 Sestets made up of Linked Enclosed Tercets,
followed by a Refrain which is the repeat of the **first line** of each Sestet,
Metered at the discretion of the poet,
lines should be similar (not necessarily exact) length.
The Rhyme Scheme is:
Abacbc Dedfef AD
The capital letters show that the **first line** of each Sestet are repeated in the Refrain of the Closing Couplet.

14. Coronet of Sonnets

This poem has 4 Interlinked Sonnet Formats - The English, Petrarchan, Spenserian, and Rubaiyat. Each is written in iambic Pentameter. Each carries its own signature Rhyme Scheme, as follows:
English: ..... abab cdcd efef gg
Petrarchan: abbaabba cddcdd
Spenserian: ababcbccdcd ee
Rubaiyat: .... aaba bbcb ccdc dd

15. Couplet Sonnet.

A Couplet Sonnet is made up of 7 Rhyming Couplets. The unique feature is that the first two lines are also the last two lines, so the Rhyme Scheme is:
AAbbccddeeff AA,

where the capital letters indicate the repeated lines.

16. Crown of Heroic Sonnets.

The Crown of Heroic Sonnets is a Sequence Poem consisting of seven Heroic Sonnets usually addressed to one person. It is concerned with a single Theme as each Sonnet explores a different Aspect of the Theme and is Interlinked to the preceding and succeeding Sonnets by repeating the Final Line of the preceding Sonnet as its First Line and by having its Final Line become the First Line of the next Sonnet.

Also, the First Line of the First Sonnet is repeated as the Final Line of the Final Sonnet thereby bringing the Sequence to a close; a Circle uniting the Beginning and End of the entire poem. Thus, the name Crown.

Each Sonnet uses a Heroic Sonnet Format to provide for a long story. I love the Form for historic presentations. A Heroic Sonnet is an iambic Pentameter based poem that adds a Heroic Couplet to either two Sicilian Octave Stanzas, or four Sicilian Quatrain Stanzas. In other words, it's eighteen lines of iambic Pentameter broken into three or five parts with the last part being a Couplet. The Rhyme Scheme has usually been;
a,b,a,b,a,b,a,b - c,d,c,d,c,d,c,d - e,e (Octaves), or
a,b,a,b - c,d,c,d - e,f,e,f - g,h,g,h - i,i (Quatrains).

17. Curtal Sonnet, written in the more ancient format of the form.

There is a bit of controversy about the format as to its true Structure, its Pedigree, and even if it can be called a Sonnet. Most sources (including Wikipedia, Poetry Soup, The Poet's Garret, Sonnet Central, and even Webster's dictionary) identify it as a "curtailed" Sonnet, and identify the creator of the Form as Gerard Manley Hopkins in 1877 using his radical "Sprung Rhythm." His Format has 10.5 Lines that are arranged in two Stanzas. The first Stanza has Rhyme Scheme abcabc, and the second is either dbcdc or dcbdc. The very last line is indented and shorter. It is, depending on what expert say about the Curtal Sonnet, either described as a Half-Line or a single Spondee. Hopkins described it as the former, but usually executed it as the latter. He described it as a contraction of the Petrarchan Sonnet, whereby the 8 line Octave becomes 6, while the Sestet is reduced to 5. It should have a Pivot between the Sestet and Quintet.

However, a site called Poetry Through the Ages, described it this way.

"The 10-line, two-Stanza Curtal Sonnet actually pre-dated the Petrarchan form, but was only used by the more masterful structural poets. A good example is embedded within the 29 movements of Dante's, La Vita Nuova."

Dante's Curtal Sonnet predates Hopkins by 400 years. It had a Rhyme Scheme of aabbba cddc, in a more typical Pentameter. Hopkin's format used a weird Meter he called "Sprung Rhythm." From what I can tell he paid no attention to meter at all, but rather the accent. In his poem "Pied Beauty", the Meter was Variable and the Syllable counts were: 9,12,12,10,11,10,10,11,14,10,2. The Poet's Garret described it as follows:

"Sprung Rhythm; that has 1-to-4-syllable feet, each starting with a Stressed Syllable (sometimes a foot by itself), where the Spondee replaces the iamb as the dominant measure, and rests and multiple Non-Stressed Syllables discounted in scansion."

18. Dante's Variation Sonnet

The most common Italian Sonnets are written in the Petrarchan format of a 14 line set consisting of two Quatrains (or an 8 line Octave), with two Closing Tercets (or a Sestet), having the Rhyme Scheme:

abba abba cdc cdc.

Dante wrote a 20 line deviation to this style. Most Sonnets in Dante's La Vita Nuova are Petrarchan. Chapter VII gives sonnet "O voi che per la via", with two Sestets (aabaab aabaab) and two Quatrains (cddc cddc), and Ch. VIII, "Morte villana", with two Sestets (aabbba aabbba) and two Quatrains (cddc cddc).

I am recreating his variation using the aabbba form of his Chapter VIII. I chose that because, I personally like 3 consecutive repeated lines. So this intrigued me when I read about it. The total rhyme scheme is:
aabbba aabbba cdddc cdddc.

Done in iambic Pentameter, of course.

With only 4 unique Rhyme choices (a,b,c,and d) covering 20 lines, the choice of Rhymes is crucial.

19. Double Acrostic Cleaved Petrarchan Sonnet/Rondeau in an If/Then Format.

Written as inspired by Pantygynt's Poem, The Sirelei Songs, where there are actually five different Poetic Formats amalgamated in this poem: an Acrostic, a Cleave, A Petrarchan Sonnet, a Rondeau, and an If/Then Poem.

An Acrostic poem is one where the First Letter of every line spells out a Word or Phrase vertically down the front of the poem. This is a Double Acrostic, because there are two separate poems, each with their own Phrase. The two poems are color-coded so that the reader can see them more easily. The Acrostic Phrases have been bolded with enlarged letters, for the same reason.

The red side is a Petrarchan or Italian Sonnet with the rhyme scheme of:
abbaabba, cdccdc
in mixed Tetrameter. The red Acrostic reads: IF MEN WERE WITTY. The blue Acrostic reads: THEN WOMEN WOULD. The right hand blue poem is a Rondeau in mixed Tetrameter, save for the Repeated Line which is in Dimeter. The rhyme scheme here is: aabba, aabR, aabbaR.

A Cleaved poem is a poem that is read in two halves, each being a poem in itself, then read as one complete poem.

An If/Then poem is one that poses an If-Then hypothesis of cause and effect. Punctuation is limited as it would differ depending on which poem is being read.

20. Dual Sonnet.

A Dual Sonnet is very similar to the Beymorlin Sonnet, in that both contain In-line Rhyming, The Beymorlin requires the Second Syllable to match the End-line Rhyme, as I noted before. The Dual Sonnet requires a Rhyme Scheme in the center of the Hexametered lines of the Stanza, but not necessarily matching the End-line Rhyme Scheme. In fact, there are two Intertwining but separate Rhyme Schemes within the poem. The two schemes are as follows:

Stanza 1	Stanza 2	Stanza 3	Couplet
a - a	a - c	c - e	e - g
b - b	b - d	d - f	e - g
b - a	b - c	c - e	
a - b	a - d	d - f	

21. Duo Sonnetino

The Sonnetino is a Five Line Poem, written in iambic pentameter. The rhyme scheme is: aaabb.

The first three lines bring up a topic and the Closing Couplet has a Turn or a strong closing thought.

She named this form Sonnetino - a teeny tiny sonnet. The word Sonnet is already a diminutive for song. So this is a tiny song. The Duo designation refers to having two Sonnetinos.

22. Echo Sonnet.

The ECHO SONNET is a relatively new form devised by the well-respected English Poet, Jeff Green. It takes its shape from three Envelope Quatrains and a Couplet, the last line of each Stanza is a Refrain that links the Quatrains and gives us a Rhyme Scheme of: A, b, b, A1, a, c, c, A1, a, d, d, A1, A, A1

Where the first A sets the A Rhyme and repeats once in line 13. The A1 of line 4 matches the Rhyme set in A, but is a distinct Repeating Line that Echoes 3 more times in lines 8, 12 and 14. This type poem, then, has 4 Rhyme Sets of A, b, c, and d.

The Echo Sonnet is based on French Repeating Forms, but unlike those Forms which are normally Syllabic, the preferred Meter is Iambic Pentameter, or similar. Being a Typical Sonnet, it should be presented as a 14 line poem.

23. English Sonnet.

A traditional English Sonnet is a poem of 14 lines. It follows a strict Rhyme Scheme. It is often about love. It consists of 14 lines, each line containing ten Syllables and is written in iambic Pentameter, in which a pattern of an Unstressed Syllable followed by a Stressed Syllable is repeated five times. The rhyme scheme in a English Sonnet is:
a-b-a-b, c-d-c-d, e-f-e-f, g-g.

The last two lines are a Rhyming Couplet.

24. Faux Free Verse Sonnet.

Another format created from my imagination. Of course, it uses my favorite Triple Rhyme Scheme layout. In a Faux Free Verse Sonnet, the text is laid out just like any Free Verse poem, except it has a Rhyme Scheme and a Syllable Count. It is actually Structured, but in disguise. Each Stanza is really just a single line in the Sonnet, so there are 14 Stanzas, rather than 14 Lines. They actually read as iambic Tetrameter. So the poem is pretending to be a Free Verse poem, because it looks like one. The Rhyme Scheme is: aaa bbb ccc ddd ee.

25. Fusion Sonnet.

This falls under the auspices of the Modern Sonnet genre. As such, it breaks several Sonnet rules. Most notably, it has 21 Lines rather than the typical 14. The Fusion comes from blending in 4 lines of Free Verse at lines 11 through 14. It has a strict Structure and Rhyme Scheme, but is more flexible in the area of Meter. Here are the complex rules:

14 line Poem followed by a Half Sonnet of 7 lines acting as a Coda or Tail to add additional stability to the poem. No particular Meter is followed, "Fusing" it with the modern Free Verse style.

First Fourteen Lines:
Same Rhyme in 1st, 5th, 9th & 10th Lines.
Same Rhyme in 2nd, 3rd & 4th Lines.
Same Rhyme in 6th, 7th & 8th lines.
Rhetorical questions in 9th & 10th lines.
Negative and pessimistic note in the first 10 lines.
Free Verse carrying Optimistic Tone in 11th, 12th, 13 & 14th Lines.
Volta gradually through 9th, 10th and 11th lines.
Next Seven Lines:-The Half Sonnet acting as a Coda.
Same Rhyme in 16th and 17th lines.
Same Rhyme in 18th and 19th lines.
Volta in the 20th line.

26. Heroic Sonnet.

The Heroic Sonnet is the Cornerstone Format of the Crown of Heroic Sonnets, which links a string of seven of them together. Unlike other Sonnets this Format does not require a Volta (or Turn), in that it is meant to convey large amounts of information, or a story.

It consists of four Quatrains typically in iambic Pentameter, using one of two classic Rhyme Schemes throughout, either aabb or abab. It is closed with the usual Rhyming Couplet. So it contains 18 lines, rather than the usual 14 lines of a Sonnet, in order for it to tell a longer story. That's where the "Heroic" designation comes from, that extra Quatrain.

27. Hex Sonnetta.

The Hex Sonnetta, created by Andrea Dietrich, consists of two Six-line Stanzas (Sestets) and a finishing Rhyming Couplet with the following set of rules:
Meter: Iambic Trimeter (6 Syllables)
Rhyme Scheme: abbaab cddccd ee

This particular Form uses six Syllables of iambic Trimeter per line. Thus, the name Hex Sonnetta, as it keys off the number 6. The first part of the Form's name refers to the Syllable Count per line, as well as six lines per Stanza. The second part of the name, Sonnetta, is to show this to be a Form similar to the Sonnet, yet with its shorter lines and different Rhyme Scheme, it is not the Typical Sonnet. Not only does this poem have six syllables per line, it also has a set of two six-line Stanzas, giving an extra "Hex" to the meaning of Hex Sonnetta. The Rhyme Scheme, with the two 6-line Stanzas has more of an Italian feel. The Rhyming Couplet completes the classic 14 line format of the Sonnet.

28. Inverted Sonnet.

An Inverted Sonnet is one of what is known as one of the Modern Sonnets.

A specific type of Modern Sonnet, it was most famously penned by Elizabeth Bishop, and christened the Inverted Sonnet. While the Traditional Sonnet is classified as having exactly 14 lines and a strict Rhyming Scheme, an Inverted Sonnet will also have 14 lines but with an Opening Rhyming Couplet rather than a Closing Couplet. It may start with an Opening Couplet, but the remaining lines could be written in Free Verse. A Sonnet that's been split in half, with each section having its own tone and style, might also be referred to as an Inverted Sonnet. The Meter and line length may vary in this Format. Source: The WiseGEEK and Wikipedia.

29. Italian Sonnet

An Italian sonnet is composed of an Octave, rhyming abbaabba, and a Sestet, rhyming cdecde or cdcdcd, or in some variant pattern, but with no Closing Couplet. Usually, English and Italian Sonnets have 10 syllables per line, but Italian Sonnets can also have 11 syllables per line.

The Italian sonnet is divided into two Sections by two different groups of Rhyming Sounds. The first 8 lines are called an Octave, which rhymes:
a b b a a b b a.

The remaining 6 lines are called a Sestet and can have either two or three rhyming sounds, arranged in a variety of ways:
c d c d c d (two Rhymes)
c d d c d c (two Rhymes)
c d e c d e (three Rhymes)
c d e c e d (three Rhymes)
c d c e d c (three Rhymes)

The exact pattern of Sestet Rhymes (unlike the Octave pattern) is flexible. In strict practice, the one thing that is to be avoided in the Sestet is ending with a Couplet (dd or ee), as this was never permitted in Italy, and Petrarch himself (supposedly) never used a Couplet Ending; in actual practice, Sestets are sometimes ended with Couplets (Sidney's "Sonnet LXXI given is an example of such a Terminal Couplet in an Italian sonnet).

The point here is that the poem is divided into two Sections by the two differing Rhyme Groups. In accordance with the principle, a change from one Rhyme Group to another signifies a change in subject matter. This change occurs at the beginning of Line 9 (L9) in the Italian Sonnet and is called the Volta, or "Turn." The Turn is an Essential Element of the Sonnet Form, perhaps the Essential Element (unless otherwise defined in the Format). It is at the Volta that the Second Idea is introduced,

30. Japanese Sonnet.

The Japanese Sonnet actually blends several Japanese Formats into a 14 line Structure that also contains other Sonnet features, such as a Rhyme Scheme. The Format begins with a 5-7-5 Haiku followed by a 5-7-5-7-7 Tanka. It then executes a 3-5-3 Haiku and closes with a Rhymed 1-6-1. Because I want to emphasize the Japanese correlation, this Format must end with the word **"Hai."**

A Sonnet usually carries a "Volta", so mine is in the 3-5-3 (lines 9 - 11). Still the Haiku and Tanka require a similar turning point, called a "Kiru", in each of its Formats, so I tried to achieve that too.

The total Rhyme Scheme Is:
aba bcbdd eec ddd.

The Syllable counts are:
5-7-5, 5-7-5-7-7, 3-5-3, 1-6-1

31. Jazz Sonnet.

A Jazz Sonnet has the familiar layout of a Traditional Sonnet with its first 12 lines separated into 3 Quatrains and a closing Rhymed Couplet. However, none of the lines in the Stanzas have an even Syllable Count, making iambic Verse difficult. This promotes Discordance (blue notes?). But there is Rhyme, it's just not what you'd typically find. You'll see Elements that play against each other, while others blend. After all, Jazz sought to be different. Each Jazz Sonnet is unique in Style, Meter, and Rhyme.

32. Kyrielle Sonnet.

This Sonnet is made up of three Rhyming Quatrains and a Non-rhyming Couplet. Just like the Traditional Kyrielle Poem, the Kyrielle Sonnet also has the Repeating Line or Phrase as a Refrain (usually appearing as the last line of each Stanza).

Each line within the Kyrielle Sonnet consists of only 8 Syllables. French Forms have a tendency to Link back to the beginning of the poem, so common practice is to use the First and Last line of the First Quatrain as the Ending Couplet. This would also reinforce the Refrain within the poem.

Therefore, a good Rhyme Scheme for a Kyrielle Sonnet would be:
AabB, ccbB, ddbB, AB or, AbaB, cbcB, dbdB, AB

33. Limerick Sonnet.

According to the dictionary, a Limerick Form consists of 5 Lines (two long, followed by two short, and closed by 1 long). The first, second and fifth Lines must have matching lengths of seven to ten Syllables (8 or 9 is most typical). The third and fourth Lines only have between five and seven Matching Syllables. So there is a bit of flexibility.

The long Cadence is either: da DUM da da DUM da da DuM da; or, da DUM da da DUM da da DUM.
The short cadence is either: da DUM da da DUM; or, da DUM da da DUM da.

The Limerick Sonnet uses a Quintet (5 line) structure with two Closing Couplets rather than one, in order to achieve the classic 14 lines. The Volta comes at the first Couplet (lines 11 and 12).
The Rhyme Scheme is: aabba ccddc ee ff.
The syllable count is: 9,9,5,5,9 – 8,8,5,5,8- 9,9 – 5,5.

34. LyriCat Sonnet.

The LyriCat Sonnet creates three Quatrains with a Repeating Line, and a Couplet. It mimics the 7-5-9 meter of the LyriCat Poem with the following Meter Structure:
7/5/9/5 - 7/5/9/5 - 7/5/9/5 - 5/5.

The rhyme scheme is:
abAb acAc adAd ee,
where the A represents the repeated line. Volta on line 9.

35. Modeled End Rhymes of Shakespearean Sonnet

A Sonnet using the End Rhyming Words from Shakespeare Sonnet. Then using those same End rhymes to create a new unique Sonnet. This is basically a Poetic Exercise to hone the skills of a Poet, using the genius of the Master.

36. Modern Sonnet

Modern Sonnets, don't necessarily follow the same rules as the more Traditional Sonnets. While there were once Strict Rules about how many Lines could be in a Sonnet, how many Syllables had to be in every Line, and the Rhyme Scheme the Sonnet had to follow, the writers of Modern Sonnets have much more freedom when it comes to Structure, Meter, and Rhyme. It can be difficult to distinguish different types of Modern Sonnets because the purpose of the modern poetry writers who write these types of poems is often to "break the rules." In fact, Modern Sonnets have a lot in common with Free Form, also known as Free Verse, poetry. However, while similar to Free Form Poetry in many ways, Modern Sonnets tend to have a bit more Structure and will have certain Characteristics that will classify it as a Sonnet.

37. Nonet/Cinquain Sonnet

The Nonet/Cinquain is a Sonnet created from two Forms. It falls under the category of Unusual and Complex Sonnets. So it is a Blend of Two Formats creating a whole. The top half is a Nonet, while the bottom is a Cinquain. Together they mesh to give a Sonnet's 14 lines.

A Nonet is a Nine Line Poem. The First Line containing nine Syllables, the next line has eight Syllables, the next line has seven Syllables. That continues until the Last Line (the ninth line) which has one Syllable. Nonets can be written about any subject. Rhyming is optional. There is no limitation to the number of Words per line, only Syllables per line. This provides a great deal of flexibility. Ideally, when centered, the work will form a nice Reverse-Triangle. A perfect Nonet has a nice set of nearly Straight Lines on each side.

A Cinquain is a Five Line Poem. The Format, inspired by Adelaide Crapsey in 1915, has a Fixed Syllable Count of: 2,4,6,8,2. Rhyming is also optional.

38. Pantygonnet

This Format is a variation of the Standard Sonnet and was created by fellow Fanstory site poet Pantygynt (James Bartlett), by modifying his Form – the Pantygynt. The original Pantygynt Poem consists of a Quatrain in Ballad Meter and Rhyme followed by a Rhyming Tercet in iambic Tetrameter. The Cycle concludes with a single line of iambic Tetrameter on the "b" Rhyme. So the Rhyme Scheme runs:
abab, ccc, b.

By running the eight lines together and putting the whole thing into Tetrameter a typical Octave, not too unlike that in a Petrarchan Sonnet, is created. Two Tercets are run together to create the Sestet with one of the many Rhyme Schemes acceptable in the Petrarchan form. The Rhyme Scheme in the octave is:
a B a B c c c B, where the B rhyme is Feminine.

The Petrarchan Sestet can be any of the following:
c d d c e e, or
c d c d e e are most used.

39. Pantoum Sonnet.

A Pantoum Sonnet combines the characteristics of the two Formats. A Pantoum is a Repeating Poem who's Second and Fourth Lines become the First and Third lines of the next Stanza. The Sonnet is a 14 line poem with 12 lines of abab Rhyming and two Closing Rhymed Lines. It can be formed in the contemporary manner of three Quatrains with Closing Couplet, of the traditional way of 14 lines together. In either case, the Rhyme Scheme for this Pantoum Sonnet is:
A1/B1/A2/B2/, B1/C1/B2/C2/, C1/D1/C2/D2/, A2/A1.

40. Petrarchan Sonnet.

The Original Italian sonnet form divides the poem's 14 Lines into two parts, the first part being an Octave and the second being a Sestet. The Rhyme Scheme for the Octave is typically:
a b b a a b b a.

The Sestet is more flexible. The Sestet and can have either two or three rhyming sounds, arranged in a variety of ways:
c d c d c d (two Rhymes)
c d d c d c (two Rhymes)
c d e c d e (three Rhymes)
c d e c e d (three Rhymes)
c d c e d c (three Rhymes)

In strict practice, the one thing that is to be avoided in the Sestet is ending with a Couplet (dd or ee), as this was never permitted in Italy, and Petrarch himself (supposedly) never used a Couplet Ending; in actual practice, Sestets are sometimes ended with Couplets (Sidney's "Sonnet LXXI given is an example of such a Terminal Couplet in an Italian sonnet). One ending with such a Terminal Couplet would be an Italian Sonnet, but not a Petrarchan Sonnet. Therein lies the distinction.

The Octave and Sestet have special functions in a Petrarchan Sonnet. The Octave's purpose is to introduce a problem, express a desire, reflect on reality, or otherwise present a situation that causes doubt or conflict within the speaker. It usually does this by introducing the problem within its first Quatrain (unified four-line section) and developing it in the second. The beginning of the Sestet is known as the Volta, and it introduces a pronounced change in tone in the Sonnet; the change in Rhyme Scheme marks the Turn. The Sestet's purpose as a whole is to make a comment on the problem or to apply a solution to it. The pair are separate but usually used to reinforce a unified argument - they are often compared to two strands of thought organically converging into one argument. This attention to a Thematic Structure is another distinction between a truly Petrarchan Sonnet and just an Italian Sonnet.

41. Pushkin Sonnet written in the English version.

The Pushkin Sonnet (aka: Onegin Sonnet), contains a couple of unique features.

The first is in its Meter, and the second is in its Layout. It was popularized (or invented) by the Russian poet Alexander Pushkin through his novel completely written in verse, Eugene Onegin.

The English Format features the Pushkin signature rhyme scheme:
aBaBccDDeFFeGG,

where the lowercase letters represent Feminine Endings (i.e., with an additional Unstressed 11th Syllable) and the uppercase representing the typical Masculine Ending (i.e. Stressed on the final 10th Syllable). So that is the first feature mentioned. However, the English Version is written **in iambic pentameter** (as opposed to the original Italian Version in iambic Tetrameter).

The second unique feature involves the lack of Stanzas. Unlike other Traditional Forms, such as the Petrarchan Sonnet or Shakespearean Sonnet, the Pushkin Sonnet does not divide into smaller Stanzas of four lines or two in an obvious way. If analyzed in a Stanzaic Format the structure would look like this:
abab ccdd eff egg,

which reveals some interesting aspects. Note that the Quatrains shift Rhyme Scheme from Alternating (abab) to Coupled (ccdd). Furthermore, the two Tercets contain an Interlocking "e" Rhyme.

A Tercet of effegg is a very Italian feature.

42. Pushkin Sonnet done in the Italian format.

The Pushkin Sonnet is also called the Pushkin **Stanza**., It contains a couple of unique features.

The first is in its meter, and the second is in its layout. The work was mostly written in verses of **iambic tetrameter** (distinct from the English format) with the rhyme scheme:

aBaBccDDeFFeGG,

where the lowercase letters represent Feminine Endings (i.e., with an additional Unstressed 9th Syllable) and the uppercase representing the typical Masculine Ending (i.e. Stressed on the final 8th Syllable). So that is the first feature mentioned, making the Italian Version recognizable by the **Tetrameter.**

The second unique feature involves the lack of Stanzas. Unlike other Traditional Forms, such as the Petrarchan Sonnet or Shakespearean Sonnet, the Pushkin Sonnet does not divide into smaller Stanzas of four lines or two in an obvious way. Thus, the entire poem is referred to as a Stanza from which comes the designation as the Pushkin Stanza. .

If analyzed in a Stanzaic Format, the Structure would look like this:
abab ccdd eff egg,

which reveals some interesting aspects. Note that the Quatrains shift Rhyme Scheme from Alternating (abab) to Coupled (ccdd). Furthermore, the two Tercets contain an Interlocking "e" Rhyme. A Tercet of effegg is a very Italian feature.

43. Qautern Sonnet

A Quatern is a poem consisting of four Quatrains, where the First Line of the poem Ripples through each Stanza. It becomes the Second Line of the Second Stanza, the Third Line of the Third Stanza, and the Last of the Fourth. It makes for a lovely Waterfall Effect as the line Ripples from beginning to end of the poem. This creates a rhyme scheme of:
Abab bAba abAb babA, or
Abab cAca adAd aA,

where the capital letter signifies the Repeated Line. The first choice uses only two Rhymes, while the second uses four.

Written in Tetrameter.

Therefore, to make a Quatern Sonnet, you merely turn the last Quatrain into a Rhymed Couplet, using the Repeated Line as the LastLline of the poem, but retaining the Waterfall Effect. The trick is to use the Repeated Line in various ways, changing its aspect, while still being a repeated Refrain. The Rhyme Scheme becomes:
Abab bAba abAb aA.

44. Rondel Prime Sonnet

A Rondel is a poem with two Quatrains followed by a Sestet where the First Two Lines of the poem become Repeated as the Last Two Lines of the next two Stanzas (the second Quatrain and the Sestet). Sometimes the Second Line is dropped in the Last Stanza. It is usually in Tetrameter, but is always iambic. So, the rhyme scheme would be:

ABba abAB abbaAB (Prime), or
ABba abAB abbaA (Classic).

The conversion to a Sonnet is quite simple. Change the Meter to Pentameter and separate the Last Two Lines of the Sestet to make it a Couplet. The Rhyme Scheme then for the Sonnet becomes:

ABba abAB abba AB.

45. Roserian Sonnet

The Roserian Sonnet was created by Jose Rizal M. Reyes of the Philippines. It consists of two Quintets or Quintrains (5 line Stanza) plus a Closing Quatrain. The two Quintrains are Interlinked with a shared Rhyme in the third line (middle) of each. So there are two Rhyming Couplets in the first Stanza with another Rhyme sandwiched between them that matches the one in the center of the second Stanza. It's almost like a Peek-a-Boo Rhyme. The Closing Quatrain uses an Enveloping Rhyme. It's usually written in iambic. Volta somewhere after line 8.

So it's a Quintet + Quintet + Quatrain, using a Rhyme Scheme of:
aabcc ddbee fggf

Its big departure from the usual Sonnet format is the lack of a Closing Couplet, but it still maintains the integrity of 14 lines, and requires an iambic Meter.

46. Rubaiyat Sonnet.

To make a Sonnet, combines the attributes of a Sonnet, having 3 Quatrains and closing Couplet, with a Rubiyat, having Quatrains that Interlink Rhymes.

The Rubaiyat Mono-rhymes line 1, 2, and 4 of each Stanza, while line 3 creates (establishes) the Rhyme for the following Stanza, thus Interlinking them. So, the Rhyme Scheme for the Sonnet is:

aaba bbcb ccdc dd.

47. Sapphic Sonnet.

This Sonnet has the classic 14 line Format of 3 Quatrains and a Rhyming Couplet, but the Meter follows the Sapphic Structure as outlined below for a Sapphic Verse.

Sapphics are made up of four-line Stanzas with three long lines, frequently of 11 Syllables, followed by a short line of typically 5 Syllables.

The main building blocks of the Sapphic are Trochees and Dactyls. The Trochee is a Metrical Foot with one Stressed Syllable followed by an Unstressed one, while the Dactyl contains a Stressed Syllable followed by two Unstressed ones. The first three lines of the Sapphic contain two Trochees, a Dactyl, and then two more Trochees (making 11 syllables). The shorter fourth, and final, line of the Stanza is called an "Adonic" and is composed of one Dactyl followed by a Trochee (making 5 Syllables). Hence the

Syllable Count is:
11/11/11/5 -11/11/11/5 -11/11/11/5-11/11

So, if you characterize a Stressed Syllable as "-", and Unstressed as "/", the Metric for a Sapphic line would be:
-/-/-//-/-/

and the Adonic would be:
-//-/

However, there is some flexibility with the Form, as when two Stressed syllables replace both the Second and Last Foot of each line.

While most Sapphic lines are Unrhymed, because this is a Sonnet, it is Rhymed in a classic Rhyme Scheme of:
abab cdcd efef gg.

48. Saraband Sonnet.

A Saraband Sonnet is a Form that consists of a Tercet + Quatrain + Tercet + Closing Quatrain. It can be configured in various styles: English, Italian, Spanish or French, making it extremely flexible. Each Stanza can be unique, but here are the basic rules.

Stanza 1: a Tercet, Rhyme aba or aaa.
Stanza 2: a Quatrain, any Quatrain form or rhyme.

The Stanza Forms may be mixed, taking on any of the Classic Forms as shown below.

English: abab or abcb.
Italian: baab.
Spanish: bcbc.
French: bbcc.

Stanza 3: a Tercet, but must be same Tercet form as Stanza 1, and line 2 of both Tercets to Rhyme.
Stanza 4: a Quatrain, any Quatrain Form and Rhyme.

Any Metrical Foot and any Metrical Line. Some authorities insist on eight Syllables but this is not cut and dried. Rhyme Scheme: depends on the Form chosen. The Volta the first line of the second Tercet.

49. Septillian Sonnet.

The Septillian Sonnet was created by fellow Fanstorian, Nancy E. Davis.

It is an elongated version of the basic Sonnet Format, having 17 lines versus the typical 14 lines. Nevertheless, it carries all the features and recognizable Structures of a Standard Sonnet, with: three Stanzas followed by a Closing Couplet, in iambic Pentameter, and a Volta (but at line 11, rather than 9). The Elongation is due to using Quintains (5 line Stanzas) instead of Quatrains. The Rhyme Scheme is set at a strict aabbb scheme.

The name is derived from the 17 lines Sept being 7 in French, and tillian being a play on "teen"). The total rhyme scheme is therefore:
aabbb ccddd eefff gg.

50. Sestet Sonnet.

A Sestet Sonnet still has the 14 lines, like the Traditional Sonnet, but instead of the first 12 being done in 3 Quatrains (4 line Stanzas), this Format uses 2 Sestets (6 line Stanzas). Both Forms are followed with a Rhyming Couplet. The Rhyme Scheme of a Sestet Sonnet is:
abcabc cdecde ff.

With the Rhymes spaced a little further apart, they are a bit more subtle. Some think this adds to the eloquence of the Format.

51. Sestina Sonnet.

A Sestina is unusual in that it doesn't use Rhyme, but instead uses the same Words repeated in different Sequences for each Stanza. So it Mimics Rhyme by repeating (or parroting) the same Words, only in a specific Sequence. Normally, the Sestina has 6 repeated Words Sequences over six Verses and a Closing Tercet that uses all six Words. But, in order to accommodate a Sonnet, it has been modified to have only 4 Words ending each line of a Quatrain repeated over three Verses, plus with a Couplet that incorporates all four of the Key Words. It is not necessary to choose Words that Rhyme, but I like to, as it then gives a nice Rhymed Sequence. Note also that the Fixed Sequence causes the Last Word of each Stanza to repeat as the first End-Word of the next Stanza.

So, if you identify the four Words with the letters A, B, C, and D, the Word Sequence for the Sonnet is:
ABCD DCAB BADC (BC)(DA),

Where the letters in parens represent two words in each line of the Couplet.

52. Shadow Sonnet.

The Shadow Sonnet was created by Amera M. Andersen. It may be written in any Sonnet Style. The Shadow takes place at the Beginning and Ending of each Line as the words are either Identical or Homophonic. Since all poetry was originally meant to be sung or recited out loud, Homophonic words are acceptable. These are words that sound alike such as "see and sea," or "be and bee."

Rules: 14 lines, 8, 9 or 10 syllables per line. The poem should have a Volta or pivot; iambic Pentameter is not necessary.

53. Shakespearean Sonnet.

A Shakespearean Sonnet is written according to the following rules:

1. The Sonnet consists of 14 lines. It must have three (3) Quatrains and one (1) Closing Couplet.

2. The Sonnet must be written in strict iambic Pentameter.

3. The Sonnet must follow a specific Rhyme Scheme as follows: First Quatrain: abab; Second Quatrain: cdcd; Third Quatrain: efef; Closing Couplet: gg. This rhyme pattern requires seven different Rhymes.

4. The development of a Shakespearean Sonnet requires attention to detail. The Sonnet must be developed in the following Thematic Format:

......a. First Quatrain: The Main Theme and main Metaphor are introduced in this Quatrain.

......b. Second Quatrain: The Theme and Metaphor extended or complicated; often, some imaginative example is given.

..... c. Third Quatrain: Peripeteia (a Twist or Conflict, Turn, Volta), often introduced by a "but" (very often leading off the Ninth Line).

......d. Couplet: Summarizes the Sonnet and leaves the reader with a new, concluding image and feeling, often times one that leaves the reader pondering the Sonnet's meaning.

54. Slide Sonnet.

Like most Sonnets, it has 14 lines. It is composed with eight, ten, or twelve Syllables to each line. The unique feature of this Format is, that the First Half of the First Line of each Stanza "slides" to the Last Half of the Third Line, creating a unique Poetic Repetition. The Rhyme Scheme may be in any of the Standard Sonnet Rhyme Schemes, either: aabb ccdd eeff gg (Coupled), or abab cdcd efef gg (Alternating), or abba cddc effe gg (Enveloped). It is typically done in iambic. The Volta, or Turn, occurs at line 9.

55. Sonnet Trilogy

This is another Sonnet Format that I created. It is really quite simple. There are three consecutive Sonnets, **not** Interlinked, all of which have the same Rhyme Scheme and Meter, but tell a continuing story.

56. Sonnet Cycle

A Sonnet Cycle is a group of Sonnets, arranged to address a particular person or Theme, and designed to be read both as a collection of fully realized individual poems and as a single poetic work comprising all the individual Sonnets.

A Sonnet Cycle may have any Theme. The arrangement of the Sonnets generally reflects Thematic concerns, with chronological arrangements (whether linear, like a progression, or cyclical, like the seasons) being the most common. A Sonnet Cycle may also have Allegorical or Argumentative Structures which replace or complement chronology.

While the Thematic Arrangement may reflect the unfolding of real or fictional events, the Sonnet Cycle is very rarely Narrative; the Narrative Elements may be inferred, but provide Background Structure, and are never the Primary Concern of the poet's art. They typically are a collection of 20 or more Sonnets.

57. Sonnet Sequence

A Sonnet Sequence is a Group of Sonnets, Thematically Unified to create a long work, although generally, unlike the Stanza, each Sonnet so connected can also be read as a meaningful Separate Unit.

The Sonnet Sequence was a very popular genre during the Renaissance, following the pattern of Petrarch. But English models also emerged. They typically include 50+ Sonnets.

The subject is usually the speaker's unhappy love for a distant beloved, following the courtly love tradition of the Troubadours, from whom the Genre ultimately derived. An exception is Edmund Spenser's *Amoretti*, where the wooing is successful, and the sequence ends with an "Epithalamion", a marriage song.

58. Sonnetino.

The Sonnetino is a very short, Sonnet-like Format, modeled after the 10 Line Curtal Sonnet. Here are the instructions.

-A five line poem (Quintrain), comprising a Tercet and Couplet
-Rhyme Scheme, aaabb
-Written in iambic Pentameter.
-The Tercet presents a scene or conflict,

and the Closing Couplet offers conclusion or resolution (with an optional Turn).

59. SonnTriolet (aka: Triolet Sonnet)

This Form was my own invention, after seeing other poets stretching the limits of what it means to be a Sonnet. There are Key Elements to any Sonnet, and anyone of them can be stretched to accommodate a creative Variation.

A Triolet is a French Form with Double Refrain. It consists of 8 lines (Octave) with a Rhyme Scheme of:
ABaAabAB,

where the capital letters represent the Repeated Lines. It can be written in any Meter. But being French in origin, iambic Tetrameter is the favorite, while iambic Pentameter is a favorite of the Sonnet form. So it should be either one or the other.
To convert to a SonnTriolet, requires three Triolets followed by a Rhymed Couplet.

60. Spenserian Sonnet.

The Spenserian Sonnet is a third Major Type of Sonnet, (along with the Italian and English Sonnets). It was invented in the sixteenth century by the English poet Edmund Spenser. It has the same Structure as the English Sonnet, but it employs a different Rhyme Scheme of:
abab, bcbc, cdcd, ee,

The "b" Rhyme carries from the first Stanza to the second, while the "c" Rhyme caries from the second to the third Stanza, which links the Rhymes within the three Quatrains together.

This puts less pressure on the final Couplet at the end to resolve the argument. The three Quatrains develop separate ideas, but they are closely related to each other. The Couplet then simply provides a different idea or commentary.The Spenserian Sonnet is written in iambic Pentameter, like the other two Major Sonnet Forms.

61. Super Sonnet

A Super Sonnet is composed of several Quatrains closed by a Rhyming Couplet. It generally utilizes all four of the primary Rhyme Schemes:
Alternate Rhyming - abab
Coupled Rhyming - aabb
Enveloping Rhyme - abba

Skipping Rhyme - abcb

So, the poem writes with a set of the Four Types, and then repeats them as many times as the author wishes. The Four Sets are necessary in every four Stanza series, but not necessarily in the same Sequence. One required feature though, relates to the very Last Stanza, which is always done with the abcb Skipping Rhyme Type. The Unrhymed third line of that Stanza sets the Rhyme for the final Rhyming Couplet, thereby linking the last Quatrain to the Couplet.

62. Swannet Sonnet (or just Swannet)

The Swannet Sonnet is a straight forward Form comprised of 14 lines with 3 Quatrain Stanzas of Enveloping Rhyme (abba) and a Rhyming Couplet. The key feature is the Repeat of line 1 and 4 to also become the Closing Couplet. The Rhyme Scheme is: (A1)bb(A2) - cddc - effe - (A1)(A2),

where A1 is the First Line of the First Stanza, as well as the Couplet, and A2 is the Last Line of the First Stanza, and the Last Line of the poem.

The Meter is not specified but is usually Tetrameter or Pentameter.

63. Terza Rima Sonnet.

A Terza Rima is a Rhyming Verse Stanza Form that consists of an Interlocking three-line Rhyme Scheme. It was first used by the Italian poet Dante Alighieri, who wrote The Inferno. The literal translation of Terza Rima from Italian is 'Third Rhyme'. Terza Rima is a three-line Stanza using Chain Rhyme in the pattern:
A-B-A, B-C-B, C-D-C, D-E-D.

There is no limit to the number of lines, but poems or sections of poems written in Terza Rima end with either a single line or Couplet repeating the Rhyme of the middle line of the final Tercet. The two possible endings are either
d-e-d, e; or
d-e-d, e-e.

There is no set Rhythm for Terza Rima, but in English, iambic Pentameter is generally preferred. So, a Terza Rima Sonnet combines that Rhyme Pattern in 4 Stanzas of 3 lines each, using the Couplet option to create the signature 14 lines of a Sonnet. The Sonnet's Rhyme Scheme, therefore is:
aba bcb cdc ded ee.

64. Tiara of Sonnets.

A Tiara of Sonnets is based on the concept of the Crown of Sonnets, which has a Sequence of seven Sonnets, Interlinked by Last-to-First Lines, and concluding with the Final Line being the same as the First Line of the First Sonnet. Thus creating a Circle that is the Crown.

The Tiara of Sonnets, then, has the same concept, but with only three Sonnets. Thus a much smaller circlet, like a Tiara, rather than a Crown.

An option is to write each Sonnet in a different Format, but that is not a requirement.

65. Tirrell Sonnet.

The Tirrell Sonnet (an American model), is quite different and has a unique feel to it. It starts with a Couplet followed by a Tercet, followed by a Quatrain, adding the Turn with a following Tercet and then reversing the order of the Repeated Couplet as a Refrain.

So it is: Couplet + Tercet + Quatrain + Tercet + Reversed Couplet.

It features only 3 Rhymes (a,b,and c). It is written in iambic Pentameter. Volta at line 10.

The rhyme scheme is:
A1, A2 - b,c,b - c,b,b,c - b,c,b - A2, A1,

where the capital letters indicate the Repeated Verses and the numbers provide identification.

66. Tory Hexatet Sonnet.

The Tory Hexatet Sonnet consists of an Octet + Couplet + Quatrain, with a Rhyme Scheme of:
ababcdcd ee ffgg.

The Format features the first eight lines (the Octet) in 12 syllable iambic Hexameter, but the Rhyming Couplet holds to eight Syllables (iambic Tetrameter), located at line 9, rather than at the end. The last four lines of the Closing Quatrain revert back to 12 Syllables. So the poem retains the signature total 14 lines of a Sonnet. The Couplet in the center provides the "changing point", or Volta. The shorter Meter provides a visual, as well as oral impact. Thus, It makes a direct statement and could be read by itself.

67. Tricet Sonnet.

The name Tricet derives from Triple-Rhymed Tercet (tri-cet). A Tricet Sonnet has the usual 14 lines, but consists of four Tercets with a Rhyming Couplet, and a Volta at line 10. The lines of each of the Tercets Mono-rhyme. The Rhyme Scheme is:
aaa bbb ccc ddd ee

What is also unique is the Meter. It is written in Dactylic Dimeter. A Dactyl is a Meter with a Hard Stress followed by two Soft Stresses. This Form repeats it twice in each line.

68. Trilonnet Sonnet.

The Trilonet, is a 14-line poem made up of four each three-line Verses of 8 Syllables (iambic Tetrameter) and one Rhyming Couplet, or alternately, four each three-lined Verses of 10 Syllables (iambic Pentameter) and one Rhyming Couplet.

Each 3 line verse is an Unrhymed Triplet. Each Triplet has a Rolling Rhyme Scheme of abc. It is a Sonnet in that it made up of 14 lines, although the Volta may occur on a line other than line 9. There are 2 possible Rhyme Schemes for this form:
abc abc abc abc dd (here the rhyme repeats), or,
abc cba abc cba dd (here the rhyme rolls, or undulates)

This form is written in either iambic Tetrameter or iambic Pentameter.

69. Triptic Sonnet.

The name Triptic derives from the Triple Rhyme Scheme. A Triptic Sonnet has the usual 14 lines, consisting of three Quatrains with a Rhyming Couplet, and a Volta at line 9. What distinguishes it is the Rhyme Scheme and Meter. The first lines of each Quatrain Rhyme with each other, Interlinking the Stanzas. The next 3 lines of the Stanza all

Rhyme, creating a elegant Echo Effect. The Rhyme Scheme is:
abbb accc addd ee.
It is written in any iambic Meter.

70. Tuckerman Sonnet

Frederick Goddard Tuckerman (February 4, 1821 - May 9, 1873) was an American poet, remembered mostly for his Sonnet Series. Tuckerman wrote Sonnets with free abandon and with virtually no regard for any kind of Pattern at all. His Sonnets burst from the gate in a flurry of Rhyme, without any Stanzas, then, after the first few lines, Rhymes fall seemingly at random, as in his "Sonnets, First Series," which Rhymes:
a b b a b c a b a d e c e d,
with a volta at L10.

71. Visser Sonnet. (aka: Hidden Rhyme Sonnet)

It was created by Audrae Visser, Poet laureate of S. Dakota, (1974-2001). It reads much like a Blank Verse poem, in that it is done in iambic Meter (12 Syllables, or Hexameter), and has no End Rhymes. However, it does indeed have a Rhyme Scheme, but it is hidden in the middle of each line, rather than at the end. So it becomes extremely subtle. In fact, it takes the Scheme of a typical Petrarchan Sonnet, with its Rhyme Scheme of:
abbaabba cdecde.

The Volta also remains at line 9.

It is so subtle that it can be easily missed, being buried in the middle as it is.

72. Welsh Sonnet.

The Welsh Sonnet uses three Awdl Gywydds with a Cyhydeddfer attached to the third one to give me the recognizable 14 lines of a Sonnet.

So, what are those strange terms?

The Awdl Gywydd consists of a four line Quatrain using a 7 Syllable Meter with a unique Rhyme Structure, where the End Rhymes form a recognizable abcb pattern, but **line 2** carries an In-line Rhyme to match the **first line's** End Rhyme (the "a" rhyme) at either the second, third, fourth, or fifth Syllable, while the **fourth line** similarly carries the End Word of the **third line** (the "c" End Word) as an In-line Rhyme somewhere between the second and fifth Syllable. So the Awdl Gywydd's rhyme can be represented as follows:
xxxxxxa
xXaXXxb
xxxxxxc
xXcXXxb,

where the large X represents the **alternate positions** of the In-line Rhymes. This is a very Welsh style, and is known as Cross Rhyming.

The third Awdl Gywydd, is closed with a Cyhydeddfer, which is simply an 8 Syllable Rhyming Couplet, often used as a Cauda (Tail) for one of the Welsh forms.

73. Wreath of Sonnets

A Wreath of Sonnets sometimes also called a Garland of Sonnets, consists of 15 Sonnets and is enriched with an Acrostic in the Concluding Sonnet. Besides the complex and sophisticated content, A Wreath of Sonnets has an Format where the Last Line of one

Sonnet becomes the First Line of the next one (just like the Crown does, making all fourteen Sonnets of the Circle an intertwining "garland" of lyric poetry; one Sonnet cannot exist without the other. The First Lines of all the single fourteen Sonnets form in turn **another Sonnet**, called the "Master Theme" or the Magistrate, linking all the Sonnets together. In the more modern versions, this Master Sonnet becomes the First Sonnet.

74. **Word Sonnet.**

The Word Sonnet is a variation of the Traditional Form that was championed by Seymour Mayne, a Canadian poet who teaches at the University of Ottawa. Its One-Word Structure has a strong resemblance to Chinese poetry. It is a fourteen line poem, with **one Word** for each line. This "Miniature" Sonnet can contain one or more sentences, as articulation requires. If you are interested in learning more about the Style, here are two links. The first is an overview by Seymour. The second is dissertation on how to make it into a 14 Word Shakespearian Sonnet.

http://poemsand poetics.com/2014/02/seymour-mayne-hail-15-word-sonnets.html
http;//stephenfrug.blogspot.com/frank-sidwicks-fourteen-word-sonnet.html
I find the format very flexible and playful. Although with only one word per line, it is amazing what you can do.

GLOSSARY OF SONNET TYPES

1. **Acrostic Sonnet**…Sonnets 31,32.
2. **Alfred Dorn Sonnet**…Sonnets 49,53.
3. **American Sonnet**…Sonnets 20,21,22,142,160,165,167.
4. **An 11-9 Anapestic Heroic Sonnet**…Sonnet 138.
5. **Arabian Onegin Sonnet**…Sonnet 69.
6. **Asean Sonnet**…Sonnet 70.
7. **Beymorlin Sonnet**…Sonnet 71.
8. **Blank Verse Sonnet**…Sonnets 29,30,148,161,168.
9. **Byron's Sonnet**…Sonnets 43,151.
10. **Carrett Sonnet**…Sonnets 61,153.
11. **Caudate Sonnet**…Sonnet 62.
12. **Compound Sonnet**…Sonnet 63.
13. **Cornish Sonnet**…Sonnets 82,110.
14. **Coronet of Sonnets**…Sonnet 129.
15. **Couplet Sonnet**…Sonnets 111,112.
16. **Crown of Heroic Sonnets**…Sonnets 130.131,132,133,134,135.
17. **Curtal Sonnet**…Sonnets 99,107.
18. **Dante's Variation Sonnet**…Sonnets 44,64.
19. **Double Acrostic Cleaved Petrarchan Sonnet/Rondeau If/Then**..Sonnet 138.
20. **Dual Sonnet**…Sonnet 72.
21. **Duo** Sonnetio…Sonnet 109
22. **Echo Sonnet**…Sonnets 113,145.
23. **English Sonnet**… Sonnets 1,2,3,4,141,143,149,154,159,162,163,164,166.
24. **Faux Free Verse Sonnet**…Sonnet 83.
25. **Fusion Sonnet**…Sonnets 65,84.
26. **Heroic Sonnet**…Sonnets 66,124
27. **Hex Sonnetta**…Sonnets 54,85.
28. **Inverted Sonnet**…Sonnet 56.
29. **Italian Sonnet**…Sonnets 10,11,12,13.
30. **Japanese Sonnet**…Sonnet 86.
31. **Jazz Sonnet**…Sonnet 87.
32. **Kyrielle Sonnet**…Sonnet 33,114
33. **Limerick Sonnet**…Sonnets 34,88,100.
34. **LyriCat Sonnet**…Sonnets 89,115.
35. **Modeled End Rhymes Sonnet**…Sonnet 139.
36. **Modern Sonnet**…Sonnets 23,24,25,26,27,28,152,156,158,170.
37. **Nonet/Cinquain Sonnet**…Sonnet 140.

38. **Pantygonnet**…Sonnet 73.
39. **Pantoum Sonnet**…Sonnets 35,36,116,117.
40. **Petrarchan Sonnet**…Sonnets 15,16.
41. **Pushkin Sonnet English version**…Sonnets 45,101.
42. **Pushkin Sonnet Italian format**…Sonnets 46,102.
43. **Qautern Sonnet**…Sonnets 37,118.
44. **Rondel Prime Sonnet**…Sonnets 38,119.
45. **Roserian Sonnet**…Sonnets 55,.169.
46. **Rubaiyat Sonnet**…Sonnets 39,157.
47. **Sapphic Sonnet**…Sonnets 90,103.
48. **Saraband Sonnet**…Sonnets 56,91.
49. **Septillian Sonnet**…Sonnet 67.
50. **Sestet Sonnet**…Sonnet 57.
51. **Sestina Sonnet**…Sonnets 40,74.
52. **Shadow Sonnet**…Sonnet 75.
53. **Shakespearean Sonnet**… Sonnets 5,6,7,8.9,144.
54. **Slide Sonnet**…Sonnet 76.
55. **Sonnet Trilogy**…Sonnet 125.
56. **Sonnet Cycle**…This Book.
57. **Sonnet Sequence**…TBD.
58. **Sonnetino**…Sonnet 108.
59. **SonnTriolet (aka: Triolet Sonnet)**…Sonnets 42,122.
60. **Spenserian Sonnet**… Sonnets 17,18,19,147,150,155.
61. **Super Sonnet**…Sonnet 68.
62. **Swannet Sonnet (or just Swannet)**…Sonnet 120.
63. **Terza Rima Sonnet**…Sonnet 41.
64. **Tiara of Sonnets**…Sonnets 126,127,128.
65. **Tirrell Sonnet**…Sonnets 47,51,121.
66. **Tory Hexatet Sonnet**..Sonnets 52,58,92.
67. **Tricet Sonnet**…Sonnet 59.
68. **Trilonnet Sonnet**…Sonnet 60.
69. **Triptic Sonnet**…Sonnets 77,78,79,146.
70. **Tuckerman Sonnet**…Sonnets 48,93.
71. **Visser Sonnet. (aka: Hidden Rhyme Sonnet)**…Sonnet 80.
72. **Welsh Sonnet**…Sonnets 81,94.
73. **Wreath of Sonnets**…Sonnet 136.
74. **Word Sonnet**…Sonnets 95,96,97,98,104,105,106.

www.ingramcontent.com/pod-product-compliance
Lightning Source LLC
Chambersburg PA
CBHW060409010526
44107CB00005B/638